Maverick

*An independent individual who does not go along with a group or party

Maverick*

A Life in Politics

Lowell P. Weicker, Jr.

with Barry Sussman

6/4/95

Little, Brown and Company

BOSTON   NEW YORK   TORONTO   LONDON

First Edition

Library of Congress Cataloging-in-Publication Data

Weicker, Lowell.
  Maverick : a life in politics / Lowell P. Weicker, Jr., with Barry
Sussman.
      p.   cm.
  Includes index.
  ISBN 0-316-92814-3
  1. Weicker, Lowell.   2. Legislators — United States —
Biography.   3. United States. Congress. Senate — Biography.
4. Governors — Connecticut — Biography.   5. United States — Politics
and government — 1945–1989.   6. United States — Politics and
government — 1989–   7. Connecticut — Politics and government — 1951–
I. Sussman, Barry.   II. Title.
E840.8.W43A3   1995
974.6′043′092—dc20
[B]   94-45709

10 9 8 7 6 5 4 3 2 1

MV-NY

Published simultaneously in Canada
by Little, Brown & Company (Canada) Limited

Printed in the United States of America

To Scot, Gray, Brian, Sonny, Tre, Mason, and Andrew
in partial payment for all the times missed

Acknowledgments

GOOD POLITICIANS get a few competent, dedicated people to stay with them over the years. I've been lucky, which is better than good, and thus have been blessed by having a full complement of bright, dogged, idealistic associates.

Some of them were very helpful to Barry Sussman and me in the writing of this book, spending hours recollecting events, providing documents, offering suggestions, and, in some instances, reviewing the text. For their assistance I extend special appreciation to Tom D'Amore, Kim Elliott, A. Searle Field II, and Bob Wicklund. Also to Dick Benson, Maureen Byrnes, Bill Cibes, Bob Dotchin, John Doyle, Tom Dudchik, Hank Harper, Pete Kinsey, Bill Shure, and Stan Twardy.

I want to thank our literary agent, Charlotte Sheedy, who approached me with the idea that I issue "a call to arms" in writing. She was helpful throughout, as was Jim Silberman, our editor.

There would have been no book without Barry Sussman. He was patient, creative, and thorough, and he managed to slip into my brain without my even feeling it. We spent perhaps a hundred hours together, and I speak for both of us in saying that it was a most enjoyable collaboration.

Finally, I am indebted to my loving wife, Claudia, for her encouragement, suggestions, critiques, and general assistance, and for her sharp, accurate memory.

— Lowell P. Weicker, Jr.

Contents

Maverick

Introduction

WHEN I WAS SEVEN or eight years old, my father asked what I wanted to be in life. "A politician," I responded.

Around the same time, an aunt came to visit. She asked if I liked her new Easter hat. I gave her my opinion — no. My mother chastised me, saying I should have been more diplomatic.

I said, "If Aunt Bea didn't want the truth, she shouldn't have asked."

Thus started a life in politics, and a habit of being outspoken.

I became a Barry Goldwater Republican, working hard in 1964 to get Goldwater his few presidential-convention delegates from Connecticut. In 1970 he reciprocated, supporting me in my first US Senate campaign. I have always liked Goldwater. He is a constitutional conservative, unlike the Johnny-come-lately right-wing moralizing nuts of the Republican party. I also supported Richard Nixon, and, in turn, Nixon helped me in my 1968 and 1970 races with personal appearances and money. This relationship was soon to blow up in both our faces.

Today I'm an independent. Some Republicans say good riddance, as I was always independent, too independent, and that I had moved about as far as possible to the left of the ideological spectrum. I don't think so. If the contrast between me and those most prominent in my former party is striking, it is largely because they have moved so far to the right. The party of strict constitutional interpretation and balanced budgets has become a collection of constitutional lightweights and spend-thrifts.

In politics, ideological movement is a very tricky business. I believe I moved little, if at all, once elected to the Senate in 1970. Somewhere along the line, though, I got out of sync with the voters of Connecticut, and in 1988, when I ran for a fourth Senate term, I lost by the narrowest of margins to a chameleon Democrat who changed from liberal to conservative by the hour throughout the campaign.

I had remained the same persistent figure, fighting with the Jesse Helmses of this world, working for society's powerless, and protecting the Constitution. In the early years, most voters approved of that. But by 1988 Connecticut citizens were tiring of a senator who kept focusing on annoying issues like discrimination, separation of church and state, health care, AIDS. After two terms of Ronald Reagan as president, they eagerly embraced "free-lunch" government. Reagan convinced much of Middle America that you can have it all without paying for it. As an advocate of fiscal soundness, I didn't move with that tide. He also urged Middle America to take care of number one and the heck with the neighbor behind you. I didn't buy that either. So I lost. Better that than to care so much about winning as to compromise on matters of principle.

On a personal level, I am a stay-at-home family man. I'm not your typical role model in this area, having been married three times, divorced twice. Nevertheless, I would rather spend time with my seven sons and wife than be part of any social whirl. My wife, Claudia, and I both enjoy that most domestic of avocations, cooking. I sack out by ten and rise around five. I bicycle, swim, or play tennis every day before breakfast. I only wish my waistline showed it!

I'm not going to deal much with my marriages in this book. I don't advocate getting married three times; things just worked out that way, and I'll shoulder the blame. Politics is a tough, demanding profession. I should have paid less attention to it and more to my family.

Politics clearly played a damaging role in my first marriage, to

Marie Louise Godfrey — Bunny — who lives in Greenwich and who is a wonderful person who has always supported me. Bunny just did not enjoy politics, and we went our separate ways. We had two fine sons of our own, Scot and Gray, and a third, Brian, whom we adopted after his parents died.

In my second marriage, it was not necessarily politics that drew us apart. It just turned out to be different from what we both anticipated. We also had two sons of whom I am very proud. One is Tre, short for Lowell P. Weicker III. The other is Sonny Weicker, a Down's syndrome child.

When Sonny was born, some people recommended that I not take him home from the hospital. Well, today Sonny can read and write, attends public school, and is a warm, marvelous person. And I'm proud to say that legislation I helped write (before Sonny was born) enables millions of others like him to develop their abilities and have lives that are full and productive.

Claudia and I play tennis, enjoy diving and snorkeling, taking her two wonderful children, Mason and Andrew, and mine to baseball, football, and hockey games. I own trotting horses that run at Rosecroft, in Maryland, and from time to time have gotten into the sulky and put them through their paces. We love art, opera, and the theater. One of the rewards of being governor of Connecticut was that I had walk-on parts with the Connecticut Opera Company in Hartford. The Met has not contacted me.

Claudia has had her own career in politics and government. She worked for Abe Ribicoff, Tom Dodd, and Hubert Humphrey before we hooked up. I was probably the first Republican she ever talked to, never mind loved. She brought her Capitol Hill experience to bear as first lady of Connecticut, working on various initiatives, mostly for children in need of help.

Our nation, with its tradition of respect for the individual and regard for the law, is the marvel of the world and will continue to be as long as we maintain our sense of who we are and how we got here. Americans have been blessed with an extremely reliable compass, the Constitution. From the writings of the Founding Fathers, we know they intended the Constitution to be a broad and enduring statement of the rights and liberties of Americans. It has been just that. But the Constitution doesn't protect itself.

In all generations, including our own, there have been those who would trade the clamor that goes with our system for a more efficient model. Two of America's greatest dangers are from those on the one hand who would rob us of democracy in the name of efficiency and quiet, and from the majority of Americans on the other hand who are willing to stand by and watch, idly, as that occurs.

I have spent much of my political career trying to protect the Constitution. During the Watergate scandal, the problem was never Richard Nixon per se. It was, as the carefully worded articles of impeachment against him stated, that Nixon violated "his constitutional oath faithfully to execute the office of the President of the United States" and "his constitutional duty to take care that the laws be faithfully executed."

These *constitutional* abuses had to be spotlighted and ended. I helped do that as a member of the Senate Watergate Committee. My staff and I did our own investigation, along with the work done by the committee.

I met with John Dean, Nixon's main accuser, early on. I met several times with the ill-starred L. Patrick Gray, the temporary director of the FBI who got caught up in the scandal. Both these men became my good friends and deserve far better marks for courage than they have received. I spent hours with Alfred Baldwin, the person who eavesdropped from across the street on the bugged telephone conversations at Democratic headquarters. I shared the tragedy of the Cuban burglars for an afternoon in their cell at the federal prison in Danbury, Connecticut.

Some of the Watergate material included in this book has not been made public before. One example has to do with the events leading to the determination that Nixon had filed fraudulent federal income tax reports, which many regard as the final straw that turned public opinion against him and led to impeachment proceedings.

The televised Watergate hearings of the summer of 1973 made mine a household name for several generations of Americans. For the first time since the hearings, I speak out about Watergate. For younger people, who weren't around to hang on every detail, I try to explain what it was that made those events so captivating and perilous.

In retrospect, Watergate remains as nasty a business twenty years later as it was in 1972 and 1973. To me, the most surprising, profound, and meaningful revelations of Watergate were the incredible abuses committed by our law enforcement and intelligence community — the FBI, the Justice Department, the Internal Revenue Service, the CIA, the Secret Service, the military. Influenced by the White House, the abuses of these agencies have been unparalleled in the modern history of this country. (Unfortunately, the Iran-*contra* scandal of the 1980s was not far behind, and in its international aspects was even worse than Watergate. For Ronald Reagan, it seems, the lesson from Watergate was, try to leave no trace.)

During my fifteen years in the US Senate after the Watergate scandal, there was hardly a moment when the Constitution was safe from raiders. Almost every year there are high-level attempts to savage it, usually hidden in some popular or pious-sounding issue. They come not from enemies overseas but from those within who have their own narrow agendas.

The recurrent drive for school prayer is one such issue. What could be more innocent sounding than letting children pray in public schools? Well, it's not that simple.

No one is stopping children from praying in school. The humorist Art Buchwald some years ago interviewed God on the subject, and reported that He was unaware He had been banned from America's schools.

"President Reagan said that kids can't pray in school," Buchwald told God.

"If they can't, they're sure doing it," God said. "I hear schoolchildren's prayers all day long. Of course, I hear more from those who haven't done their homework, or have been caught committing some infraction. . . . And there is a lot of praying when report cards come out, and when college test scores come in. . . . I can't understand why President Reagan said I've been banned from the classroom."

One problem with school prayer is that we would end up with organized, virtually compulsory prayer and not voluntary prayer. Another is that any prayer that could satisfy the varying Christian

denominations, Jews, Muslims, Taoists, and all other interested
parties would be not much of a prayer at all. As someone said, it
would be in the order of a "to whom it may concern" prayer. Not one
I, as an Episcopalian, would want my children voicing.

It would also be the first step in demolishing the wall of separation between church and state. One has only to observe events in
Bosnia, Northern Ireland, and the Mideast in recent years to understand the nitroglycerin that results from mixing church and state.
There is no question in my mind that the unique concept of keeping
matters ecclesiastical out of our governing is America's greatest
contribution to the laws of civilization.

You would have thought that an issue like school prayer had
been settled long, long ago and that democracy had won, but that's
not the way things work in Washington. There is no such thing as a
losing cause. Proponents and lobbyists lick their wounds for a while
and come back, and a number of legislators can be counted on to
lead sham battles on their behalf. For me it was Jesse Helms. Today
it is Newt Gingrich. Losing makes no difference to these members of
Congress; with their ideological agendas, losing is every bit as worthwhile politically as winning — maybe more worthwhile.

One of the worst national problems is the eddying one of politicians who won't level with the public and a public that won't vote for
politicians who level with them. Eddying, pulling totally downward,
with fewer people voting each election cycle.

On the surface, the 1992 presidential election appeared to
break the pattern, with a 55 percent turnout of eligible voters, compared to 50 percent four years earlier. But only 45 percent of eligible
voters cast ballots for Bill Clinton, the Democrat, and George Bush,
the Republican, combined, so the two-party vote actually declined
substantially in 1992. The entire gain, and then some, was due to the
presence on the ballot of the independent candidate, Ross Perot.
Perot stood for nothing other than rejection of the Democrats and
Republicans. He was a "none of the above" candidate. Imagine how
hungry for change voters must be if they give almost 20 percent to
"none of the above."

The eddying's root cause is that the American people do not
want to face reality. In campaign after campaign anyone who advocates raising taxes loses. Our nation is in hock beyond anything the

government can live with, with a debt that is driving us to the poorhouse. Without question, the present deficit and the practices that keep it in place are the greatest threat to the national security in my lifetime. The government must use the weapons at its disposal to make the debt manageable. That means cutting spending and paring entitlements. It also means increasing taxes. All three. With the size of the national debt you don't get to pick and choose.

Except for program cuts, the people don't want to hear about these solutions. Unfortunately, there are plenty of candidates for office who are content to pander to them.

In 1993 and 1994 the Democrats and some Republicans tried to create a national health care program. That was an admirable goal, one I endorsed many years ago. But they failed terribly. President and Mrs. Clinton dotted every *i* and crossed every *t* in their health proposal except for one aspect: providing a means of paying for it. I don't know how you establish a health program without paying for it. I don't know how you pay for it unless you change health practices or pay exorbitantly for present practices, which for the most part are not conducive to good health. Indeed, there is not enough money in the world to pay for America's current health care practices.

Taxation to me is something to be used in a selective way toward whatever the problem happens to be. It is not a matter of philosophy or redistribution of the wealth. If there is any philosophy in taxation, Weicker style, it is no more complicated than if, after cuts, you are to spend money, you must raise money.

The national debt is so high that taxes alone cannot begin to solve the problem. If taxes are increased too much, economic growth will be stifled, making things worse. When I became governor of Connecticut in 1991, the problems were the same as those of the United States, in miniature but also in the extreme. With the help of some very bright people, we got out a surgeon's knife and cut a fine balance of spending reductions and tax increases. We did that in the first year. The second, third, and fourth years we had tax cuts along with further spending cuts. Lo and behold, Connecticut enjoyed four straight budgetary surpluses.

We went through the same excruciating process each time. I didn't run for governor to cut back on everything. I had real goals and ambitions, born of three decades of experience. But I had no choice.

Cuts were inevitable. So was installation of a state income tax, for which I was vilified.

On the national level the problem is that we have spent far beyond our means for much too long. In part the national economic woes date to Democratic guns and butter during the Vietnam era — pouring our treasure into warfare and setting up social programs at home without properly funding them. But the debt escalated wildly in the 1980s as a self-serving Congress rubber-stamped Ronald Reagan's weird and unsound program of building military spending to obscene levels while cutting back on taxes, especially taxes for the rich. It was Reagan, and a Congress that went along, who created the first trillion-dollar debt. But the public also is to blame.

The reason we have a debt of almost $5 trillion is that no one can campaign for office successfully on a platform that honestly tries to resolve the problem. The public cuts such candidates off at the knees. The American people are just as responsible for the huge deficit and debt as the country's leaders.

In our democracy, the people rule. But for the longest time, the people haven't been doing their job. Making hard choices is the most difficult aspect of leadership. Voting is easy. For decades, increasing numbers of Americans have done neither.

I want to go behind the scenes to show how politics really works. In these cynical times, it is necessary to reaffirm to people that government can work for them. Indeed, in America government has done better than anywhere else at any time.

I want to talk some about what I am proudest of in my many years of public life, such as helping formulate the Americans with Disabilities Act, contributing to the scientific study of AIDS, working for the powerless in all areas, building up the National Institutes of Health and the National Oceanic and Atmospheric Administration (NOAA), and, as governor, starting to put the state of Connecticut on a sound financial footing. There is an important unifying theme here: Government can work. Things get done. Politicians may have to be encouraged, but the good ones can and do improve the quality of life. It is a rare theme these days.

One message that I hope comes across is more important than any others. It is to all Americans: Care about the nation! Do so by getting off your butt to make it work for all.

Finger-to-the-wind government in Washington leads us down the wrong road too many times. We have been shortsighted where we must be bold. We cannot permit the most subtle of destructive forces, self-indulgence, to stifle our development as a people. Change is a certainty. Change is the promise for the United States and its people.

Change — its recognition, its assimilation, its implementation — is what made the United States the greatest nation in the world. Now, fear of change, avoidance of change, lack of change, is shrinking this nation to a microcosm of its stated ideals and promise.

In 1994 I went to South Africa for the presidential inauguration of Nelson Mandela, an event so sweeping as to be undreamed of even by its most ardent supporters. I was part of the American delegation. In my autograph collection I have this thought written by Alan Paton, the great South African author, in March 1957: "It is important to me that America should achieve racial justice speedily, for all of us in Southern Africa, both black and white, may need her help in the dark days that lie ahead."

We made difficult advances after that was written; we handled change in terms of race well for a time. But only for a time. Now we are handling it not at all.

We like to think of ourselves in the roles of past American heroes but we have stopped performing our own heroic acts. Revolutionary spirit these days is a dying ember. That ember must be fanned into a flame, the flame into a bonfire.

My call to fellow citizens is that they stop thinking of America as a finished product. Work for change, don't fear it.

As for the leadership in Washington: start leading; go for it! My advice to Washington is, it doesn't matter if you tax people ten cents or a dollar. If it takes a dollar, then tax them a dollar, because they'll hate you just as much for the ineffective dime as for a dollar. What's wrong with the figuring in Washington is that politicians are calculating how much they can drag out of the people and still be reelected. We have an administration and a Congress, for example, that says, "We have addressed the subject of deficit reduction."

Well, the hell with *addressing* the subject. People don't care about addressing the subject. They want the pain reflected in results. That doesn't mean spending more money on debt service than on domestic programs.

Lick the problem and get on with life.

1

The Great Tax Revolt

IT WAS THE FIRST SATURDAY in October of 1991 and a crowd that would grow to forty thousand was beginning to gather on the grounds of the capitol in Hartford. Most were there to protest a new state income tax that had been in effect one week. Some were on a more personal mission: to attack the governor. Attack verbally and physically. Spit, hang a dummy from a scaffold, compare me to Adolf Hitler, you name it.

A few politicians and media lowlifes had spent weeks getting citizens worked up for this lynch mob. A principal organizer was Thomas Scott, a former Republican state senator and defeated candidate for Congress in 1990. Scott created a citizens lobby and developed a two-part plan to rebuild his fortunes: part one, attack Weicker, part two, get the income tax repealed. He was helped along by radio talk show hosts who hyped the tax issue and the rally day after day, using hate to increase their ratings and pander to listeners.

My first stop that morning was at a conference on children in the legislative office building next to the capitol, where my wife, Claudia, was to speak. As I arrived, protesters passed by on their way to the rally, in clusters and singly, looking like early arrivals at a football game. I, however, was to be the football. Some spotted me and yelled obscenities; I responded by blowing kisses.

A tunnel with a people mover connects the modern legislative office building to the traditional golden-domed capitol. I could have used that tunnel to get to my office without going outside. My aides and Claudia wanted just that. The fact is, they wanted me to stay away from the capitol altogether. But I couldn't; for weeks I had been set on going.

More and more in recent years, I had seen people on the streets become ruder to each other, while at the same time our formal bodies, such as the Congress and state legislatures, had likewise become progressively less civil. Live and let live had dropped out of the lexicon of public discourse. Knuckling under to demagoguery was not in my character.

At about ten-thirty that morning, I walked toward the rally with my chief of staff, Tom D'Amore, and a plainclothes state policeman, Henry Semper, one of the regular security detail. We started along the side of the capitol, where the crowd was thin, aiming to swing across the front, mingle with the protesters, and go into the building through a main entrance.

Perhaps five thousand had gathered by now and it was getting noisy. As expected, there were many loudmouths and organized groups of agitators. But in the main there were decent citizens of Connecticut who thought the income tax was unfair and wanted to exercise their constitutional right of dissent. I engaged at least a dozen such people in conversation right away. Some jocular, some perplexed, some rude. Most of the questions came from persons who hadn't realized that because they did not make much money, they would pay either no income tax at all or hardly any. Others asked if I was nuts for even being there.

There wasn't a single mean-spirited comment. Honest disagreements, honest questions. Some people were pleased with my answers, some not. I was having just the kind of effect I had hoped for in terms of a dialogue that would frustrate and rout the demagogues.

We turned the corner toward the front of the capitol and continued to mix into pockets of discussion. One of the rally's organizers spotted me and hollered, "Go back to Russia." Brilliant, that.

The crowd around us began to swell. At six feet six, I stand out in a group and people came toward me on the run. In a few minutes what had been fifty or seventy-five people in our small circle expanded to about two or three thousand.

It got difficult to move, although not really worrisome. Everyone around me still seemed genuinely interested in talk. I was not at all concerned. Crowds are a politician's business. It's when you don't have them that you worry.

Then one individual, a little guy, moved in close. He cursed and made threatening motions, urged on by a few compatriots. I got the impression he was one of a small knot of agitators from Waterbury (their T-shirts proclaimed their origins) whose main purpose was to seek me out and cause trouble. Suddenly, they did. They spit, cursed, and charged at me. I was surprised, somewhat shocked. But more than anything else, I was pissed.

Almost all the people around me had been attentive, either talking or listening to the discussion. Now mob psychology took hold. Acting normally was no longer socially acceptable; many of these plain folks took on a violent, threatening air. They also began to press in so that I could hardly move.

For Tom D'Amore, still at my side, we were enacting his worst nightmare. He had urged me not to attend this rally and had warned about the potential for riot. He saw someone he knew in the crowd, a Vietnam veteran who had come to protest cuts in the budget. In frustration, D'Amore screamed, "What the hell are you doing here, you're at the wrong damned rally!"

At least one person, maybe several, lunged at me. Henry Semper and another state policeman, Paul Samuels, threw neat bodyblocks, and a few plainclothes troopers, unnoticed until then, forced their way between me and the surging crowd. People began to back off.

I continued to be more angry than fearful. I wanted to keep up the dialogue. I was sure that had many in the crowd known the details of the income tax, they would have come to praise it. I felt I was getting that message across, and I was damned if I was going to let a few rednecks stop me.

I was also aware that there might be renewed attempts to slug me. People were shouting things like "Weicker sucks," "We don't need Communists like you," the kind of inanities you expect in that situation. I had fought many, many constitutional battles in the US Senate for everyone else, so when my First Amendment rights were being abused, I said the hell with this, let them take a swing.

Had someone landed a punch, shame and revulsion would have spread across the gathering, and the protest would have turned on the rabble-rousers. I motioned the troopers to move us deeper into the crowd.

Tom D'Amore, however, was quicker. He had caught the eye of a state police lieutenant and signaled him to get us inside. That was what the troopers were wanting to hear. They moved me into the capitol and out of harm's way.

Later I asked Tom why he gave that signal, since it was exactly opposite to my wishes. More important than personal safety at that moment was the symbolic presence of the governor at this "petitioning" of the government.

"You see a crowd, Lowell, and think that here's an opportunity for a speech. I see this crowd and think, here's the potential for violence." I asked why he felt that way. "You've always been a mainstream politician," he said, "but not me. I was in Students for a Democratic Society in college. I know violence, and I've never been this scared in my life."

Tom Scott, Connecticut Republican-party chairman Dick Foley, and the trash-talkers from radio continued whipping up the crowd with fiery speeches. At one point Foley singled out a Democratic legislator, Miles Rapoport, who had voted for the income tax and who also felt it important to attend the rally. "There he is," the cowardly Foley said, and a mob went after Rapoport. But he got behind a barrier and was safe.

Coverage of the event appeared on national TV and gave the feel of a riot narrowly averted. If you are familiar with Connecticut, you know how extremely remote the possibility of a riot was. Nevertheless, I was shown jostled, hooted, burned in effigy. As in an old western, a scaffold showed up out of nowhere and a dummy looking like me was hung from it.

Mobs kept glaring up at my second-floor office, shaking their fists, thinking I was there. But I had already left for a third public appearance that day. This one was in New London, where I was scheduled to deliver the reading in Aaron Copland's symphonic tribute "A Lincoln Portrait."

Months later I learned that an old colleague from Watergate days, former US senator Howard Baker, had watched the antitax rally on television in Washington, DC. He remarked to those with him, "There's Lowell Weicker — the only man I ever met who would light a match to look into a gas tank."

Because of the crowd size and the TV coverage, some people saw this protest as extremely menacing. But the fact is, I was in much greater physical danger that night, in New London.

As Claudia and I arrived at the Garde Theater there, we ran head-on into a raucous, violent group of protesters. Some were clearly drunk; some I recognized as among those who had charged at me earlier in the day. They threw bottles, tomatoes, and cans. One bottle barely missed Claudia as we slipped in the stage door entrance.

The rabble remained outside, chanting, screaming, and cursing during the entire performance. I received a standing ovation inside and threats of bodily harm outside. At the end of the evening the state police and the New London police chief maneuvered Claudia and me through back alleys and shoved us into a waiting automobile, barely ahead of the mob. A few goons caught up and rocked the car, but the security detail was able to disperse them. As we pulled out, someone threw a rock that shattered a window.

The person most responsible for our making it to safety was a young state trooper, Steve Salvatore, who decoyed much of the mob by staying with the car we arrived in outside the theater. For two hours he took abuse and the potential of violence without flinching. We had made our getaway by the time the rabble realized their prey had left in another car.

This was a totally senseless episode. When you spend your life in politics at what are sometimes very high levels of controversy, you understand the possibility of bodily harm and come to terms with it. That was the case with Watergate, when I used to get a death threat a week, or when I spoke up for the AIDS community in the 1980s.

But such issues were far loftier than the one that put Claudia and me in danger this night. We were being taunted and threatened by a mob that acted as if they wanted to tear us to bits. And for what? For gripes over an income tax that would provide a fairer, more consistent source of revenue to meet Connecticut's needs? Never mind to bail the state off the edge of bankruptcy, that they, not I, had created.

2

Couldn't Run, Had to Fight

EVERY BOOK SUCH AS THIS is obliged to have a "human interest" chapter, a glimpse into the private life of the author. In my case the reader would be bored. The fireworks of life have been political and governmental, not personal.

Having been married three times is no more than confirmation of my failure to mesh family and political life. From these unions, however, I have seven wonderful sons: Scot, Gray, Brian, Sonny, Mason, Tre, and Andrew. They are all far more normal than I. They are smarter, better looking, and more athletic and, God bless them, none aspire to follow in my footsteps. Even I concede that one Lowell Weicker, Jr., in politics is quite enough.

I was born in Paris, France, on May 16, 1931, and lived there until I was five years old — hardly the optimum age for a sojourn in Paris. In 1952, on the eve of becoming a second lieutenant of artillery in the US Army, I rejected French citizenship, telling the gendarmes at Orly Airport that battlefield situations were far better spent in the company of Americans than the French.

From 1936 to 1953, growing up took place in New York City and Mill Neck, Long Island. I was very fortunate in terms of homes, schools, and parents. Since I hold to the belief that parents are the most important influence on any child's life, I'd like to introduce you to my father and mother:

Lowell P. Weicker. Born, Stamford, Connecticut. Educated at various prep schools. Graduated from Yale in 1926. First European sales manager for E. R. Squibb and Sons, later president and chief executive officer of the company. Built Squibb into the most prestigious and profitable pharmaceutical firm in the United States. Served in the US Army Air Force in Europe during the length of World War II. Discharged as a full colonel, he was deputy director of intelligence for the Eighth Air Force. He won a slew of decorations.

At age thirty-eight, my father was too old to be drafted into the military after Pearl Harbor but he wanted in. Preparing for this book, I came across some of his old correspondence, including a letter to John J. McCloy, who was then undersecretary of war in Washington. "Now, Jack," Dad wrote, "I really want to do something of real value for our country. . . . Believe me when I say that I don't care about title, danger, or place, if the object is important to the nation at this critical time."

Dad was inducted shortly afterward. So at a time when some people were trying to use pull to avoid military service, my father used influence *to get in.*

Returning to Squibb as CEO after the war, he was bounced in a family feud and became undersecretary general of the North Atlantic Treaty Organization during the Eisenhower years. He then returned to business as the CEO of the Bigelow Sanford Carpet Company. He took Bigelow from bankruptcy to huge profitability and a merger with Sperry and Hutchinson. As a businessman my father was without peer. As a father he was principled, fair, a man's man, and always at our side when my mother or I or my sister and two brothers needed him.

My mother: born Mary Hastings Bickford in Bangalore, India, the daughter of a British general and niece to Randall Thomas Davidson, the sixty-ninth archbishop of Canterbury. Her immediate family eventually migrated to Toronto and then Buffalo. There she came to know and marry an ardent young suitor from Yale. She made childhood a magical time for her four children. She was a devout Episcopalian, fun-loving and socially conscious.

Mother was an enthusiastic Democrat. The reason for that was basic: most of her family were in England in the late 1930s and early 1940s. Every Englishman considered Franklin Roosevelt a hero for bringing the United States to the side of Great Britain during those dark days. That started her off, and she never wavered from the Democratic line, casting her last vote for David Dinkins for mayor of New York in 1993, not long before she died.

My father was a Republican, but only in a casual sense. For him, politics was no place for anyone, including his son. It wasn't until I was elected to the US Senate that he finally accepted and was proud of my achievements. One thing I do know from observing my own father and many like him since: Most American businessmen, though brilliant in their chosen fields, don't know their ass from first base about politics. They think it a corrupt business, which it is not. They think us stupid, which we are not.

As I view the business debacles of the eighties and nineties, corruption and stupidity seem to have been corporate America's lot to a far greater extent than anything I encountered in political life. The sacrifice and integrity of those holding elected office in America are something for which this nation should be grateful. I witnessed them from the inside for more than thirty years. As much as I fault the two-party system and its addiction to excessive partisanship and winning elections at all costs, I have nothing but praise for almost all the participants. Sure, there are a few rotten apples, but no more than in other lines of work, and probably fewer.

Let me restate this: We have gone from a politics of accountability to a politics of reelectability, which is a mammoth sea change. In addition, we are suffering governmentally because extreme partisanship has created bickering and constant contentiousness in Washington. These elements of national politics are unpleasant and self-defeating when practiced ad nauseam.

At the same time, I am tired of members of the House and Senate being caricatured as feckless, corrupt baboons. These are very intelligent men and women, and almost all are honest and hardworking. At one time or another, Democrats and Republicans have tried to knock my block off, and I love, respect, and thank them all. Don't let the editorial writers and holier-than-thou activists neuter American politics in the name of good government. Remember, the one-issue activist is rarely around for the day-to-day grunt work that makes government run. As long as policymakers are elected, the citizenry should bestow accountability upon them. The problem of the past few decades is that the citizenry has become preoccupied with itself, selfish. That is the massive corruption of our times, not some isolated political hack with a hand in the cookie jar.

Back to my formative years. Grade school for me was the Buckley School in New York City. It had teachers who never allowed me to give up on myself. On almost every grade level I received the "most improved" award — which makes me wonder what course in backsliding I took each summer.

One of my sharpest early recollections is of my family returning to our Manhattan apartment from our weekend home in Oyster Bay. When we arrived, I ran through the lobby, into the elevator, and right into the apartment. A few minutes later, my father came in.

"What's wrong with you, young man?"

"Oh, the doorman will take the bags."

"How old is the doorman?"

"I don't know, Daddy."

"Don't you ever order any adult to do anything for you. You get your ass down there and bring up your own bag."

Obviously, I had an elitist attitude and thought I was a little hotshot. My father was not about to allow that. The children in the family were taught to know their place.

Aside from my parents, athletic coaches were the ones who really set me straight. To this day I firmly believe in the character-building value of sports. Anyone who feels education is complete without sports is full of beans. This needs to be said because penny-pinching adults are cutting sports out of school budgets, along with arts and libraries, on the grounds that they're not education. Bullshit! Most of my character building took place on a playing field, not in a classroom.

From Buckley to Culver Military Academy. One anecdote from this experiment in drill and discipline. Boxing was compulsory. Reporting to the first session, I was analyzed with a truth that has remained with me ever since. I had yet to grow to my present six feet six, but weighed my present 245 pounds. I looked more like a stationary object than poetry in motion.

The coach eyed this plebe and said, "Weicker, a man has to

learn to do one of two things in life: either to run or to fight. One look at you and I suggest you learn how to fight."

The lesson in retrospect is that far from having the courage that has been attributed to me in a political career, the simple fact is I don't run because I can't.

The last three years of high school were spent at the Lawrenceville School in New Jersey, starting in 1946. This became the first key building block toward a career in politics. No, it wasn't my being elected head of the dramatic society (Periwig Club) that had political implications, though there is a slice of the ham in all of us. For me, it was the geographical diversity of the student body. For a kid from Park Avenue and the north-shore estates of Long Island, I was in the same boat with young men (no women then) from all over the United States. Diversity entered my life, and I loved it. I started to learn through classmates, not classes, about Cuba and California, Panama and Puerto Rico, Chicago and County Cork. It was an eye-opener and encouraged inquisitiveness. The fun of politics is that no day is like any other. Politics, being the business of people, guarantees a different world a hundred times a day, every day.

I mentioned that I came across some of my father's old correspondence in preparing to write this book, and some of it dated back to Lawrenceville days. Sometimes Daddy goaded me on, concerned with my study habits, my weight, my discipline. Sometimes his letters were just warm and loving. And sometimes, when he felt the need, he wrote to the headmaster, as in a letter from February 1949, when he was worried about my being overweight:

"Will you please ask the school physician to insist that Lowell report to him once a week in order that his weight may be checked," the letter said. Daddy also asked the headmaster to be in touch with "the various stores in Lawrenceville that deal with food products, cutting off Lowell's charge facilities as far as any food product is concerned." (At age sixty-three it must be confessed that I lost the battle to milkshakes, Spam, and McDonald's long ago.)

From Lawrenceville to Yale University. I cannot report to you that either in academics or athletics I led my peers. Let's just say I got through, having a good time all the way, with neither blemish nor academic honors.

My father saw some spark in me, though. In a letter dated January 1951, he said the key to happiness, success, even greatness was the use of personal discipline as a guide. "When a man really has the opportunity to compete with the very top flight, it is amazing how few survive. I want you to be one of the few who survive. I have very great expectations for your future."

A couple of events did occur at Yale that clearly gave hints of things to come.

The forum of campus politics, then as now, was the Yale Political Union, composed, from right to left, of the Conservative party, the Bull Moose party, the Liberal party, and the Labor party. Not yet the raving "left-winger" — the perception that brought about my expulsion from Republican ranks — I joined the Bull Moose party.

A senior by the name of William F. Buckley was the head of the Conservative party (*plus ça change,* as they say). At a particular session of the union, Buckley, in line with so much of his behavior in future years, accused the head of the Labor party of being a Communist. That was a bit much for many, this freshman included, and thus took place my first impassioned debate on behalf of freedom to think and speak without being smeared. I remember receiving a standing ovation. It was, as I look back, my first foray against the prejudice of a majority.

Mr. Buckley does not need me to recount his life's successes. It is sufficient to say we met in debate again at Yale. This time he was there to defend Richard Nixon; I, as a United States senator, to condemn the excesses of the Nixon administration. Buckley's brother James was elected to the Senate, from New York, the same year I was. He was a fine person intellectually and personally. Later, after losing reelection, he tried to make the grade in Connecticut and indeed did get the Republican nomination for the Senate. He lost in the general election, and my lack of support is one of the reasons relations with the Buckleys have been strained.

William F. Buckley has maintained a consistent patter of verbal hate since those days. Sometimes he wins (support of Democrat Joseph Lieberman against me in the 1988 US Senate campaign), sometimes he loses (support of Republican John Rowland against me for governor in 1990). But some things never change: Buckley is the same ass today as he was in 1949 when he tried to portray liberal thought as being "Communist."

The second event that pulled me toward politics at Yale also occurred while I was a freshman. I volunteered as a Young Republican in the reelection campaign of New Haven mayor William Celentano, who faced a formidable challenge from a young man named Richard Lee. Celentano won by two votes. One lesson there, the obvious one, was that "every vote counts." In a rematch two years later, Lee won overwhelmingly, and the lesson that time had to do with tenacity, a virtue in politics as in all endeavors.

Most important for me in this early experience was that my suspicions were confirmed: I found enormous satisfaction in the vitality of local politics.

The natural next step was to become active in Greenwich, and to adopt a highly personal and vigorous style of campaigning. Only once after I got into public office did I ignore that style, and that, in 1988, was the only election I lost.

Upon graduation from Yale I married Bunny Godfrey of Rye, New York, and started active duty in the army as a second lieutenant of artillery at Fort Sill, Oklahoma. The next six years were spent at Sill and Fort Bragg and then at the law school of the University of Virginia. These were wonderful years for both of us. No, I didn't prefer Lawton, Oklahoma, or Fayetteville, North Carolina, to my native Northeast, but my admiration for the military lives to this day. Every youngster should have the experience of military service, if only it could be gained without its companion, war.

The Eighty-third Field Artillery Battalion taught me leadership and responsibility. I got used to hearing, "That's your problem, Lieutenant," and found it easier to accept the idea than to shirk things off on someone else.

One incident at Fort Sill that I've recounted many times deserves repeating here as a lesson in "a rose by any other name," et cetera.

Oklahoma was a dry state in the fifties. Young officers bought their booze on base and had the habit of going off the post with bottled refreshments, much to the irritation of the local authorities. One evening, before dismissal, an old army regular, Sergeant William Belke, pulled us together to relay the complaints of Lawton law enforcement. He concluded his admonition by stating the following: "And remember, gentlemen, nothing looks so much like a bottle of whiskey in a bag as a bottle of whiskey in a bag." I suspect that truism explains why today's public is not as taken in by political semantics as my colleagues might like to believe.

My affection for the University of Virginia law school is unbounded. Here were laid the foundations of my struggles over the Constitution, first during Watergate, and then during the constitutional battles with the "New Right" during the eighties.

And yet it was by the proverbial whisker that I crossed the finish line in law school. My first year was almost my undoing. When the standings were posted, everyone below me was out, and I had to attend summer school in order to continue. From then on, I climbed in the standings to finish respectably. Graduation meant a diploma, coupled with a firstborn, Scot, and a decision to seek employment in Seattle.

Bunny and I were attracted to Seattle because it offered city life and the great outdoors at the same time, something unobtainable in most places. So west we went.

The only unforeseen problem was that the Boeing firm was in a shutdown mode. In those days, when Boeing shut down, Seattle shut down. For six months I pounded the streets from one law firm to the next. No hires. I hadn't yet passed the bar; perhaps that was part of the problem. Finally an offer — not from anyone in the state of Washington — but from Connecticut.

And so the lifestyle of the Northwest was not to be for us; instead of Seattle it was Greenwich. The irony of this came home to me after I was in the US Senate for a while. Two of my colleagues there for more than ten years — indeed, my good friends — were Scoop Jackson and Warren Magnuson. They also were institutions in the state of Washington, and it is highly unlikely I would have ever gone to the US Senate had I gotten that first job in Seattle and lived out my life and dreams in the Northwest.

In Connecticut, on the other hand, time and again I was in the right place at the right time. I worked hard but I also was lucky. Don't ever underestimate luck in politics. Whatever my allotment, believe me, that ingredient is a key to success.

Ivey, Barnum, O'Mara, and Nickerson. A name and a job never looked so good. Most important, I was in Greenwich, the community whose people were to be my teachers and supporters for the career in public life that was to follow. Shortly after we arrived there, our second son, Gray, was born. Gray became an all-American hockey player at Saint Lawrence University and signed with the Hartford Whalers, playing minor-league hockey for two years. How I would have loved to have that experience!

There would be many elections and positions, another law firm, several houses, more children, grandchildren, two additional marriages, a stint of more than a year out of politics in the private sector. But the constant was Greenwich, which gave me my start and to which I return at every opportunity.

I'm sure the reader has little interest in local contests and infighting, but they are to politics what the minor leagues are to baseball. And so, as I close this chapter, a few anecdotes of transition are in order as I went from being a multifaceted young adult to a man totally consumed by politics.

If the question were asked as to who started me in real politics, I would have no hesitation in naming Peter deStefano. Pete was a pharmacist who was the Republican boss of the Third Voting District in Greenwich. His district was almost 100 percent of Italian origin and was comprised of working people who in many different ways built the town of Greenwich. Along with the Fourth and Ninth districts, this is the Greenwich of which little is known or written. No glamour, big business, or international financiers inhabit these streets. Just decent, hardworking, down-to-basics families. This was my first power base.

It was from deStefano and a couple of others that I learned the importance of constituent access and services. Snow removal, traffic lights, through truck traffic, clean beaches, adequate policing — certainly not national issues, but the mother's milk of political success. Had I been raised as a typical Republican in the salons of Fairfield County, discussing international issues at teas and cocktail parties, I know my career would have been a short one once off the Greenwich electoral scene. I was lucky to be a Republican raised as a Democrat.

My first venture was a defeat, yet, in the long run, a lesson in victory. In 1960 I aligned myself with Albert Morano, a candidate for the Congress who was opposed by the controlling faction of the Greenwich Republican Town Committee. Morano, a protégé of Clare Boothe Luce, had served several terms in Congress, only to get swallowed up in the Ribicoff gubernatorial landslide of 1958. He was opposed in his comeback attempt by the Bush family of Greenwich — Senator Prescott Bush et al. — who made common cause with his opponent in the primary, state senator Abner Sibal. According to the party line, Morano was "not representative" of Fairfield County. ("Not representative" — meaning a non-Wasp.)

When Morano was defeated I was quickly on the outs with the Republican town committee. I sought the nomination for state representative and lost by forty-seven to three. The three votes were from Pete deStefano's district. Two years later, 1962, I again sought the nomination and this time I won, fifty to nothing. For a Republican in Greenwich, nomination is tantamount to victory, and so I was elected to my first public office. The lesson learned here was to ask one-on-one for support. To turn around an entire political organization in a year and a half — that's a lot of asking. But that's what my business is about.

I also learned early on the bitterness of primary contests. In 1963 I went after the Republican town committee and its titular head, Griff Harris, the first selectman (mayor) of Greenwich. I won the primary principally because I outcampaigned Harris in the one-on-ones. I then went on to win the general election with my running mate, Bob Holbeck. But for a Republican in Greenwich, my election night totals were abysmal, the lingering, nasty effects of the primary battle. Eventually Harris and I once again became friends. But in retrospect, I'm not sure I would advise budding politicians to go for the jugular so early in their careers.

When I was elected first selectman, the local papers referred to me as a Goldwater Republican. That may make people snicker today, but it had more than just an element of truth at the time. I was responsible for getting Barry Goldwater the four Connecticut delegates he took to the Republican national convention in 1964. Also, I beat Griff Harris by coming at him from the right, in part by criticizing him for proposing that the town of Greenwich establish regional contacts with New York City.

My leanings toward conservative positions, however, were even at that formative stage countered by a pull from the opposite direction, brought on, in part, by a very liberal colleague, a Quaker named Agnes Morley.

Agnes represented the liberal wing of the Democratic party in Greenwich. She was totally against United States involvement in Vietnam at a time when most people had not yet started paying attention. I have never met anyone in my political career who was as kind as Agnes, and as dedicated to bringing that kindness to bear through governmental decision making.

Agnes was concerned about public housing problems in Greenwich, about the elderly, about virtually every local social issue. Greenwich was concerned with the causes of the nation and the world, but it sometimes tended to disregard the needy at home.

We had low-income housing in Greenwich, we had middle-income housing in Greenwich, we had elderly housing in Greenwich, yet those never captured the interest of most influential people in Greenwich. They captured Agnes Morley's interest, though. To me, she was a conscience: She made me think and care about issues I otherwise might well have dismissed.

3

Going Where the People Are

I SERVED IN THE STATE legislature and as first selectman of Greenwich until 1968, when I ran for Congress in Connecticut's Fourth District. We worked up a slogan — "I'm a Weicker liker" — to get people to remember my name. Two nights before the election, Governor Nelson Rockefeller of New York campaigned for me in a multistation radio hookup, and referred at least three times to his "close friend Lowell *Wicker*." So much for that slogan.

The incumbent was a conservative Democrat, Donald J. Irwin, who was elected to the House in 1958, lost in 1960, then won again in 1964 and 1966. The Vietnam War was the key issue in our campaign. Irwin backed Lyndon Johnson's handling of the war and I criticized it, recommending that the United States take the initiative to get peace talks going and get out of Vietnam according to a schedule. I suggested halting bombing in key areas and having the South Vietnamese hold an election in which Vietcong candidates could be on the ballot. I proposed that the United States withdraw its forces after such an election.

I staked out a plowshares-type foreign-policy position: "Our main thrust toward convincing people that democracy is the best system should be made in the areas of peace," were the words of one of my campaign releases. "And the programs of peace are food to eliminate starvation, medicine to combat disease and education to provide leadership for nation building."

While the United States was using force of arms in Vietnam, I pointed out, Communist China was building a university as a gift to Singapore — a school that would be used for years to capture people's minds to the Communist philosophy.

The 1968 campaign is probably as good an example as any of the truth of the maxim "Some things never change." In this instance, it was the importance of personal campaigning. The immense role of television, advertising, negative campaigns — all these were largely developed after 1968, and I'm sure there will be many other changes long after I'm gone. But today, as in 1968, if you can shake someone's hand, your chances of getting that person's vote are very high, higher than as a result of any other type of contact.

The biggest annual gathering in my congressional district was the Barnum Festival parade in Bridgeport every Fourth of July. Incumbents were allowed to ride in the parade, challengers weren't. No one ever really contested this inane rule; it was just a given that if you weren't an incumbent, you weren't in the Barnum Festival parade. I said all right, we'll abide by the rules. I promptly proceeded to walk the four miles of the parade route along the sidelines, shaking hands and doling out campaign materials to people in the crowd. No one could stop me from doing that, and I could see the frustration on Don Irwin's face. He was sitting in a convertible waving to people, but he had none of that personal contact. He looked as though he wanted to jump out of that car. Incumbency had become a millstone.

From then on, I pretty much applied the style I learned in Greenwich to the new, wider constituency. I spent the summer and fall at bars, bowling alleys, parades, beaches. We had one rule: wherever there were people, that was where we would be.

In those days, voters often went to where the politicians were, and not vice versa. If the candidate had a rally, the public was expected to attend. We totally turned that around, going where the people were. Riding the commuter trains in and out of New York, campaigning on station platforms, all of that which is now commonplace was very new back in 1968.

My main adviser was my press secretary, Hank Price, who had been a political writer for the *Bridgeport Sunday Herald* and was probably the best reporter in the state. He understood the state and district, and was in reality a campaign manager as much as a press secretary. For my advertising, I relied on Pete McSpadden. McSpadden, in fact, did all my political advertising, from the time I ran for selectman through my senatorial career and gubernatorial election. And with one short-lived exception, there was no such thing as a negative campaign ad, either.

Bridgeport, the largest city in Connecticut, traditionally delivered huge margins to the Democrat, in effect overriding Greenwich, Darien, and New Canaan. Not in that election, however. I cut Irwin's victory margin there to almost nothing, and the game was over.

I won with 52 percent of the vote. Again: the real story of the '68 election was taking the campaigning, the one-on-one, to the streets.

I was one of nine new Republicans elected to the House that year, and one of five to defeat an incumbent Democrat.

I saw right away that my six years in the Connecticut state legislature would prove very helpful. The only real difference, as I used to say at the time, was that in Washington you add nine zeros to the end of every figure. The human emotions and the relationships were identical to the ones experienced in the representative town meeting in Greenwich and in the capitol at Hartford. I was very comfortable on the floor of the House of Representatives from the day I walked in; I wasn't awed by debate and had no compunction about standing up and speaking my mind.

I was in the House for one two-year term. Looking back, some of my actions there seem to be those of a different person, not the Lowell Weicker of today. I cosponsored a constitutional amendment calling for prayer in the schools — a bill very similar to ones I worked hard to defeat in later years. I went along with a drive led by the House minority leader, Gerald Ford, to impeach William O. Douglas, one of the most liberal Supreme Court justices, and, in retrospect, one of the best.

On occasion, I have been asked to reconcile these actions with my subsequent political record. My explanation is that I matured and changed. It's as simple as that.

While I did some things in the House that I now regret, I am proud of other actions. At the time, federally funded urban-renewal projects were being developed in many cities. Large parts of old downtowns and slums were leveled, often replaced by municipal government centers or business and shopping areas. Left out of the equation were the poor whose homes had been razed. Many had no place to go.

I introduced legislation requiring renewal programs to provide housing for those who were displaced. It was beaten back at first, then enacted. Observers called it a stunning achievement for a first-termer, especially for a minority-party member. So if my early prayer amendment and anti–William Douglas stands made me look like a young reactionary, well, the urban-renewal legislation gave a different impression.

As a member of the House, I also focused on transportation problems. They were severe in the Northeast, and getting worse in other parts of the country.

I was active in a big battle of that time, the fight over ABM, the antiballistic missile system that was promoted by Richard Nixon. I opposed Nixon on the ABM because both its cost and effectiveness were open to question.

On the humorous side, while in the House I was asked to play in a charity tennis match. It was Republican senator Jacob Javits of New York and I against Vice President Spiro Agnew and Joe Blatchford, the head of the Peace Corps. We played at the Washington Hilton Hotel with hundreds of people watching. At one point, Agnew smashed the ball right into his partner Blatchford's head! Javits and I won, 6–1, 6--1. I thought I had never played better tennis in my life.

Everyone has a secret ambition; mine was to be number one in sports. That day I felt I had reached the top of the ladder. And of all things, going home in my car I heard a reporter describing the match on the radio, and how Agnew had beaned Blatchford.

She said of Blatchford that he was "the best-looking man you've ever seen in your life," and that "he plays a beautiful game of tennis." Of Javits she said, "He is getting along in years but plays a very steady game." Of Agnew, "he's enthusiastic."

I felt she was saving the best for last, that she was preparing to say which individual really played best in that match. And then it came. What she said was, "I can't remember the name of the fourth guy."

Early in 1970, it was widely assumed that Thomas Meskill, the senior Connecticut Republican in the House of Representatives, would run for the Senate seat that had been held by Democrat Thomas Dodd. Dodd had been censured by the Senate for alleged misuse of campaign funds, and said he was retiring from politics. The Democratic nomination went to the Reverend Joseph Duffey, an antiwar, liberal activist who was head of ADA, Americans for Democratic Action.

Meskill's office was down the hall from mine in the Longworth Building. One day he called and asked me to meet with him, and out of that session came one of the biggest shocks of my life.

As we sat down, Meskill said, "I'd like to talk to you about the forthcoming election." I figured he was asking my help in his quest for the Senate, and I was prepared to say that I would work as hard as I could. I thought he would be a fine senator.

"I want to tell you something, Lowell. I'm going to run for governor."

I was stunned. Like everyone else in the state of Connecticut, I thought he was going to make the run for the Senate. The governor's race seemed illogical because a popular Democrat was expected to run, and be unbeatable.

"I think you're nuts, Tom," I said. "You've got this Senate seat in the bag."

"Lowell," he said, "I want to be governor of Connecticut. It has been my life's ambition. I want to go back to Connecticut; I want to be in Connecticut, and I think I can win."

I told him again, "I admire you but I really think you're making a mistake here."

"No, it's really what I want to do; I've made up my mind," Meskill said. "But there's a second part to this. One of the things that has to happen is we have to have a balanced ticket, in terms of philosophy and geography." Meskill was conservative; by that time I had come to be known as a moderate-to-liberal Republican. Meskill said, "I want you to run for the US Senate."

I said, "My God, it never even occurred to me. I'm here now, I love it." Everyone could see I would have been reelected, that things were going well for me in the Fourth District.

"I can't give you an answer right now," I said. "Let me think about it."

"I've got to know in the next several days," he said.

I agonized for a week. The question was, do I give up a safe seat on a gamble? Not many Republicans had been elected statewide in Connecticut since the ascendancy of Abe Ribicoff as governor and then senator. I finally came to the conclusion that I had been fortunate in having a life in which many things were given to me on a silver platter. If there was anyone who could afford to roll the dice, it was me. That was the basis for my decision: the fact that I could afford to gamble because if it didn't work, I was in a better position than others to go on with life outside politics.

I went back to Meskill and said that if he was crazy enough to run for governor, I supposed I had the guts to run for the Senate. At that time I was very partisan, and I saw my decision as helping the Republican party as well as advancing myself.

As a new House member, I was not very well known across the state, although I was beginning to attract some attention. In February 1970, for example, an editorial in the *Westport News* urged me to make the Senate bid. "In less than two years," the editorial said, "Lowell Weicker has emerged as a lawmaker of concern, conviction and courage. His votes on critical issues have surprised and/or pleased many constituents. He has remained independent of those 'pressures' which seem to control so many of our men in Washington."

The editorial said that "with moving examples, Rep. Weicker makes us realize in terms of people what happens when a nation spends $417 for armaments and only $68 for all the other areas of health, education, water pollution, railroads and drugs, out of every $1,000 of tax revenue."

Meskill had more than just the geography and political philosophy worked out; he also understood the practical workings of the system. Running together in a Republican primary, he and I presented a balanced ticket, and we both won handily.

On the Democratic side, Joe Duffey got the nomination by

virtue of a primary victory over a conservative, Al Donahue, who had been the favorite at a state party nominating convention. Duffey had forced the primary and won as young people all over the state worked their tails off for him. The fight caused a sharp Democratic-party split, inducing Tom Dodd to reenter, as an independent.

The lineup in the general election was Duffey the liberal Democrat and Dodd the conservative independent, leaving me, the Republican, as the moderate.

Before Dodd announced his candidacy, I was approached by Murray Chotiner, who was best known as a longtime hatchet man for Richard Nixon. Chotiner did not enjoy a savory reputation in Washington, but for one reason or another he had been good to me. When I opposed Nixon on any issue, or from time to time said things as a House member that weren't complimentary, Chotiner always took up my cause in the White House. He was not just a friend but a good friend.

Chotiner came to me and said, "Lowell, if you would like, we will encourage Tom Dodd to get in this race. Do you think you can profit by a three-way race?" The idea was that Dodd would siphon Democratic votes from Duffey.

I said, "Listen, Murray, I don't want you guys laying a finger on this race, I don't want you doing anything. Nothing; I can win on my own. I don't need a three-way race." Chotiner said, "If that's your wish, I'll convey it."

Chotiner later was badly injured, hit by a car, and died not long afterward. When I attended his funeral, at a synagogue on Massachusetts Avenue in Washington, some people in the Nixon camp were surprised to see me. He was known for tough politics, but he protected me.

The 1970 Senate campaign stayed absolutely divided, one-third, one-third, one-third until two weeks before Election Day. The voter polls simply wouldn't budge. In 1970 you didn't have the massive television coverage of political races that you now have. And you didn't have the multiple debates that today are all over the airwaves for the last month of any campaign. But there was one debate scheduled in New Haven between Dodd, Duffey, and me, and I was determined to make the most of it.

Up to then, I had not laid a glove on Tom Dodd. I just let him be and allowed the facts to speak for themselves. I never mentioned Congress's censure of him, never personally criticized him. But the campaign situation was going absolutely nowhere, and if you let things stay static for too long, you can pretty much write off any change. In a static situation, voters are most likely to stay with the devil they know rather than the devil they don't.

Duffey in the meantime was making the most outrageous statements about the United States, typical of the antiwar critics circa 1970. I like Joe Duffey; he's a good guy personally. But during that election campaign, I took him on as a creature of the left and went after him regularly.

In the New Haven debate I tried to knock off both Dodd and Duffey together, two birds with one stone. I think a comment I made there took hold and turned the election for me.

Looking at Dodd, I said, "It's the Tom Dodds of this world that create the Joseph Duffeys." I was trying to establish myself as the only middle-ground candidate; portraying Dodd as out of touch and suggesting that the result of his inattention might be to put a radical in office.

Within forty-eight hours of the debate, polls showed that I had jumped out ahead. Today I regret having made the remark. In the passion of the times, my tactic and my statement were acceptable. Nevertheless, I have to say I wouldn't have made the comment had I known as much about Dodd then as I came to learn later on. Dodd had given a great deal to America, both as war crimes prosecutor and senator.

It may have been correct politically to attack Dodd that way. But I think anyone familiar with Lowell Weicker knows I don't make those kinds of political moves. Dodd was an elder who had served well, and to this day I regret saying what I did even though it was the stick of dynamite that broke the logjam.

As Murray Chotiner had foreseen, being in a three-way race helped. I won with 41.7 percent of the vote.

4

The Great Cover-up

I WAS ON TOP of the world when sworn in to the US Senate in January 1971. I was thirty-nine years old, one of the three youngest members, positioned exactly where I had dreamed of being since boyhood.

I quickly got close to Jacob Javits, my erstwhile tennis partner. Our beliefs were much the same: conservative on spending, progressive on social issues. He, I, and a few others were almost the last of the moderate Republicans. Clifford Case, Ed Brooke, Charles McC. Mathias, Mark Hatfield, Bob Stafford, Mark Andrews, and Jim Pearson stand out.

My first speech of some length on the Senate floor was on behalf of the War Powers Act, which Javits introduced and I cosponsored. Aimed at reducing a president's unchecked foreign-policy authority, the act would have limited the situations in which armed forces could be used without congressional approval. I pointed out that the Founding Fathers had made the president commander in chief with the power to *wage* war, but that Congress was given the power to *declare* war and *control the purse strings* needed to raise and equip the army and navy.

The War Powers Act got nowhere in 1971, but it was enacted in 1973 when President Nixon, weakened by the Watergate scandal, lost his hold over Congress. He vetoed the legislation but Congress overrode him in November 1973, not long after the Saturday Night Massacre, a climactic Watergate episode.

Presidents Ford, Carter, Reagan, Bush, and Clinton disregarded the War Powers Act when it suited their purpose, and Congress did not move to constrain them, as it could have. The record in this regard has been shameful. But at least the mechanism is there, to be used in a crisis if members ever work up the courage.

When I entered the Senate, Nixon, in office for two years, had been satisfying a lust for secrecy and political spying. In March 1969, weeks after his inauguration, he began bombing Cambodia in violation of that country's neutrality in the war in Southeast Asia. Only a handful of members of Congress were told of the bombing despite the requirement that Congress approve such action in advance.

In May 1969 an account of the Cambodian bombing appeared in the *New York Times*. That report, and others regarding arms limitation talks with the Soviet Union, infuriated Nixon. He authorized illegal wiretaps on the telephones of four news reporters and thirteen executive-branch officials in hopes of getting to the source. Some of the spying in these early stages was done by private detectives reporting to John Ehrlichman, Nixon's first White House counsel.

In August 1969 the Internal Revenue Service, at the request of the White House, set up what was called an "Activist Organizations Group," later named "Special Services Group." Its stated function was to crack down on extremists. In practice, it made the IRS a lending library, a spying and harassment agency, turning over confidential tax files on so-called enemies of Richard Nixon to the White House.

In 1970 Nixon approved a plan drawn up by a twenty-nine-year-old presidential aide, Tom Charles Huston, that called for stepped-up spying and suppression of the antiwar movement. Nixon's approval came even after Huston said, in writing, that much of the plan was illegal.

One tactic to be used, Huston wrote to Nixon, would be burglary, even though "this technique is clearly illegal." He said there would be intensified wiretaps and the lifting of all restraints on surveillance of mail. Including the Central Intelligence Agency in domestic intelligence work, as Huston proposed, also was illegal. But Huston said that CIA director Richard Helms "was most cooperative," and that the only stumbling block was FBI director J. Edgar Hoover.

On July 14, 1970, Huston got a memo back from Nixon's chief of staff, H. R. Haldeman, saying the recommendations "have been approved by the President." Later, when the Huston plan came back to haunt him, Nixon said it had never been implemented and that he ordered it rescinded because of Hoover's objections. But there was no paper of any kind showing it had been rescinded. Instead, there was strong evidence that it had been put into effect.

In addition, Nixon and his aides extorted enormous amounts of cash from special-interest groups and individuals. On December 14, 1970, for example, a dairy group promised to contribute $2 million to Republican coffers in return for curbs on dairy imports. Lo and behold, two weeks later Nixon placed an import quota on certain dairy products.

In June 1971, Nixon was infuriated when the *New York Times* began publishing the so-called Pentagon Papers, a closely held, Defense Department–sponsored history of US government involvement in Vietnam. One result was his creation of a White House spying unit called "the plumbers," whose job, as the name suggests, was to find and stop leaks.

Nixon also sought and won a federal court injunction ordering the *Times* to stop further publication of the Pentagon Papers. The *Washington Post* then started printing them, but it too stopped after an injunction. These were the first instances in US history of the government seeking and winning prior restraint of publication.

It was revealed that the Pentagon Papers were leaked by a think-tank analyst, Daniel Ellsberg, who had helped put them together. At that point the White House plumbers were expanded and sprang to action in an attempt to defame Ellsberg. Charles Colson, best known as a tough, dirty White House political operative, called a friend, a former CIA agent named Howard Hunt, and asked if he had any ideas on how they could go about "nailing" Ellsberg. Hunt said he did.

Hunt the plumber was put on a special White House payroll as a consultant to Colson. Immediately afterward, John Ehrlichman asked a deputy director at the CIA to give special assistance to Hunt on what he described as an important project. In short order,

Hunt linked up with another recent White House plumbing acqui-
sition, G. Gordon Liddy. This was the pair that, less than a year
later, were to direct the flubbed Watergate break-in.

I myself was settling in, getting comfortable in the Senate in this
period shortly before the 1971 summer recess. It would have been
fair to say that I was a happy and a lucky man. Lucky that Thomas
Meskill had encouraged me to run for the Senate, lucky to have
two fine sons after a period in which it had been difficult for
Bunny and me to have children. The older boy, Scot, was then
thirteen, and Gray was eleven.

That August we went to Marion, Massachusetts, on Buzzards
Bay, for our vacation. I flew from Washington to Providence,
Rhode Island, where I met the family, and we proceeded to drive
from there. Naturally, I thought I was now very well known, but I
got my comeuppance quickly when we stopped to buy groceries
and filled a shopping cart at an A&P. I had no money. No problem
for a US senator, right?

I went to the check-cashing booth and showed my Senate ID
card, with my picture on it, signed by the president and vice president of the United States. I handed it to the man in the booth, with
a check for him to validate.

"What's this?" he asked.

"I'm Senator Weicker and this is my ID card."

"That doesn't mean anything to me. Where's your A&P
charge card?"

So much for privilege and visibility.

That was a reminder not to get too high and mighty. But there
was a worse comeuppance for my family, a terrible scare, soon
afterward.

One sunny morning Scot, with my permission, set out for a
fishing trip on a Boston whaler. I went to play tennis. Not long
afterward I heard sirens wailing all over town but didn't think
twice about them. Then I got a call saying my son had been fished
out of the water and was in the hospital. He must have fallen out of
the boat, and the propeller slit his head viciously. Scot went
through a whole year of hospitals before he could really get back
on his feet. He had microsurgery on his eyes — the blade appar-

ently missed his eyeball by a millimeter — and had a plastic plate put in his head. But he made a full recovery, and for that I thank God to this day.

The reason I tell this story is that in 1971 I was Mr. Hotshot, having achieved much at a comparatively early age. Well, what happened to Scot gave me some perspective on what is important in life. People used to come to me and say, "Listen, Lowell, if he doesn't make it, it is probably for the best, because Scot would be a vegetable." My answer was: "I'll take the vegetable and leave the US Senate. I want my son." That "almost" tragedy is responsible for an attitude I maintained throughout the rest of my political career — sacrifice of family and ideals aren't worth the job.

Looking back, I think Scot's condition in the period after the accident and other events yet to come in my family life made me sensitive to the needs of people who need help, who have no access to power. I came to regard them as my special constituency.

On Labor Day weekend, 1971, Gordon Liddy and Howard Hunt supervised several Cubans in a burglary at the California offices of Daniel Ellsberg's psychiatrist. Their aim was to get material that would help defame Ellsberg.

Later on, during the Watergate scandal, White House strategy was to maintain that Liddy was a self-starter, that no one above him knew of his illegal activities. But in a memo to Charles Colson before the Labor Day break-in, Ehrlichman referred to the break-in as "Hunt-Liddy Project number one" and asked Colson for a "game plan" on how and when to use the materials obtained.*

This break-in was one of the first major activities of the White House plumbers. Political spying and sabotage were no longer assigned to private detectives but instead became the sole assignment of White House aides who were quartered, like proper bureaucrats, in the Old Executive Office Building next door.

The burglars failed to find anything useful, but the break-in was not exactly wasted, serving as a rehearsal for Watergate.

---

* Ehrlichman and Colson were indicted, convicted, and imprisoned in connection with the break-in at the psychiatrist's office.

Also in September 1971, Dwight Chapin, an appointments secretary for Nixon, hired an old acquaintance, Donald Segretti, to work as a political saboteur in the 1972 election campaign. He was paid $30,000 to $40,000 by Nixon's private attorney with funds left over from the 1968 campaign. Aside from his own activities, Segretti was assigned to recruit spies to play other dirty tricks against the Democrats.

The break-in at Ellsberg's psychiatrist's office and Segretti's lowlife work for the White House were revealed later on, as separate but integral aspects of the Watergate scandal.

Watergate!

Watergate was the worst constitutional crisis in the nation's history, but most people today have no idea what the scandal was about. Watergate resulted in Nixon's forced resignation, a terrible humiliation. By rights, it could have led to his being put on trial like a common criminal and to his imprisonment as well. Nixon was saved from that by a reluctant prosecutor, Leon Jaworski, who chose not to indict, and by Nixon's successor as president, Gerald Ford, who took no chances on the legal system. Ford pardoned Nixon for any crimes he may have committed even though no charges were even contemplated.

Because of their involvement in Watergate, more than twenty men who worked for Nixon, including his attorney general and several of his closest associates, people who had spent years at the seat of power, who had been blessed with many of the highest honors the nation can bestow, went to prison. Others left Washington in shame, their reputations ruined.

My own career and reputation are inextricably tied to the uncovering of the Watergate scandal. I was in the third year of eighteen years in the Senate then; most of whatever good I accomplished came afterward. But even now, so long after the events, it is the televised Senate Watergate Committee hearings in the summer of 1973 through which many Americans know me.

The Watergate scandal started as a botched break-in at the Washington headquarters of the Democratic party on June 17, 1972. Those headquarters were in the Watergate office building, part of a high-rent, office-hotel-apartment complex overlooking the Potomac River. Five men on the payroll of the Nixon 1972 re-election committee were caught red-handed in the middle of the night with bugging equipment and cameras. Their connection to Howard Hunt in the White House was revealed in a day or two, and to Liddy in about a month.

"A third-rate break-in," Nixon called it. Had the Watergate scandal been limited to the burglary itself — which is what Nixon and his chief aides wanted — it would have been a soon-forgotten episode. But the break-in was not to be forgotten, for it served to open the door on the wide array of political spying, bribery, un-precedented campaign-finance fraud, and other illegal and uncon-stitutional activities at the White House since 1969.

A vast cover-up was begun in fear that these activities, includ-ing the burglary at Ellsberg's psychiatrist's office, would be re-vealed in any unfettered FBI investigation of Watergate. Nixon personally set the cover-up strategy. He told Haldeman to explain the situation to the director of the CIA, Richard Helms, and to Helms's deputy, Vernon Walters. Helms and Walters were then to maneuver the FBI into curtailing its investigation on the grounds that certain leads, if pursued, would jeopardize the national secu-rity. Of course, the only security threatened was Nixon's.

At the beginning, the cover-up worked as Nixon outlined it. But the acting head of the FBI, L. Patrick Gray III, the temporary successor to J. Edgar Hoover, was balky. He asked Helms and Wal-ters to explain in writing just why certain interviews were off limits. When they would not comply after constant urging, Gray gave agents the go-ahead to conduct the interviews that so frightened the cover-up schemers.

Gray, from Stonington, Connecticut, was chosen by Nixon after Hoover's death in May 1972. In the spring of 1973, as I per-sonally began looking into the scandal, Gray told me details of the cover-up that made my hair stand on end.

Before the 1972 election Watergate was a big story inside the Washington Beltway but of only mild interest elsewhere. It had little effect on voters. For one thing, the Nixon camp denied most assertions and charged that others were nothing more than politics as usual, and that they too, not just the Democrats, were victims of campaign sabotage and harassment. For another, the Democrats had managed to offer up for president one of the weakest candidates they could find, George McGovern, the South Dakota senator. In subsequent years I came to know McGovern well. He was a decent man and a good senator, but a poor presidential candidate.

Richard Nixon was never a great crowd-pleaser, but McGovern made him look like Will Rogers. With McGovern as the alternative, few people wanted to hear about scandal in the White House. So in November 1972, Nixon won reelection with what was, until then, the greatest majority ever in a presidential contest.

Soon afterward, some political leaders began to focus more on the scandal, laying the groundwork for hearings in the Senate. Seven men had been arrested and went on trial in January 1973. Two of them were the White House / reelection committee aides Hunt and Liddy. A third, James McCord, also worked for the reelection committee. The other four included two Cubans and two Americans who had spent a good deal of time in Cuba. At least one of them had worked for the CIA.

When the trial opened, government prosecutor Earl Silbert said he would show that Liddy was the leader of the Watergate venture, but few experienced Washington hands thought the case stopped there. For one thing, it had been reported that one of the burglars had more than a hundred thousand dollars of reelection committee funds go through his bank account in a money-laundering operation. The men running the reelection committee, former attorney general John Mitchell and the finance chairman, former commerce secretary Maurice Stans, were not the type to let that much money be passed around without one of them knowing about it.

On the first day of the trial, Hunt tried to avoid testifying by pleading guilty to three of the six charges against him. The judge, John J. Sirica, said he would accept a plea only if Hunt admitted guilt on all charges. Three days later, he did. Shortly after that, the four men with Cuban backgrounds also pleaded guilty, leaving only McCord and Liddy. The trial ended on January 30 with their conviction, but perjury had kept the cover-up running strongly, with no testimony — only suspicions — that higher-ups were involved.

Judge Sirica, frustrated at the court's failure to implicate anyone higher than Liddy in Watergate, made this statement: "I would frankly hope, not only as a judge but as a citizen of a great country and one of millions of Americans who are looking for certain answers, I would hope that the Senate committee get to the bottom of what happened in this case."

On February 7, 1973, the US Senate created the Select Committee on Presidential Campaign Activities by a vote of 77 to 0. The following day the names of committee members were announced. Heading it up was Sam Ervin, the Democrat of North Carolina. It has been stated, I believe correctly, that Ervin was chosen for the job by Democratic leaders because he was not viewed as an extreme partisan. The other Democratic committee members were Herman Talmadge of Georgia, Daniel Inouye of Hawaii, and Joseph Montoya of New Mexico.

On the Republican side, Howard Baker of Tennessee was named ranking member. Minority leader Hugh Scott, who made the appointments, said Baker was a good lawyer, a good interrogator, and in the middle of the road ideologically. At the outset, however, some viewed Baker as the White House's man on the committee. A second Republican member was Edward Gurney of Florida, who made it no secret from the get-go that he was there to defend Richard Nixon. And then there was me, the junior member. Scott said Gurney and I were chosen because we were the only two Republicans who volunteered.

The Watergate affair subverted faith in the democratic process, in politicians in general, and in Republican politicians in particular. I volunteered for several reasons. I had been trying to develop a shield law to protect reporters, and the press, in particular the *Washington Post,* was being put under improper pressure by a number of Nixon's allies. I had been interested in campaign financing, and Nixon's reelection drive seemed to be a model for abuse of the system. And as a politician and a Republican, I felt, to use Sirica's words, that I had a stake in "getting to the bottom of what happened."

As I delved into Watergate with that attitude, a few Republicans began calling me a maverick, as though I had taken a position somewhere outside the party. But my position was not a maverick position, it was a pro-Republican position.

Two days after the committee members were named, White House aides met at the La Costa resort in California to plan strategy for dealing with the Ervin committee, to keep the cover-up going and keep us in the dark.

On February 21, Sam Dash, a former Philadelphia district attorney who now teaches law at Georgetown University, was named counsel and staff director for the committee. Later, Fred Thompson, a trial lawyer and assistant US attorney in Nashville, was named minority counsel by Senator Baker.*

At that point just about the only public day-by-day Watergate-related activities were procedural ones relating to staffing of the Ervin committee. With Judge Sirica's trial in limbo, there were hardly any newsworthy disclosures; the story was disappearing. But on February 28, events seemingly unrelated to Watergate shattered the quiet.

That morning Abe Ribicoff, the senior senator from Connecticut, and I went before the Senate Judiciary Committee to praise Connecticut resident Patrick Gray as hearings opened on his appointment as permanent FBI director. Ribicoff gave Gray his unqualified support; I said I believed Gray to be "a man of absolute integrity," which certainly was true of my feelings at that moment.

The hearings could have been perfunctory. A few senators on the committee, including Sam Ervin, Edward Kennedy, the late Philip Hart of Michigan, Robert Byrd of West Virginia, and John Tunney of California, asked fairly provocative questions, but not on Watergate. For the most part, the issues they cared about had to do with the safekeeping of FBI records, allegations that the FBI kept files on members of Congress, infiltration of the FBI in radical groups, fingerprinting records, and other matters.

The senators seemed satisfied with bland responses, such as statements by Gray that he was unsure of certain events or would have to check the record to recall others. They seemed to want

* In 1994, Thompson was elected to the Senate as a Republican from Tennessee.

Gray to succeed. The only one who didn't was Gray himself. He was acting out a death wish.

Gray had been used in a terrible way by Watergate conspirators John Ehrlichman and John Dean. They had emptied Howard Hunt's White House safe and found in it extremely damaging papers showing the illegal, surreptitious work Hunt had been doing as a White House plumber. They gave the papers to Gray, asking him never to let them see the light of day. Gray took them home, put them in a bureau drawer. About five days later he took them to his FBI office, tore them up, and put them in a burn bag without ever having read them.

Gray had served his country well, most recently as an assistant United States attorney general and, for twenty-six years before that, as an officer in the submarine service, including a stint as a submarine commander. But by the time of his nomination to head the FBI, Gray knew that he had let himself be used by Watergate cover-up conspirators, and it weighed heavily on him.

In the following months, I got to know Pat Gray very well. He told me about having burned the Hunt papers before he told anyone else. He was so distraught then that I feared for his life. But that's getting a little ahead of the story.

One of the first to question Gray at his confirmation hearings was Senator Ervin. He asked about reports, printed in the *Washington Post* the previous year, that a White House aide had prepared political saboteur Donald Segretti for a grand jury appearance by showing him copies of FBI interviews with him.

Ervin lobbed questions like softballs. "I take it you give the committee your reassurance that if any such event happened, that is, if any copy of the FBI interview was given to Mr. Segretti, it was not given by you or with your knowledge or consent?"

"It was not done with my knowledge or consent, that is true," Gray said. He could have concluded his answer there and avoided controversy. He didn't. "But I can go into it further if you want me to explain how it possibly could."

"Yes, I would like to have that," Ervin said.

Gray said that in July 1972 he began forwarding material on the FBI's investigation to John Dean, at Dean's request as counsel to the president. "So you see the possibility here, Senator," Gray said to

Ervin, "the allegation is really being directed toward Mr. Dean having one of these interview reports and showing it to Mr. Segretti."

It was the first time John Dean's name had been linked to any hint of wrongdoing. Other senators pounced on Dean's possible activities and on Gray's forwarding sensitive FBI material to him. On the second day of the hearings, March 1, Gray dug his hole a little deeper, with more incriminating testimony regarding Dean and the revelation that John Mitchell had told FBI agents not to interview his wife, Martha Mitchell. Senator Kennedy asked Gray what questions the FBI had put to Herbert Kalmbach, Nixon's personal attorney. Gray said he was unable to answer that, but that he would enter the FBI reports of the Kalmbach interviews in the hearing record.

That day Ehrlichman and Dean discussed Gray on the telephone in a conversation taped by Ehrlichman. "You ought to read the transcript. It just makes me gag," Dean told Ehrlichman. Dean said the Judiciary Committee might not act on Gray until they got testimony from White House officials like himself, and conjectured that Gray's nomination would be left hanging because Nixon had said he would not allow aides to testify.

"Let him hang in there?" Ehrlichman asked. "Well, I think we ought to let him hang there. Let him twist slowly, slowly in the wind."

On March 7 Gray entered into the record the FBI reports he had promised Senator Kennedy. The material was explosive, confirming the authenticity of some of the most important Watergate stories that had been printed in the press and that had been so hotly denied by the White House time after time.

Gray's hearings were then put in recess by the Judiciary Committee chairman, James Eastland of Mississippi, a friend of Nixon's, "to allow things to cool off," as Ehrlichman put it to the president. They never did resume.

The disclosures made by Gray gave Nixon cause for concern about the upcoming Senate Watergate hearings. With the scandal suddenly heating up again, the president announced that he would not allow aides to testify. He gave executive privilege as a reason — the need for a president to maintain the confidentiality of his conversations and remarks.

Because I was a member of the Watergate Committee, some reporters asked me for comments on Nixon's executive-privilege assertion.

"My reaction is of course that the 'executive privilege' which he chooses to invoke is supposed to be based on the 'national interest,'" I said in a statement. "I think the national interest in the case of Watergate is a restoration of faith by the American people in the integrity of their political system, and I think the national interest is achieved by opening, not closing, the White House doors. . . .

"The White House staff is not a side issue. The people around the President and in the White House *are* the issue."

A reporter asked if I would vote to subpoena presidential aides to testify, and my response was: "Absolutely! Can anybody tell me how the national interest or national security is served by having those persons who are suspects not appear?"

By making these remarks and seeing to it that they were disseminated, I began to assume a role that I was to hold until the end of the Watergate scandal, that of independent participant rather than partisan chorister.

The record shows that not many elected leaders criticized Richard Nixon during the two years that Watergate dominated the nation's political screen. It may be difficult to realize that now, but it is true, and it is one of the most frightening aspects of the scandal. The allegations made against him came first and foremost from the press, and later on through testimony, such as that of John Dean, and after that, through incontrovertible evidence presented in White House tapes of conversations.

Generally, elected officials either stayed quiet or rallied to Nixon's side. In March 1973 I was just starting my own investigation. I didn't suspect Nixon of any wrongdoing, but I knew political fakery when I saw it, and that is what the claim of executive privilege was — fakery imbedded in a legalism.

It is the job of political leaders to quell such fakery, not help it along. People aren't experts on public affairs; they need a little assistance in interpreting events. In all my years in politics I never shrank from letting people know what I believed and why I believed it. That's part of the job. You rise or fall, get elected or defeated, on the stands you take. That accountability is sadly lacking in many government leaders today. Politicians' caution and timidity is a main reason for the growth of cynicism in our country.

A few days later, events took a turn for the worse as far as getting to the bottom of things was concerned. At his confirmation hearings, Pat Gray had offered to let every US senator review the FBI's Watergate reports. However, Attorney General Richard Kleindienst, Sam Ervin, and Howard Baker overruled Gray, arranging it so that only Ervin, Baker, Sam Dash, and Fred Thompson were authorized to see the FBI reports.

Once again, I felt called on to express my discontent. In a speech on the Senate floor on March 20, I said Gray's nomination as permanent FBI director was being jeopardized by "wrongdoers within the Executive branch who . . . have seen fit to cut the ground from underneath him."

I also pointed out, in regard to the arrangement worked out by Kleindienst, Ervin, and Baker, that "the Senate did not create a two-man committee with five spectators. On the contrary, Senate Resolution 60 provides for full participation by all committee members."

I announced that I would be adding investigators of my own to the Watergate inquiry because of lack of cooperation from the executive branch. Nixon's invocation of executive privilege and Kleindienst's refusal to produce FBI files obviously were making our job much harder. Finally, I said that no agony over shortcomings in government programs could be as great as the agony of a nation living with and operating under a political system it does not trust. That, not the separation of powers, I said, was the problem confronting us in Watergate.

By then, I was pretty sure from my own digging that I knew more about the scandals than either Ervin or Baker. I was not about to let this deal remain in effect, and it didn't. A face-saving compromise was arranged so that all senators and staff members they selected could look at the FBI reports. The face-saving part was a stipulation that they not be allowed to make copies of the reports. In reality, they made copies whenever the need arose.

In the early going, some of my colleagues on the Ervin committee looked on me with amusement and irritation because I was outspoken. But I was picking up solid information, and before long I think they knew that I was not showboating but fact-gathering.

On March 23, 1973, a main prop in the great Watergate cover-up collapsed. It was the day Sirica was to sentence James McCord, Gordon Liddy, and the other defendants. I asked one of my chief assistants, Searle Field, to go to Sirica's court for the proceedings.

Searle said he had other work to do, but I had a feeling something was about to blow up, and I asked him to get down there. He did — and he just happened to sit in on one of the most dramatic moments in the entire scandal.

The courtroom was packed, and Sirica got to the drama right away. He said a probation officer had brought him a letter from McCord three days earlier stating that "political pressure had been applied to the defendants to plead guilty and remain silent," that "perjury occurred" in highly material matters, and that "others involved in the Watergate operation were not identified during the trial, when they could have been by those testifying."

Sirica told all the defendants they would serve maximum sentences unless they came clean. "You must understand that I hold out no promises or hopes of any kind to you in this matter, but I do say that should you decide to speak freely, I would have to weight that factor in appraising what sentence will finally be imposed in each case." He gave provisional sentences as high as forty years, with final sentences to be issued in three months.

Had someone asked me if this was high-handed behavior by a judge, I would have said yes, it certainly was — and wasn't it great! The day of the sentencing I sent a letter to Sirica, congratulating him for his handling of the Watergate case. I admired him for his guts in taking things into his own hands. He was a great American, God bless his soul.

It was largely due to John Sirica that the long and odious list of crimes that made up the Watergate scandal came to be known. Every major substantive part of the Constitution had been violated, abused, and undermined, either at the direction of the president of the United States or on his behalf by close aides. What a list it was: breaking and entering, illegal wiretapping, perjury and suborning perjury, bribery, lying to the FBI, contempt of court, contempt of Congress, destruction of evidence, campaign-finance violations, falsifying government documents, income tax violations, defrauding the United States, embezzlement, extortion, distributing false campaign literature, slander, libel, malicious mischief and malicious use of the courts, intercepting mail, and theft.

Caught up in or abetting criminal activities in some way were two attorneys general and other ranking executives in the Justice Department, the FBI, the CIA, and the Congress, aside from those in the White House and the Nixon reelection committee who led the break-in and cover-up. For many, their crime was to be overly loyal, to follow Nixon wherever he took them.

5

Investigating Watergate

AT ONE O'CLOCK on Friday afternoon, March 23, 1973, just after Judge Sirica's explosive disclosures, a lawyer for James Mc-Cord called the Senate Watergate committee and offered to make McCord available for hearings. That afternoon and the next day McCord met with Sam Dash, and the following week he testified in a closed session at the first official meeting of the full committee.

On Saturday, March 24, I met with a member of the Republican National Committee from California. His name was Ed De-Bolt, and he knew nothing about Watergate but a lot about Nixon. I was basically an easterner who had not followed Nixon's career closely even though he had been supportive of my 1968 and 1970 campaigns. Of course, I had read about him waging a nasty campaign against Jerry Voorhis and Helen Gahagan Douglas to get his start in politics, and about his work in the Alger Hiss case.

DeBolt opened my eyes wide. In sum, what he said was that many people in California Republican politics considered Nixon a chronic gutter fighter. If that had reached the East, I didn't know about it.

Even though it was the weekend, I also met with three of my staff aides, Bob Herrema, who was in charge of my office, Dick McGowan, my press secretary, and William Wickens, who had been loaned to me by Senator Robert Taft of Ohio to work on Watergate.

McGowan started putting in enormous amounts of time on

the scandal, as did two other aides, Searle Field and Bill Shure. Field was my chief Watergate assistant; Shure was a young New Haven lawyer who was about to join the Ervin committee staff. Shure in effect was half committee aide, half Weicker aide.

For all concerned, the work was extremely demanding. Twenty years later, as several of us met to go back over the Watergate story in preparation for this book, Shure, by then a prominent Connecticut attorney, said that neither before nor since Watergate had he ever worked as hard or put in as many hours. It was an intense period. We worked seven days a week. I usually began by six in the morning; there were few nights when we left before ten-thirty.

I tried to keep my investigation focused more on the misuse of government than on the personalities involved. I didn't want to get so hung up on John Dean or Richard Nixon that I might overlook a point about misuse of the Justice Department, the Internal Revenue Service, the CIA, or the FBI.

The kinds of questions my aides and I were asking had to do with why an internal-security division had been set up in the Justice Department, what led to the IRS auditing of people for purely political reasons, and so on.

By this time I had picked up enough information to know that others beside the seven original defendants were involved in Watergate and the related abuses, and I was quoted as saying so in an article in the *Washington Star-News*. Behind the scenes, President Nixon and others in the White House began to express concern about me. That Sunday I got a call from Attorney General Kleindienst asking that I fork over any material I had regarding criminal violations.

Nixon and his chief aides kept using Kleindienst as a front man to do dirty work. Around this time he was urged to put pressure on me to slow me down but he resisted, saying Weicker is just "an excitable kid."

A few days later, on March 27, 1973, I was the subject of discussion in an Oval Office meeting between Nixon, Haldeman, and Ehrlichman that was made public later as one of the many White House tapes of Nixon's conversations.

"Weicker is out today with another statement," Haldeman said.

"What did he say today?" Nixon asked.

"He has absolute proof that it goes to the White House staff and he isn't going to name names until he gets his evidence in hand. . . ."

"Well, who is Weicker?" Nixon asked. "Where is he getting this?"

Also on March 27, a lobbyist for Nixon on Capitol Hill telephoned Howard Baker, I was to learn much later on, and asked how Weicker could be shut up.

As it happened, I talked some with Baker that day on the floor of the Senate. I shared information that my staff and I had picked up; he reciprocated with information that was new to me.

I also met for a while with Ben Bradlee, executive editor of the *Washington Post*. I wanted to know him a little better because the *Post* had made more Watergate disclosures than any other news organization; he was interested in me because of the views I had started to express and because I was moving into a key investigative position. I mentioned to Bradlee that from information I had gathered, I was convinced that Haldeman knew about Watergate-type campaign activities that violated the letter and the spirit of the law.

My efforts were becoming noticed more back home. On the same day, the twenty-seventh of March, the *Bridgeport Post* praised me in an editorial. "His perception of right from wrong is luminous and free of influences which have no place in the thought process of a man in whom the public has placed a special trust," the editorial said. "He is willing to shake the White House and the Republican establishment, caring not about any political chastisement which may be visited upon him. . . . What more could be asked of a United States Senator?"

That editorial and scores like it elsewhere were samples of what were to become one of the more pleasant aspects of my political career: favorable press reviews. Not totally favorable, of course. But by and large, I have been well treated by members of the press, both editorial writers and reporters. I've given them good copy and they have given me a pretty fair shake.

Implicit in the observation that I was not afraid of "political chastisement" was the thought that such chastisement might lie ahead. Indeed it did. The Nixon White House manufactured dirt to use against me and I was criticized by those Republicans who thought the party was better off pushing Watergate under the rug. But what I lost among Republicans was more than made up for in my newfound popularity among Democrats and independents. In future years it was support from these voters that kept me in office. As a politician I wasn't hurt by Watergate, I was made by it.

McCord met in private hearings with the Senate committee several times toward the end of March 1973. After each, there was a burst of leaks to the news media. In part these leaks were aimed at making it appear that Gordon Liddy was the Watergate mastermind, and that blame for the scandal stopped with him. It was a repeat of the ridiculous approach that had so infuriated Judge Sirica in the Watergate trial.

Because of these leaks, I called a news conference in which I was critical of the committee.

I had smelled the Liddy tactic coming and said so: "Four days ago I told my own staff of my concern that a tactic would be used to lead the path of Watergate to Mr. Liddy's doorstep. . . . We would be negligent in our duties if we were to succumb to this Liddy tactic. . . . It is my analysis, and the analysis of my staff, that we are not going to carry this case on the back of this man, now being tossed out as the trail to follow."

As for the leaks, I had this to say: "To his credit, even Mr. McCord was willing to have the hearings open. It demeans all of us, as well as the free exercise of intelligent judgment by the American people, when our procedures require closed doors. . . . The committee rules as to our own confidentiality were not honored yesterday, and such a breach has no place in the search for truth with justice," I said.

Let me make a distinction regarding leaks. As recently as 1993, twenty years after the fact, a Washington lawyer who had been on the Watergate staff said I was the biggest leaker on the committee. What a long memory! And what a distorted one!

It is true that I worked closely with members of the press at times; they were the only people we could count on. I had very clear standards and goals in this regard. For example, during the hearings, I never asked questions at a reporter's request; it was not my function to carry their water. At the same time, however, some of the reporters my staff and I talked to had been working on Watergate almost since the day of the break-in and had good knowledge of details and good sources. Occasionally they had reports that seemed correct but which they couldn't confirm. They wouldn't print or air such reports but they could — and sometimes did — share them with my staff as leads worth pursuing.

A memo from one of my assistants toward the end of March 1973 is illustrative of our relationship with the press. In it was an analysis of the scandal as written by one newspaper reporter, a copy of a Justice Department investigative report on Watergate that had been given to us, a suggestion from another reporter that we interview Hugh Sloan (a Nixon reelection-committee official who was an important source in the *Washington Post*'s Watergate coverage) — and one or two other recommendations from reporters. And that was just one memo from one aide on one day.

Often the material my staff and I were coming up with put us far out on a limb, and it was at such moments that they or I would meet with trustworthy reporters. The idea was to ensure that as the material became public, our point of view was aired and represented as much as possible. I had to make damned sure that I could at least have some say in what the press would report regarding my findings. Had my staff and I made even a single mistake, we would have been ripped to shreds by both the Republicans and the Democrats; it was important, therefore, to present our fact-finding to the press. Watergate was no game. It was a deadly serious matter whose resolution, one way or the other, would have great impact on the course of national and world events.

Why make the material public at all at this stage? a reader may ask; why not let the investigation take its course? The answer gets to the heart of what was happening. As the Watergate Committee was getting started, there was ample reason to be concerned about how thorough a job it would do. In private conversation, John Dean told Nixon that Sam Ervin could be handled without much difficulty if his aides weren't around; Ervin's agreement preventing most senators and staff members and aides from seeing FBI reports was a sign that Dean was correct. So the first problem was that Ervin might unintentionally give away the store. I say unintentionally; no one in his right mind would question Ervin's sincerity in this investigation.

Second, there were the questions in the early stages about Howard Baker's role. In February Baker had met with Nixon without informing any of us. It was legitimate to wonder whether he was Nixon's mole on the committee.

I had a few particularly touchy moments with Baker. One came after he fired an aide of his. Earlier, the aide had mentioned to me that Baker was being fed material from the White House, even told me some of what was involved. The firing left me more than a little upset and I expressed that sentiment to Baker.

As the facts of the scandal became known, Baker could see that his friends in the White House had been misleading him, and he changed accordingly. But at the beginning of our collaboration, I had suspicions about him, and in return he wondered what in the world I was up to.

Lacking total confidence in Ervin and Baker, my staff members and I thought it possible that the committee's investigation might be coopted. Certainly that was what the plotters in the White House wanted. Even as we were starting to investigate, they were engaged in various contortions to continue the cover-up. They sought an extremely narrow investigation, limited only to the Watergate break-in. Because I was holding my own inquiry and getting close to some of the players, I knew it would have been adding to the cover-up had we circumscribed the committee's work in such a manner.

Of course, I wasn't alone in feeling that way, so I don't want to assume the role of being the one person who saw to it that the Senate inquiry got to the bottom of Watergate. One of several people, maybe, but not the only one. Nevertheless, having my findings aired in the press was a way of ensuring that the Ervin committee's investigation be as wide-ranging as necessary. As Searle Field puts it today, there was a delicate point sometime in April 1973 when it was not clear how forthright the inquiry would be.

One problem with the Senators on the committee, including me, was that we didn't expect to find so much fire behind the smoke. Surely, I did not; I didn't go into this as an anti-Nixon man, a tough prosecutor. I sat there openmouthed when Ed DeBolt told me what was already known to everybody in California.

Once I got into it, I ran a "let the chips fall where they may" inquiry. Because I did, I knew I was opening myself to attack.

A case in point was a nasty incident that lasted about a week over the role of H. R. Haldeman, Nixon's chief of staff in the White House.

On March 31, 1973, I met for eight or ten hours in Connecticut with Alfred Baldwin, a former FBI agent who had been recruited by the Watergate culprits to listen to the bugged conversations from a Howard Johnson's hotel room across from the Watergate building. As you'd expect, I got a lot of information from him.

The next day, a Sunday, I was on the CBS TV program *Face the Nation*, and I said on it that the Nixon reelection committee had been engaged in political espionage that went well beyond the Watergate break-in. I mentioned that Baldwin had outlined a broad range of surveillance on Capitol Hill, watching and reporting who went in and out of the offices of senators Charles Percy, Jacob Javits, Ted Kennedy, William Proxmire, and a few House members.

Baldwin and a high campaign official had told me by this time that Haldeman had been involved in planning and carrying out Watergate-type activities, if not the burglary itself. So I said on TV that day that there seemed to be an attitude at 1600 Pennsylvania of "who can do the dirtiest deed," and that "the time has come for Haldeman to step forward and explain. It is an absolute necessity that he testify before the committee."

As the chief of staff, it was Haldeman's obligation to accept the blame if it fell on him or, if he were guiltless, to at least explain what had happened. He was the top guy except for the president; he and Nixon set the tone.

"It's not just Watergate," I said. "It's not Watergate at all. It's whether or not we as Americans are going to accept a new standard for our presidential elections. . . . We've had a strength way beyond our numbers because we had ideals." (Did we? Do we still?)

Behind the scenes, the cover-up was breaking wide open

then. About a week earlier John Dean had tried but failed to have Nixon stop hush-money payments that were buying silence from the Watergate burglars. "God damn it, get the money!" Nixon told Dean. Dean, already implicated by Patrick Gray, was stuck more and more in the middle. Finally, on April 2, convinced that he was going to be made a fall guy, Dean began telling his story to the Watergate prosecutors. Of course, I had no idea that anything like that was taking place.

On April 3, I was the guest at one of the lesser-known Washington institutions, a "Sperling" breakfast. Named for Godfrey Sperling of the *Christian Science Monitor,* these sessions were held regularly in a hotel near the White House with fifteen or so well-known members of the press corps. I was asked to talk some more about Haldeman. Pointing out that I had no evidence of Haldeman directly ordering any illegal activity or committing any, I said, nevertheless, that "he has to accept responsibility as chief of staff. I think it would be quite proper for Mr. Haldeman to offer his resignation."

I spent a good deal of the day responding to reporters who wanted me to elaborate. The clamor was upsetting to some people, including Sam Ervin and Howard Baker. On April 4, without mentioning it to me, they put out a two-paragraph statement that repudiated my remarks.

"The Committee is concerned with certain news media accounts attributable to this Committee inferring that Mr. H. R. Haldeman, of the White House staff, was involved in the break-in and bugging of the Democratic National Committee Headquarters at the Watergate and other illegal activities in connection with the Presidential Campaign of 1972," the statement read. "In the interest of fairness and justice, the Committee wishes to state publicly that, as of this time, it has received no evidence of any nature linking Mr. Haldeman with any illegal activities in connection with the Presidential Campaign of 1972."

This unusual statement was a criticism of me for having the audacity to say that people at the top set the tone and should be accountable for the activities of those under them.

"Weicker Target of Senate Rebuff" was the headline in the April 5 *Washington Star-News.* The body of the article said that "the joint statement was being read in the Senate as a direct rebuff to Weicker. . . . It caused some uplifted eyebrows in the Senate cloakroom, where it was being read as a public chastisement of the junior member for his performance. A senior Democratic senator met a reporter outside the Senate and commented, " 'Did you see what they did to Lowell Weicker?' "

The news article also said that the statement had been drafted by Sam Dash at Ervin's request, and that Baker agreed to sign it willingly.

I was then promptly attacked in a *Washington Post* editorial that said, "The Connecticut Republican has been making quite a splash over the past few days, and in our estimation it has been regrettable." Things could get out of hand that quickly.

By then, many officials were in effect supporting Nixon by saying it was time to stop wallowing in Watergate. California governor Ronald Reagan said the people involved weren't really criminals and shouldn't be treated like criminals because they were not criminals at heart. Exactly what these fine gentlemen were if not criminals Reagan did not spell out. The fact is, politicians were setting a terrible example for the public. More and more, events were making it clear that the Nixon White House was a cauldron of corruption. And even as disclosures kept coming, more and more national leaders were acting as though nothing especially unusual had happened.

This failure of so many in the Washington establishment to even show indignation served to increase public cynicism sharply. Many people were so skeptical that they just turned off government, and Watergate, altogether. At the beginning, despite speaking out consistently, I got hardly any mail regarding Watergate. I can't tell you how upset that made me. Nobody seemed to care.

I made that point in an interview at the time with the *National Observer,* a now defunct publication. "I know this is going to sound naive and foolish," I said, "but I'm still young enough to remember that this seat is everything I dreamed about when I was a kid. I looked upon politicians as I looked upon baseball and hockey players. They were my idols. That isn't the case today. . . . Does the politician stand alongside the rock star now? No. No way. The politician has become almost a laughable type."

At this point someone in the White House tried to discredit me once and for all. The method was to claim, falsely, that I had taken illegal campaign contributions in my 1970 Senate campaign. At issue, almost incredibly, was a contribution of $71,000 to my election drive, directed to me by people working on behalf of Richard Nixon. Thus, had I been guilty of taking an illegal contribution, the person at least as guilty, the donor, was the president!

What had occurred was this: Under the campaign-financing laws of the day, a candidate could not personally accept cash gifts but staff members could. Six thousand dollars of the $71,000 was in cash, and had been accepted by an aide of mine, Phil Drake.

My recollection is that the person who distributed the money, a man named Jack Gleason, called my campaign headquarters and said, "I have a contribution for Congressman Weicker and I have to give it to him personally." He talked to Drake, who told him I was campaigning in Connecticut and could not go to Washington. So Gleason sent the contribution to Drake, and I never got any cash in my hands.

Receipt of all the funds was publicly disclosed, as the law required. Nevertheless, on April 10, 1973, Jack Gleason visited my office and warned that the White House was going to maintain that I had not reported all the funds I had received. Gleason had worked out of a Washington, DC, townhouse in 1970 when he distributed funds to me and other Republican candidates, including an unsuccessful Senate candidate in Texas, George Bush. Because of the location, the money came to be known as the "townhouse funds," or the "townhouse operation."

A few days afterward, reporters were tipped by someone in the White House that if they approached Gleason, they would find out about illegalities in the 1970 Weicker campaign. Some did, Gleason stated later on, but he told them there was no basis in fact for the allegations.

Subsequently, when the townhouse fund once again was used in an attempt to silence me, I asked the Watergate prosecutors to conduct an investigation, knowing I would be cleared. According to a *New York Times* article nine years later, in June of 1992, Gleason, interviewed by prosecutors, explained the cash part of the donations this way: "The purpose of these contributions was to set up possible blackmail for these candidates later on." The *Times* article quoted a 1974 prosecutors' memorandum as saying that the Nixon White House hoped to gain political leverage over the candidates "by placing cash in their hands which they might not report."

Watergate events now began to dominate the national news; it was as though nothing else was happening. But what was playing out in public was minor compared to what was transpiring in the investigators' office and in the White House.

By April 14 John Dean had told prosecutors in the US attorney's office that President Nixon was involved in the Watergate cover-up. On Sunday, April 15, Dean met with Nixon in the Oval Office and told him what he had done. Nixon kept standing near a curtain, leading Dean to suspect he was taping the conversation. (It was Dean's suspicion that led an Ervin committee staff member to ask and find out a few weeks later that there was a White House taping system.)

On April 16 Dean told Assistant US Attorney Earl Silbert about the break-in at Ellsberg's psychiatrist's office. From then on, it was just a matter of time for the political ruin of Richard Nixon. Once investigators knew about the Ellsberg break-in, White House officials could no longer maintain that Watergate was a stupid, isolated act planned and perpetrated by such a low-level figure as Gordon Liddy.

Dean also told prosecutors that day about the papers from Howard Hunt's safe that he and Ehrlichman had given to Pat Gray. Silbert immediately told his boss, Assistant Attorney General Henry Petersen, and that afternoon Petersen told Gray. The next morning, Gray phoned me, sounding almost panicky but not relating what his concern was.

On April 17 Nixon, his defenses crumbling, announced that there have been "major new developments in the case." No longer holding any good cards, he decided to bluff the rest of the game. Having claimed executive privilege for so long, he now said he would allow his aides to be questioned by the Watergate Committee. "Real progress has been made in finding the truth," he said on this date.

I, like many others, was pleased by the announcement but wary. "I think the spirit of getting at the truth which has slowly but surely been building in this country, whether by the citizens or the Senators, now has everybody in its grip," I said at the time. "Believe me, there will be no coverup. We are going to have the truth. We are going to have that story."

A couple of days later, John Dean made his first public statement about the Watergate scandal, saying he would not be made a scapegoat. "Anyone who believes this does not know me, know the true facts, nor understand our system of justice." Dean had not yet spoken to Sam Dash or anyone from the Watergate Committee.

Through one of those loose Washington connections — an associate of mine who knew an associate of Dean's lawyer — I began trying to set up a meeting with Dean. Like everyone else in Washington, I had lots of questions for him.

Before I got to see Dean, however, I got another call from Pat Gray. It came on the morning of Wednesday, April 25. I went to his office immediately, and out came the story of Ehrlichman and Dean giving him the Hunt papers and telling him they should never see the light of day.

The more I heard, the more infuriated I became that Gray, such a steady, reliable person, had been used in such a way. At our meeting Gray was desperate and frightened. As I left, I promised to get back to him quickly.

The more I thought about his situation, the more convinced I was that the only thing to do was go public with the story. I met with him again that afternoon to tell him so. "Pat, I'm going to do you the greatest favor in your life. You're not going to understand it now because you don't understand politics. We are going to put this story together from A to Z and we are going to go public with it."

Understandably, Gray was not enthusiastic, but he went along. He had no better alternative: the events had occurred, they were known to have occurred by a number of people, and, therefore, they were sure to get out. It would be best if they were presented in the most favorable light for Gray.

The next morning, the twenty-sixth of April, I talked with Gray on the phone and met later with several reporters to get the story out. I told them Gray had been abused by White House aides and I criticized him for being overly loyal and not independent enough. I said that Dean, Ehrlichman, Kleindienst, and Petersen had important questions to answer, such as why Dean gave the papers to Gray in the first place, and why Ehrlichman permitted it when he knew it was wrong.

The story appeared in newspapers and on TV on April 27, and Gray immediately resigned. Nixon named William Ruckelshaus as his replacement.

Gray was shamed by the disclosures, but I could see no way around that; what he had done would have been made known sooner or later, and with a worse spin. The next Sunday, for example, the White House press secretary falsely said that Gray had been forced out when he wasn't. There would have been a lot more of that kind of thing had we not gone to the press ourselves.

Coming clean probably helped Gray greatly. Others who had done no more were charged with crimes and disbarred as lawyers. Neither happened to Pat Gray. Now retired and living in Florida, he practiced law with his old Connecticut firm for ten or fifteen years after the Watergate scandal.

On April 25, the day Gray told me about having destroyed the Hunt papers, a more startling Watergate development was taking place, having to do with the Ellsberg case.

Word of the Ellsberg psychiatrist's break-in went from John Dean to the prosecutors to their boss, Henry Petersen, who mentioned it to Nixon. Nixon said the Ellsberg case was not Watergate-related, and to stay out of it. But Petersen told Kleindienst, and Kleindienst took it upon himself to tell Nixon that it was for investigators, not the president, to decide what was Watergate-related.

Kleindienst had been a loyal servant of Nixon's for a long time. But when he met with the president the afternoon of April 25, 1973, it was not to ask permission but to tell Nixon that word of the 1971 break-in was already en route to Judge W. Matthew Byrne, who was presiding over the Ellsberg trial.*

---

* Ellsberg had been charged with theft, violation of the Espionage Act, and conspiracy for taking and releasing the Pentagon Papers.

In Los Angeles the following day Judge Byrne sent jurors home, saying evidence in the case had been withheld. Two weeks later he called a mistrial and disclosed publicly what the evidence was.

The walls of the cover-up had crumbled, but Nixon kept trying to put the clamor to rest. On April 30, 1973, he announced the resignations of Haldeman, Ehrlichman, Dean, and Kleindienst. To succeed Kleindienst as attorney general, he chose someone already in his cabinet, defense secretary Elliot Richardson, and he gave Richardson authority to name a special Watergate prosecutor. Nixon hoped these moves would be interpreted as a signal that he had cut loose the perpetrators, that he was putting Watergate behind him and that everyone else should, too. It didn't work that way.

A few days later, on the evening of May 3, I had my first meeting with John Dean. It was at the home of Charles Shaffer, Dean's attorney, in suburban Rockville, Maryland, and had been set up by my aide Bob Herrema.

Dean was becoming a central figure in the scandal; it was natural for me to want to see him. He and Shaffer met with me, as Shaffer explained it later, because they thought of me as "a loose cannon" and wanted a firsthand impression.

"In the beginning," Shaffer said years afterward, "my feeling was that Weicker's posturing was not genuine but was being done for political capital. So we wanted to meet with him, to feel him out."

Our session lasted about twenty minutes. I had met Dean once before, apparently, but didn't remember it. As soon as the introductions were made, he said, "Lowell, I want to talk to you alone before we discuss anything."

We went to another room and he asked, "Are you sure you are going to be able to survive the attack of the White House on your campaign finances?" Once again, it was the townhouse operation aimed at me — something in which I hadn't done anything even remotely wrong.

I said, "Jesus, John, I don't remember doing anything illegal. I don't know anything about it."

He said, "Okay, as long as you are aware of it."

We then rejoined Shaffer and my assistants McGowan and Herrema. Dean synopsized everything that had occurred in the entire Watergate scandal. He was in a good position for that. Not only was he a key figure in the cover-up, but he had been reviewing details for his sessions with the prosecutors. When I say Dean synopsized *everything,* I mean everything, including Nixon's role in the cover-up.

In the short time our meeting lasted, Dean went a long way toward satisfying my curiosity about him and establishing a bond of trust. I thought of him as terribly unfortunate for having got caught up in such a tragedy. I had no reason to doubt his word then, or later. By coincidence, sometime earlier I had rented, but not yet moved to, a townhouse on Quay Street in Alexandria, Virginia. Dean lived on the corner when I first moved in and then bought the house across the street from me. We would run into each other and even dine out once in a while. I also became friendly with his wife, Maureen. When the Deans moved to California, I bought their house.

On May 17, 1973, the Ervin committee began holding its long series of televised hearings. It was not until June 25 that Dean began testifying, and by then he had been debriefed secretly for six weeks by Sam Dash. My encounter with him at Shaffer's home was the first Dean had with any representative of the Watergate Committee. As a result, I had as good an understanding of the fullness of the scandal as any of my colleagues, and certainly a better understanding than most.

6

Stealing Our Precious Heritage

ALL HELL was breaking loose as we prepared to open the Ervin committee hearings.

On May 11, Judge Byrne in Los Angeles announced a mistrial in the Ellsberg case.

On May 14, the number-two man at the CIA, Vernon Walters, testifying before another congressional committee, said pressure had been put on the CIA to cooperate in a cover-up of the Watergate scandal. In my office, I got a round of phone calls asking when I was going to switch political parties and become a Democrat. It was the second such series of calls in recent weeks.

On May 17, the new attorney general, Elliot Richardson, appointed the first Watergate special prosecutor, Archibald Cox. That day, our hearings began.

Senator Ervin had an eloquent opening statement: If what was charged about Watergate turned out to be true, he said, then what the burglars "were seeking to steal was not the jewels, money, or other property of American citizens, but something much more valuable — their precious heritage, the right to vote in a free election."

I saw the scandal in a similar light. "The gut question for the committee and country alike," I said as the hearings opened, "is and was, 'How much truth do we want?' A few men gambled that Americans wanted the quiet of efficiency rather than the turbulence of truth. . . . The story to come has its significance not in the acts of men breaking, entering and bugging the Watergate but in the acts of men who almost stole America."

What people had forgotten, I strongly believed at the time, was that it wasn't only Richard Nixon and his aides who were responsible for Watergate. Their actions had been taken because, with so much loud dissent taking place over the Vietnam War, many Americans had exhibited a yearning for quiet. The Congress and the press had become sheepish.

At the same time, I was beginning to notice a positive effect of Watergate as our hearings got under way. The debasing of the president had restored some balance to the three branches of government. For the first time in six years, the House of Representatives had asserted its control over war powers by limiting funds for operations in Cambodia. Through Judge Sirica, we were seeing the same signs of strength in the court system. And elements of the press that had been docile earlier were no longer bending to White House wishes.

My staff members and I spent hours preparing for every day of the Watergate hearings. In advance of a witness's testimony, all the senators got briefing papers from the committee counsel on what that person had said in closed session. My assistants supplemented these papers with material from our own inquiry, giving me lists of questions. Almost immediately, this special preparedness made a difference and was noticed.

The late columnist Joseph Kraft (whose telephone was among those tapped by the White House in 1969), wrote a highly complimentary column that appeared in newspapers on May 22, 1973.

"The point man on the committee," Kraft wrote, "the senator who has forced the pace of investigation, all along, is the Connecticut Republican, Lowell Weicker. . . . Weicker has made the big points so far in the Senate hearings. On the first day, he elicited the information that Jeb Stuart Magruder had files removed from his desk at Creep the day after the Watergate burglars were apprehended.* On the second day, Weicker showed that the Internal Security Division of the Justice Department . . . was collecting

---

* Magruder was the number-two person at the Committee for the Re-Election of the President, or Creep, reporting to John Mitchell.

security information and passing it out on a regular basis to Creep."

My actions and press plaudits were sticking in the White House craw. About this time a newspaper reporter got a call from a lobbyist who said he had contributed to my 1970 election campaign. The lobbyist said he had been approached by Charles Colson with the request that he call me and demand that I start acting like "a real Republican." Needless to say, the lobbyist never did call; I heard of the incident through the reporter. I had heard a good deal about Colson by then; the only thing complimentary was that he had a lot of nerve. Too bad it was so misdirected.

One of the first witnesses before the committee was James McCord, who got us off to a dramatic start, describing how he had been instructed to go to a pay telephone near his home and how, once there, the phone rang and he got a message: "Plead guilty. One year is a long time. You will get executive clemency. Your family will be taken care of and when you get out you will be rehabilitated and a job will be found for you."

Witnesses after McCord included Hugh Sloan, Maurice Stans, Jeb Magruder. Sloan was penitent; Stans denied any wrongdoing and was skewered in questioning by Sam Ervin.* Magruder implicated former attorney general John Mitchell in the planning of the Watergate break-in and the cover-up. The testimony of each was fascinating, and each helped raise the theme, expressed time and again by Senator Baker, that the real question was, "What did the president know and when did he know it?" That question became a drumbeat as the time neared for John Dean to take the stand, for it was no secret that he was going to implicate Nixon in the cover-up.

There was a one-week break in the hearings, brought about by a visit to Washington of Soviet leader Leonid Brezhnev. Almost everyone seemed to think that tact and delicacy demanded the hiatus. Everyone except me. The committee voted, and sure enough

---

* "Do you not think that men who have been honored by the American people as you have, ought to have their course of action guided by ethical principles which are superior to the minimum requirements of the criminal laws?" Ervin asked Stans at one point. When Stans pointed out that there was a history of transgression in American politics, Ervin responded, "There has been murder and larceny in every generation but that hasn't made murder meritorious or larceny legal."

the vote came out six in favor of a break to one — me — against. I still think I was on the right side here.

"There is no reason why we can't accomplish both the work of the committee and Mr. Brezhnev's visit," I maintained. "Both are important. But it is also important that Mr. Brezhnev understand that the real strength of this country and its democracy is that we do these things out in the open and don't tailor them to any individual. The hearings would not in any way diminish the importance of Mr. Brezhnev's visit nor our negotiations."

Our republic is a hell of a lot more robust than a lot of the politicians in Washington believed then or believe now!

On the twenty-fifth of June, John Dean began testifying before the Senate Watergate Committee. (Even as he did, the phones in my office were ringing off the hook with a third harassing round of calls suggesting that Lowell Weicker switch political parties.) With Maureen seated behind him, he began by saying that President Nixon was involved in the cover-up but that he "did not realize or appreciate at any time the implications of his involvement." Then, for more than six hours, Dean read from a prepared statement of 245 pages. He described the atmosphere in the White House from the time he arrived in 1970 — the concern about antiwar protests, news leaks, the desire for political intelligence.

"A do-it-yourself White House, regardless of the law," was the way Dean described it. It was such a climate that led to Watergate, he said. He told of the early days of the cover-up, said he was a go-between for Haldeman, Ehrlichman, and the reelection committee; he went over his talks with Patrick Gray, with Richard Kleindienst and Henry Petersen; told how the CIA was brought in to obstruct justice. In closing, he described his concern that he was being set up as a fall guy.

Along with his testimony, Dean introduced dozens of memoranda and other documents. From my meeting with him in early May, I had a good idea of where he was taking us. On day two of his testimony, under questioning from me, he described in some detail the Huston plan for domestic spying. I encouraged him to continue speaking about abuses in various executive agencies, and eventually he mentioned the existence of a so-called enemies list maintained at the White House.

"I'm not going to ask who was on it," I said; "I'm afraid you might answer." The next day Dean entered the names for the record, along with his own previously made recommendations on "how we can use the available federal machinery to screw our political enemies."

Lawyers have a maxim about not asking questions in court unless they know the answer; that was how it was with my questioning of Dean and other witnesses. A reader may say, why ask a question if you know the answer? Well, in most court cases it would be for the effect the answer has on a jury. In the matter of the Senate Watergate hearings, the jury was the American people, and it was extremely important that they knew the extent of the corruption in the White House.

In questioning Dean, minority counsel Thompson and Republican senator Gurney tried to cast doubt on his credibility, blackening his motives and his interpretation of events. On the other side, majority counsel Dash and Senator Ervin were extremely protective of Dean.

Dean testified for five days. By the end, the matter of whether there would be a narrow or a broad Senate investigation had been put to rest. It was very broad. I no longer had any concern whatsoever about our inquiry being improperly contained, and I turned my efforts to the interpretive side, trying to explain the significance of Watergate. I did that at every opportunity — in questioning, in comments at the hearings, in interviews with the media.

After Dean's second day of testimony, for example, I was interviewed on the *Today* show and asked if I believed Dean's story. "Yes," I responded. "I'm not saying I believe one hundred percent of John Dean's story, and I'm sure there are many self-serving statements in the testimony; I'm sure he's motivated by a variety of considerations. But is he getting facts out before the American people that never would have come out were it not for John Dean? — And the answer is yes."

The interview continued in this fashion:

Q. You seemed to be suggesting yesterday that you had a feeling the president had set up a sort of little personal or private secret police force hidden in the Justice Department. Were you getting at something like that?

WEICKER: As you know there was the [Huston] plan of 1970. It called for bugging and wiretapping and breaking-and-entering and mail cover and all the rest. Now we know that the director of the FBI objected strenuously to such a plan being put in force. Here was just one example of the actual apparatus being set up by Mr. Dean with the approval of the White House.

We already have examples of the FBI engaging in activities of hiring student informers, which they hadn't done prior to the 1970 plan being raised. We already see the security arms of the government — sure, independent of this particular group, the IEC (Intelligence Evaluation Committee) — engaging in activities of threat and almost blackmail against American citizens.*

While Dean was on the stand, attacks on me, put out by the White House, continued. On June 26, a reporter called my office to say that Charles Colson had told him I was involved in campaign-fund illegalities in 1970. It was the same old canard. I must have been pretty clean, if this was all the White House could come up with. But I was annoyed by the pestering, and I mentioned on the *Today* show that there were some public and private pressures put on members of the committee.

Just before nine that same morning I got a call from Leonard Garment, an attorney for Nixon, asking if I could back up the charges. I reviewed the exact comments I had made, described the phony allegations over my 1970 campaign, and suggested that if the White House wanted to do something constructive, it should disavow Charles Colson. I could see that we were getting into something of a skirmish here, so instead of simply playing a game for the media, I formally notified the senior members of the committee, Ervin and Baker, and Special Prosecutor Archibald Cox

---

* The IEC, formed in December 1970, included representatives of the White House, the CIA, the FBI, the National Security Agency, the departments of Justice, Treasury, and Defense, and the Secret Service.

of attempts to influence a member of the committee. My request to Cox was that he investigate for possible criminal action.

Thursday, June 28, was Dean's fourth day of testifying. That afternoon, in my round of questioning, I let it all hang out. I mentioned Colson by name as having spread malicious, false rumors about campaign-funding illegalities. I elicited as testimony from Dean what he had told me back on May 3, that there would be a White House attempt to embarrass me over campaign contributions. I read from a transcript of a taped phone call between Ehrlichman and Kleindienst in which President Nixon was quoted as saying "it wouldn't be too bad . . . to take a swing" at Weicker's comments on the scandal.

I mentioned some of the crimes the executive branch had been implicated in: "Conspiracy to obstruct justice; conspiracy to intercept wire or oral communications; subornation of perjury; conspiracy to obstruct a criminal investigation; conspiracy to destroy evidence; conspiracy to file false sworn statements; conspiracy to commit breaking and entering; conspiracy to commit burglary; misprision of a felony; filing of false statements; perjury; breaking and entering; burglary; interception of wire and oral communications; obstruction of a criminal investigation; attempted interference with administration of Internal Revenue laws; attempted unauthorized use of Internal Revenue information."

And finally, I made a fairly emotional soliloquy.

There are going to be no more threats, no more intimidations, no innuendoes, no working through the press to go ahead and destroy the credibility of individuals.

If the Executive branch of government wants to meet the standards that American people set for it in their minds, then the time has come to stop reacting and to stop playing this type of game, and either disavow it completely or make very specific charges that apparently are being leaked either against the Committee members, or against the witnesses appearing before this Committee.

I am going to conclude this way, Mr. Chairman, and then I am done, and I have tried, as I say, to accomplish one role that I think needed accomplishing in these hearings: Among the rumors that are floated around — and this isn't hearsay — there have been, on three different occasions, plants to the effect that I am a disloyal Republican and that I am going to switch to the Democratic Party.

In your memorandum, Mr. Dean, you had me described, whether it was you or Mr. Haldeman or whoever was there, as an independent who would give the White House trouble. But I say before you, and I say before the American people and this Committee, that I am here as a Republican and, quite frankly, I think that I express the feelings of the forty-two other Republican Senators whom I work with, and the Republicans of the State of Connecticut and, in fact, the Republican party, far better than these illegal, unconstitutional and gross acts which have been committed over the past several months by various individuals.

Let me make it clear, because I have got to have my partisan moment, Republicans do not cover up; Republicans do not go ahead and threaten; Republicans do not go ahead and commit illegal acts; and God knows Republicans don't view their fellow Americans as enemies to be harassed but rather, I can assure you, this Republican, and those whom I serve with, look upon all Americans as human beings to be loved and won. Thank you very much, Mr. Chairman.

If I had gotten a little carried away, so did the audience, which broke into rare, sustained applause. Moments later the committee adjourned for the day. That evening I had dinner out with Bill Shure, the committee staff member who also reported to me. As we entered the restaurant, diners saw me and began applauding. It was a heady feeling.

My comments of June 28, 1973, drew an amazing reaction from all across the United States. The first thing that happened the next morning was that Charles Colson showed up in my office, bright and early. Colson had left the White House upon Nixon's reelection in 1972 and gone into law practice with a highly regarded Washington attorney, David Shapiro. The two of them appeared at my door before eight, ostensibly to tell Colson's side of the story.

But I knew too much about Colson, and they weren't going to soft-soap me. I just wasn't interested in listening to garbage.

Our conversation got heated right from the beginning. Colson was a former marine, a tough guy. He said he had nothing to do with the drafting of the enemies list. He said he had come to my office because he wanted to tell me the truth, and that he had brought a statement.

I said I had seen his statement and asked if he would also disavow a memo saying that the income taxes of a certain administration opponent should be audited. He admitted writing it. "That's disgusting," I told him; "you can just get your ass out of my office." I said to his face what I had brought up at the hearing — that I knew he was spreading false stories about my 1970 campaign.

The meeting got very tense. In one sense I have to hand it to Colson; most people would have got the idea and left. Not him.

I asked if he had called my father in an attempt to bring me in line. Dad hadn't told me of such a call, but someone else did. "I never called your father; I don't know your father," Colson said.

"I know you don't know my father, because if you did, you wouldn't have made that call."

Colson said he was proud of what he had done for the president, and was sorry if I had a grudge against him.

"How could you be proud after the disservice you've done him?" I asked. At that point both of us started shouting. We stood up, squared off as if to fight. I once again told him to get out, and this time he did.

During the rest of the day I got 1,143 telegrams and mailgrams regarding what I had said the day before. Of them, 18, or 1.6 percent, were critical of me. A woman from Texas wrote, "With friends like you and John Dean Mr. Nixon does not need an enemies list." A California man wrote, "You should resign. You do not practice what you preach. President innocent until proven guilty."

Most were quite different.

From a woman named Kelly in Colorado: "No longer am I embarrassed that some of my best friends are Republicans. Thank you, sir."

From a couple in Ohio: "Thank God for Americans like you."

From Vermont: "Washington, Lincoln, Teddy Roosevelt and God are proud of your actions today."

From Wisconsin: "Your pursuit of truth and resistance to pressure from high places have been beautiful for us to behold. . . . Your independent Republicanism is in the finest tradition of our nation's history in which truth is our foremost legacy. Thank you for your vigor, your heat and your concern."

From Oregon: "As I watched your angry impassioned stand re Watergate, etc., I was thrilled beyond words. I too gave you a standing ovation. In my living room all alone today I saw a tall, tall man. . . . I have never been so moved, so thrilled, and so stunned. Never have I been so awed in man's honest fury."

The sincerity, depth of emotion, and the nature of the observations moved me more than I can say, and June 29 was just the first day. Letters came at a furious pace. One that I am proud of was from retired US army general Matthew B. Ridgway, the noted World War II hero who replaced Douglas MacArthur as the leader of the American troops in the Korean War.

Ridgway asked that I show his letter to his friends, Senate leaders Mike Mansfield and Hugh Scott, and that I publish it if I thought it proper. He said he had watched me on TV "and thought at long last here was one highly placed official in our government with the moral courage to restate Americanism at its best; to rise to the stature of those great patriots — Washington, Franklin, Jefferson, Madison and their colleagues — whose vision, moral courage, wisdom, and integrity brought out of the Constitutional Convention of 1787 the finest instrument for the government of men which has yet been devised."

7

The Tragedy of Watergate

AFTER JOHN DEAN, the main witnesses to come before the Ervin committee were John Mitchell, H. R. Haldeman, and John Ehrlichman. I had unpleasant exchanges with each of them. On July 16, after Mitchell was done but before the other two were to testify, the Watergate scandal suddenly was pointed in a new direction. That day a former White House aide, Alexander Butterfield, said a taping system had been installed in 1970 to capture every conversation in the Oval Office and elsewhere in the White House. For those following Watergate as a criminal case, the question became "What did the President say and when did he say it?"

Despite that turn, there was still some startling testimony before the committee. On July 23, 1973, Gordon Strachan, an aide to Haldeman, said that in the 1972 elections, a hundred Democrats, mostly from the South, had the blessing of the White House because they either supported Nixon on the Vietnam War or for some other reason.

I knew what Strachan had to say because I had heard it in his closed-door testimony, but I wanted the American people to hear it also.

> STRACHAN: The goal was not to give a tremendous amount of support to Republicans that would oppose these Congressmen. . . .
>
> WEICKER: In other words, in the instance of certain Republican candidates in the South, support was withheld from

them because their Democratic opponents had supported the President on the war, would that be a fair
paraphrase?

STRACHAN: Yes, that is my understanding.

The arithmetic of it meant that Nixon the Republican was
covertly supporting 42.5 percent of all the Democrats running for
Congress. Things like this drove me nuts. I don't remember anyone
else commenting or complaining about Strachan's testimony, but I
sure did. What we had were Republicans doing in Republicans,
and it was infuriating. "Put in the bluntest terms," I said, "the
Republican party took a dive in the 1972 congressional races at
White House direction." Yet those of us who disagreed with Richard Nixon on issues were supposed to be the bad Republicans.

On July 27 John Ehrlichman and I went at it for about fifteen minutes while he was on the stand. I asked him why he had
hired Anthony J. Ulasewicz, a former New York City policeman, to
be an undercover agent for Nixon. Ulasewicz, paid by Kalmbach in
California, had started a bunch of sleazy investigations in 1969,
only months after Nixon took office. Ehrlichman said politicians
had an "affirmative obligation" to investigate their opponents' private lives.

"Do you mean to tell me and this committee," I asked, "that
you consider private investigators going into sexual habits, drinking habits, domestic problems and personal social activities as a
proper subject for investigation during the course of a political
campaign?"

Ehrlichman said he did, that it was important for the American people to know if members of the Senate had serious drinking
habits, for example.

I mentioned that I had run in eight political campaigns — two
primaries and six races against Democrats — and never had I spied
on my opponents' private lives, nor they on mine, as far as I knew.

With a smirk, Ehrlichman's response to that was, "I know
that, in your situation, your life-style is undoubtedly impeccable,
and there wouldn't be anything of issue like that."

"I'm not an angel," I said.

"I thought you were," Ehrlichman snapped back.

"Believe me, I am not."

At one point when I was being critical of Ehrlichman, chairman Ervin rapped his gavel, starting a lunch break. I went out for a quick bite with Bill Shure, who asked if I had seen the hate in Ehrlichman's eyes as the morning session ended.

"He just sat there staring at you. He wanted to kill you," Shure said.

Following Ehrlichman as a witness was H. R. Haldeman, Nixon's chief of staff. In three days of testimony he said about 150 times that he couldn't remember one thing or another. I don't know who he thought he was fooling; the American people knew President Nixon didn't choose some dunce to be his top assistant.

On August 1, 1973, Haldeman's second day, I confronted him with two documents. One concerned plans for an October 1971 Nixon rally in Charlotte, North Carolina; the other had to do with a February 1973 effort to link demonstrations and so-called Communist money to the Democrats and their 1972 presidential candidate, George McGovern.

The Charlotte memo was from a White House advance man to Haldeman and warned that demonstrators would be present for Nixon's visit and that they would be violent and carry "extremely obscene signs." In the margin Haldeman had written, "Good." The memo also stated that the demonstration would be aimed at the Reverend Billy Graham as well as Nixon. At that point, Haldeman wrote in the margin, "Great."

In other words, Haldeman thought a violent, obscene demonstration against Nixon and Billy Graham could create sympathy for the president, and therefore he loved the idea. The more violent and obscene, the better.

My question to Haldeman was, "What mentality is it in the White House that goes ahead and indicates 'good' when the word 'violence' is mentioned, when 'obscene' is mentioned, at which violence and obscenity is to be directed against the President of the United States. How in any way can that be good?"

Haldeman's explanation was that the grosser the conduct, the clearer it would be that hecklers of Nixon were violence-prone extremists.

The 1973 memo, which Haldeman took responsibility for, said, "We need to get our people to put out the story on the foreign or Communist money that was used in support of demonstrations against the President in 1972. We should tie all 1972 demonstrations to McGovern and thus to the Democrats as part of the peace movement."

The *Washington Post* account of this session said I "bristled with anger" as I raised this issue with Haldeman. "This type of business, when it emanates from the highest councils in the land, I think it is a disgrace," I said. "I don't think there has been any change in tactics from the election campaign of '72 as to when you sit before this committee right now, Mr. Haldeman."

As had happened with Ehrlichman, at one point when we broke for lunch, a live TV camera remained focused on Haldeman's face and he could be seen staring at me. My father was watching in New York, and he called to ask if I had any extra security. No, I said. Well, he said, I should think about getting some; never in his life had he seen as much hate in a man's eyes.

Around this time I was asked on the *Today* show what my response was to criticism that I had been "a little rough" with some of the witnesses. My answer, then and now, was that "these people were a little rough on an awful lot of innocent people in the United States."

My mail kept coming. My office kept count and responded to each communication. Before Watergate I would get about five hundred letters on Mondays and another thousand the rest of the week. During Watergate, I was getting five times as much, on the average.

By this time it was clear to me that our hearings had succeeded in explaining as well as possible exactly what Watergate was, leaving little to the imagination. The Constitution had been raped. Politics at the presidential level had been reduced to a level akin to the gutter.

In July 1973 there was another unpleasant incident regarding the townhouse funds from the 1970 campaign. George Bush, who himself got $112,000 in townhouse contributions for his unsuccessful Senate campaign in Texas, had become chairman of the Republican National Committee earlier in 1973. He called me on the telephone one day and said he had in his possession the list of everyone who had gotten contributions from this fund. He then asked me if he should burn the list.

This was a very peculiar question, coming as it did not long after I had requested publicly that the special prosecutor's office investigate the townhouse fund. Destroying potential evidence is a criminal offense. It came to mind that the call might be an attempt to set me up, and I wondered if Bush was taping it. My response would have been the same whether he was or wasn't.

"Until now," I said, "Watergate has been a scandal of the Nixon reelection committee. You burn that list and you're making it a scandal of the entire Republican party."

Since then, Bush has denied suggesting that the records be burned, and that's fine with me. But that is one conversation, shall we say, that was burned in my mind. I know what he said. If there was a misunderstanding, it was on his end.

On August 13, 1973, I went to the federal penitentiary in Danbury, Connecticut, to see the four Watergate burglars who had ties to Cuba. It was Bernard Barker's daughter who invited me; once there I was met at first only by Barker, with the understanding that the others would come in later. He told me how he and his associates got involved in Watergate.

Howard Hunt first contacted him on April 16, 1971, Barker said, and then not for several months afterward. He said Hunt told him a group was being formed in the White House to operate above the FBI and CIA, that it would be working on national-security matters. Barker said, therefore, he thought he was working for the government in the Ellsberg break-in and Watergate.

Hunt talked about resuming raids on Cuba, Barker said, and even about the possible assassination of Castro. I asked if he had engaged in other break-ins for Hunt aside from that of Ellsberg's psychiatrist's office and the Watergate, and Barker said no.

Our conversation was mainly Barker telling me of the hardships he and his family were suffering. Then the others came in. One of them, Eugenio Martinez, was very dignified, articulate, and emotional. He started off by saying he never dreamed he would be able to sit down face-to-face with a US senator, but that I had been honest and frank in the hearings and that was why he wanted to talk to me. He said he also felt that I was somewhat of a romantic.

It had been reported that Martinez had worked for the CIA; he told me he had served for thirteen years, under presidents Kennedy, Johnson, and Nixon. He said he knew a lot that he couldn't talk about because it would hurt the interests of the United States. He said he had made more than 350 missions between Cuba and the United States since Castro came to power. He described taking part in the disastrous 1961 Bay of Pigs attack in a twenty-eight-foot wooden boat without gas to return, and escaping in the same boat by drifting in the current.

Martinez said Hunt represented "maximum authority" to him. He said he had languished in horrible jails in Cuba with rats eating at his feet and other tortures and difficulties but that he never complained, feeling it was done for the US government and that it was his job to put up with such things.

I will never forget Martinez's parting comment: "In my country José Marti is a great hero. He crossed the water once. I have crossed the water a hundred times for your government, and look where I am."

All four were disillusioned with Hunt. Even after they encountered him in prison, they said, he wouldn't discuss their plight or the situation with them at all.

Martinez said Cuba had over five thousand agents in the United States and that his CIA job in Miami was to screen Cuban immigrants, looking for agents, saboteurs, provocateurs. He said his highest pay from the CIA was $8,000 a year. He also said that had they not been caught at the Watergate office building, he would have quit the group because of its highly unprofessional bungling. Martinez said the Cubans had no money and were desperate.

Frank Sturgis then talked for a while. He aired a suspicion that James McCord was a double agent, involved in the break-in and deliberately seeing to it they were caught. It was reasonable for Sturgis to think that way; why shouldn't conspirators have conspiracy theories? But there was no credible evidence that McCord was any sort of double agent.

I asked the four men when they first realized that their work for Hunt was not a CIA operation. Barker said he wasn't sure yet: "I never fully realized."

I stayed with them for about six hours. I was sympathetic to these men but told them I was not exonerating them in my mind, and made no commitments to them. These were the little guys in Watergate, and they were being punished more severely than some of the big shots. Back in Washington, I communicated my views to corrections officials.*

A few days after that the special prosecutor's office cleared me of any possible wrongdoing in connection with the townhouse fund. I was certifiably clean.

In the prosecutor's office's notes of an interview with Jack Gleason on the townhouse records is a line that says, "Bush called Weicker, asked whether he should burn them."

Every now and then something totally wacky happened in the course of Watergate. In the middle of September, 1973, I got a two-and-a-half-page letter from Meldrim Thomson, Jr., the governor of New Hampshire, a person whose politics made the radical right seem only slightly off center. Thomson had one of the weirdest complaints I have ever heard. Two Watergate investigators, he wrote, had appeared in his state *without his permission* and had been asking questions of a doctor and another person. Thomson wanted such activities ceased. I couldn't resist a temptation to get a little playful, so I made a copy of his letter, put a note at the end of it, and mailed it back to him.

The note said:

Dear Governor:

I thought you should know some nut is using the official state letterhead and forging your signature to hate mail.

Sincerely,
Lowell Weicker

At one point I got an angry telegram from John Wayne because of a White House memo I had made public: "For your infor-

---

* In January 1975 Judge Sirica ordered their release. I said in a statement at the time, "Since my views were made known in a letter to Judge Sirica, I'm clearly delighted this action was taken."

mation I have never asked for nor received IRS favors nor have I
needed them. What I need is protection from cheap politicians like
you. IRS has reviewed my taxes annually for 30 years now. You will
find no difference caused by politics. I resent your using Senatorial
privilege to throw my name around."

I suggested in a response that Wayne direct his comments to
the White House, and sent him a copy of an internal executive-
branch memorandum to John Dean dated September 30, 1971,
showing a deficiency for 1966 and audits from 1966 through 1969
that were still open. "The material requested regarding John
Wayne is not yet in," the note said.

On September 21, 1973, the nomination of Henry Kissinger to be
secretary of state was voted on in the Senate. I voted against, the
only Republican to do so. I considered Kissinger a brilliant and
capable man, and I wished him success. But as Nixon's national-
security adviser, Kissinger had been deeply involved in the wiretapping of the thirteen administration officials and four news reporters in 1969; they were even called "the Kissinger wiretaps."

"I don't want the United States to accept a little law breaking,
a little spirit breaking in the name of security or the greater good,"
I said in a speech shortly before the vote.

As the result of a scandal unrelated to Watergate, the vice
president of the United States, Spiro T. Agnew, resigned from
office on October 11, 1973. I sent President Nixon a list of three
possible successors: Senator Barry Goldwater, former secretary of
state William P. Rogers, and Senator Edward W. Brooke. He chose
Congressman Gerald Ford, who, in my view, ended up being the
best president of my adult lifetime.

The Watergate Committee's role was essentially over by now, even
though hearings continued into the fall and were to resume briefly
in 1974. Through television, Senator Ervin, Senator Baker, Sam
Dash, and the rest of us had taken Americans on a venture that
would have been unfathomable to previous generations in any nation. It was the public-affairs equivalent of the first moon landing.
Into living rooms, dens, bars — anyplace there was a TV — had
come high drama and low comedy, some of the mightiest of the

mighty, the haughtiest of the haughty. I heard from citizens who said they watched the hearings all day on commercial television and then all evening as they ran again on public stations.

Always edifying was the sometimes sharp, sometimes florid rhetoric provided by Senator Ervin, hearkening back to the politics of eras past. At one point Ervin summed up the scandal in this fashion:

> I think the Watergate tragedy is the greatest tragedy this country has ever suffered. I used to think that the Civil War was our country's greatest tragedy, but I do remember that there were some redeeming features about the Civil War in that there was some spirit of sacrifice and heroism displayed on both sides. I see no redeeming features in Watergate.

Using the "reasonable person" standard, I am sure that, because of our hearings, the administration of Richard Nixon was seen as one of the dirtiest, if not the dirtiest, in the nation's history. Any reasonable person called on to judge Nixon in court, that is, would have concluded that the president and his chief assistants were up to their eyebrows in muck.

Nevertheless, Nixon seemed to persevere. In August 1973, as public interest began to wane, he had the chutzpah to say, "We must now move on from Watergate to the business of the people" — as if Watergate were nothing more than a summer diversion. What was worse, national leaders tended to go along with him, saying the country shouldn't wallow in Watergate. As far as anyone could tell, it was not clear that Nixon would suffer any punishment other than embarrassment.

That was about to change.

From the time Alexander Butterfield revealed the existence of a White House taping system, our committee and Archibald Cox, the special prosecutor, had tried to acquire some of the tapes. Was there a simpler way to determine the involvement or lack of involvement of Nixon? If so, I didn't know it. But despite court orders, the president kept refusing to turn over any tapes.

On Friday, October 19, 1973, Nixon announced a "compromise" that, if allowed, would have gotten him off the hook entirely. Called the "Stennis plan," the idea was for Nixon to review the tapes and submit to Judge Sirica a written transcript of what he said were the parts relevant to the Watergate scandal. By choosing the segments himself, Nixon ostensibly would be protecting the principle of executive privilege. Then, to verify that the transcripts were accurate, Senator John Stennis of Mississippi would listen to them. One more feature of the scheme was that Special Prosecutor Archibald Cox would not be allowed to seek other tapes or records of Nixon's conversations.

This plan was so bad, I could spend a chapter on what was wrong with it. It was incredible at that stage that anyone would trust Nixon to select the evidence to be heard in Watergate. And any fool would know that Cox could never accept the constraint forced on him. Poor John Stennis; he didn't need this headache. At age seventy-two, he was recuperating from gunshot wounds inflicted by a mugger outside his home in Washington.

As ridiculous as the idea was, it was almost a fait accompli when I heard about it. Stennis said he didn't exactly understand his role, but sure, he would review the tapes. Terrific! The real disaster was that the two chief members of the Senate Watergate Committee, Ervin and Baker, were in on the deal. The proposal, in fact, had been cooked up in the White House in an hour-long meeting that Friday afternoon. Ervin had been summoned from New Orleans, Baker from Chicago to attend.

The first reaction from many leaders, as usual, was to support Nixon. You had to wonder where these people had been! Senate Democratic leader Mike Mansfield said, "I think it's a move to avoid a constitutional confrontation." As a counterbalance, he also said that Cox's position — expected opposition, that is — "will have to be given full consideration." Overall, however, Mansfield, who had been largely responsible for creating the Watergate Committee in the first place, had made it clear even before October 19 that he wanted Watergate put behind, investigations ended.

The comments of Hugh Scott, the Republican Senate leader and a man I admired, almost made me gag: "A very wise solution has been reached," he said.

A few others joined in this bold attempt to pluck Nixon out of the Watergate fire. Senator Eastland said, "I think it's a fine compromise." Senator Wallace Bennett of Utah said it was "a joint expression of faith both in the Senate and in Senator Stennis." The Democratic Speaker of the House, Carl Albert, said the proposal was "interesting"; Gerald Ford, the vice president–designate, said it was "a reasonable, fair solution to an unfortunate problem."

I was baffled by comments from other Watergate Committee members. Senator Inouye, my friend, said he had not been consulted in advance but "there may have been some good reason for them to concur with the President." Senator Talmadge said, "I have complete confidence in Senator Stennis's integrity and I am satisfied with the President's decision in this regard."

I was stunned. It was back to square one, when Ervin and Baker agreed that they would be the only senators allowed to look at FBI reports.

As had happened several times earlier, Watergate was on the verge of disappearing. The hearings were pretty well exhausted, and the president was about to dance away, escorted by half the US Senate. I never was anti–Richard Nixon, and I'm still not. But the illegalities he was involved in and the rape of the Constitution were too vast to be put aside as politics as usual.

A few days earlier, purely by accident, I had run into John Dean in front of our townhouses on Quay Street. He had just pleaded guilty to obstructing justice in the Watergate cover-up. Nixon's status came up.

"Is there something else?" I asked Dean. "Something we overlooked?"

His answer was no, probably not. "Except for the tax fraud."

Tax fraud? Tax fraud? Tax fraud!

8

Tax Fraud? Tax Fraud!

I WAS BACK in Connecticut on October 20, 1973, as I often was on weekends, and I held a press conference that morning at my Bridgeport office. I said the Stennis plan was "a hollow deal." I pointed out that Nixon had pledged not to interfere with the work of the special prosecutor, and I said I was disappointed that Ervin and Baker had gone along.

"The old courtesies and accommodations of Washington's power structure don't sit well with a sensitive and intelligent American people," I said. "Rather than appearing wise and honorable, last night's compromise looks like what it is — a deal between an evasive president and an easily diverted Congress."

I also tried to make another point. People who followed the scandal were becoming Watergate junkies. The more news there was, the more they wanted. Yesterday's horror story was quickly put aside; as a nation we were beginning to think of low behavior as normal because there was so much of it. "The press, the public and the Congress," I said, "have over the past months been bombed into insensitivity by the absurd and deceitful being presented as the highest thought from the highest office in the land."

That Saturday lives in the Watergate annals as the day of the Saturday Night Massacre. Special Prosecutor Archibald Cox could not accept Nixon's demand that he not seek other taped White House conversations. He would not resign, so Nixon ordered Attorney General Elliot Richardson to fire him. Richardson refused and was called to the White House that Saturday afternoon to hand in his own resignation. The number-two man at the Justice Department, William Ruckelshaus, was then ordered to fire Cox and he too refused and resigned. At that point the third in charge, Robert Bork, did fire Cox.* The files in the special prosecutor's office were sealed and FBI agents put in place to see that staff members removed nothing. Richardson's and Ruckelshaus's offices also were sealed off and guarded.

These activities were not revealed until 8:30 at night, when everything had been done. Nixon's press secretary, Ron Ziegler, announced that the office of special prosecutor no longer existed and that its functions were being taken over by the Justice Department.

There was an immediate firestorm of criticism, with some people, including a number of leaders in Washington, fearing that Nixon had gone over the deep end. A few days earlier, the president, citing intelligence reports of Soviet troop movements, had put American servicemen on "red alert," the highest state of military preparedness. The Saturday Night Massacre, coming right after that, sent Senate leaders Mansfield and Scott to the military Joint Chiefs of Staff in alarm. The two were told that, in fact, there had been no intelligence reports suggesting the need for a red alert. Mansfield and Scott then became concerned that Nixon might declare martial law. They discussed that with the military leaders, and drew from them agreement to consult with Congress before acting on any rash presidential edict. We have never been close to a coup d'etat in this country. As far as I know, this is as close as we got to fear of a coup.

Millions of letters and telegrams began to descend on Capitol Hill in the wake of the Saturday Night Massacre. At my office by noon the following Wednesday had come 1,843 pieces of mail, 1,808 opposing Nixon and 35 in his favor — an opposition level of 98 percent. The first hesitant steps toward impeachment now began. In some newspapers, editorial writers asked that Nixon resign.

Nixon saw that a gesture on his part was needed. On Tuesday, the twenty-third of October, he said he would submit the tapes of

---

* Yes, the same Robert Bork, later Judge Bork (but not to be Supreme Court Justice Bork).

nine conversations to the Watergate prosecutors and our Senate committee. As public pressure grew, Nixon also agreed to restore the special prosecutor's office. A successor to Archibald Cox, Leon Jaworski of Texas, was named on November 1. Slowly the Watergate criminal investigation got back on track.

My efforts, however, had already turned in the direction pointed out by John Dean: Nixon's taxes.

For the years 1968 through 1972, Richard Nixon claimed enormous tax deductions based on charitable gifts of his prepresidential papers to the United States. In doing so, he was was following a pattern set by his predecessor, Lyndon B. Johnson. Lawyers for both, it seemed, would estimate the tax debt at the end of each year and then determine how much of a deduction they felt like claiming. It's a nice way to do your taxes, if you can get away with it.

Johnson's use of this dodge angered many of those in Congress who wrote the tax laws, so Congress set a date — July 25, 1969 — after which such a gift would no longer be deductible. There was no question of the legality of Nixon's 1968 claim, as he had presented a proper deed of the gift when it was transferred to the National Archives.

But Nixon and his agents failed to do that the next time around. They did deposit vice-presidential papers at the National Archives on March 26 and March 27, 1969, but a better case could be made that the papers were put there for storage than as a gift. Nowhere at the time was it said that the papers were to be a gift, and no deed was transferred. While it was routine procedure for archivists to record a gift in writing when they got one, no such procedure was followed this time.

Nixon's tax lawyers assessed the value of the papers at $576,000, and their plan was to deduct that amount over a six-year period.* For the years 1969 through 1972, Nixon took charitable

* How the $576,000 estimate was reached was not exactly scientific. The appraiser, a man named Ralph Newman, had been told by Nixon's tax attorney that the president wanted to claim a deduction of $500,000. Newman said he went to the archives, looked at the boxes stored there, and made a "ballpark estimate" that they were worth at least $500,000. Newman told my aide Searle Field he set the value at $576,000 to allow some margin of error if the IRS challenged the overall figure. He was surprised, he said, that Nixon claimed more than $500,000.

deductions of $482,109 based on the worth of the papers. The result was that, in 1970, Nixon paid a total of $789 in federal income taxes and in 1971 he paid $878. His combined taxable income for the two years was $525,000.

What Nixon paid in 1970 was less than what a person with $4,400 in taxable income would pay; for 1971 it was less than what someone with $5,400 in taxable income would pay. The following year, 1972, Nixon paid $4,298 in federal income taxes — less than someone with a taxable income of $19,800.

Nixon's taxes were prepared each year by the California firm of his personal attorney, Herbert Kalmbach. For a while beginning in 1970, John Dean handled the Washington end of Nixon's personal finances, including working with Kalmbach's firm on any matters that needed coordinating. As Dean's other responsibilities grew, one of his assistants, a young attorney named Roy Pete Kinsey, assumed that role.

Kinsey, as it happened, was a neighbor of Dean's and mine in Alexandria. Dean suggested that I call on him to find out more about Nixon's taxes, and I did. Kinsey got me so interested that I asked him to come to my office. When he did, I put Searle Field to work on the case.

By then, Kinsey had left the White House to work at the government's nuclear regulatory agency, then known as the Atomic Energy Commission. Dean had helped him get the new job and had, in effect, pushed him out of the White House, Kinsey said, to keep him from being tarnished by Watergate. Neither Kinsey nor Dean knew exactly what was wrong with Nixon's tax returns but both felt the claim of a $576,000 exemption simply looked fishy. In addition, Kinsey knew of other questionable items, such as the possible juggling of Nixon's taxes to conceal his daughter Tricia's interest in two lots in Key Biscayne, Florida.

As he began looking into the matter, Field told me at one point that Nixon had paid around $500 in federal income taxes in 1968. "That does sound low; what should it have been, about $800?" I asked. I thought we were talking about his tax payment each *week*. I wouldn't have dreamed he was talking about $500 for the whole year.

It was Field, working with others, who uncovered most of the shortcomings in the deductions. They also found that whoever transferred the papers specified that archivists were to have only limited access to them. The effect of that alone was to make the papers something less than a gift.

Even granting Nixon and his tax lawyers the best of intentions, it seemed to us that the circumstances ruled out any legitimate tax-deduction claim. Furthermore, at this stage of the game there really was no reason to assume good intentions on Nixon's part. Among papers in the case was an alleged deed of gift signed by Edward L. Morgan, deputy counsel to the president, and notarized by Frank DeMarco, Jr., of the Kalmbach firm. The deed was delivered to the National Archives on April 10, 1970, but the signatures on it were dated April 21, 1969. Intentional backdating of such documents would have been illegal, of course.

The existence of this document was the main reason for initial suspicions about the deduction, since it was not presented until more than eight months after the deadline.

As Searle Field pointed out in a memo to me, there were only two ways any gift of Nixon's papers could be valid. The first was for them to be presented in a timely fashion, along with a deed of gift. That had not occurred. The second was to make the gift by simply handing the papers over, which could have been acceptable under common-law rules.

Searle and I were convinced that the Nixon papers did not meet even the lax standards for a gift required under the common-law rules. We were pretty sure we could prove that in a court of law, but not 100 percent sure.

Around the time we had finished putting the facts together, Nixon went into overdrive in an attempt to leave the Saturday Night Massacre and the rest of Watergate behind. On November 17 he told newspaper editors assembled for a convention at Disney World, "I am not a crook." He then embarked on what his aides called "Operation Candor," traveling to places like the Grand Ole Opry in Nashville, where he was photographed, stiffly, with country-and-western entertainers. Operation Candor compared to what? I wondered.

On November 21 it was revealed that one of the tapes that Nixon had finally turned over had eighteen-and-a-half minutes of conversation missing. It was determined that the section had been manually erased between five and eight times. So much for candor.

The night before Thanksgiving, Searle Field telephoned Ron Ziegler in the White House. "I told Ziegler that we had the whole thing put together on the tax case," Searle recalled long afterward. "I said we were prepared to make the information public, but that we thought the president might like to come out with some sort of statement first. I said we need an answer by Friday — if he wants to come out with it or if he wants us to come out with it."

Ziegler called Searle back Thanksgiving afternoon, finding him at his parents' home in Connecticut. Ziegler said, "The president has one thing to say to Lowell Weicker: 'Tell him to go shit in his hat.' "

"When are you going to come out with this bullshit?" Ziegler asked. In about two weeks, Field said. The only item that stalled us was whether others would think the evidence was as overwhelming as we did. We feared getting caught in some legalism if Nixon's attorneys claimed the papers were a common-law gift.

On December 6 Gerald Ford was confirmed vice president by Congress to replace Agnew. On the eighth, much to our surprise, Nixon released what he termed a full explanation of his finances. In it, he said that all the papers at the National Archives that had not been earmarked as a donation still belonged to him.

To Searle and me that meant there was no way — none — that the papers deposited at the archives in 1969 could be claimed as a charitable deduction, for none had been earmarked before the July 1969 deadline. There simply had been no gift. By my office's calculations, Nixon would have to come up with about $235,000 to set his taxes straight, and he would suffer extreme humiliation as he did so.

On December 11 I turned our findings over to the Internal Revenue Service in the form of an eleven-page legal analysis, and I asked that the $576,000 deduction be reexamined. Our two-month investigation, I said, had shown "no valid gift of personal papers."

That signatures had been backdated was proved beyond doubt two weeks later in a most ironic manner. People familiar with Nixon's career may recall that his perjury case against suspected Communist agent Alger Hiss in the 1940s was greatly strengthened when, through resourceful digging, Nixon proved that Hiss was in possession of a particular typewriter at a time when incriminating material known as the "pumpkin papers" had been typed on it. Well, detective work involving a typewriter played a similar role in proving that the deed regarding Nixon's prepresidential papers had been backdated.

Jerry Brown, the former governor of California and several-time presidential candidate, was then secretary of state in California. He took a copy of the backdated deed with Frank DeMarco's name typed on it and matched it against the typewriters at the Kalmbach firm to locate the one that had been used. He then found out that the typewriter was one of a number that had been purchased months after the date on the deed. The date on the deed could not have been correct! Shades of the Hiss case, which contributed so much to Nixon's rise.

The phony tax deduction cost Nixon severely. In terms of public opinion, the extravagant, improper tax deduction was the straw that broke Nixon's back. For a president to pay no more in taxes than an indigent was more than people could bear. Parts of Watergate may have been complicated for the ordinary citizen; other parts may have been viewed as politics as usual, the Nixon interpretation. But there was no satisfactory explanation as to how the president of the United States, sitting where Washington, Jefferson, and Lincoln had been before him, a man with a $200,000 annual salary, additional income aside from that, and generous other benefits, could pay less than $900 a year in taxes.

Soon it also was revealed that Nixon paid no local or state income taxes either in the District of Columbia or in California, his state of residence. Noting that, a member of the California Franchise Tax Board accused Nixon of tax evasion.

In one of the most shortsighted actions imaginable, White House advisers reacted by urging Nixon to insist that his critics make their tax returns public. They must have figured that everybody operated the way they did! Maybe they really believed their politics-as-usual crap. If so, how blind they were. On December 14 Sam Ervin and I made our taxes public. Ervin's showed him paying more than $15,000 on an income of $63,000 in 1972; mine showed a payment of more than $14,000 on income of almost $68,000. Both of us had paid more than three times as much as Nixon for the year, and his reported taxable income was $268,000.

"Quite frankly, it makes the President's tax return look all the more ridiculous," I said at the time. In his homey way, Ervin said, "I don't know who this unidentified person is who tried to do a little character assassination, but if he identifies himself I'll let him come to North Carolina and memorize my tax returns for the last 50 years."

As for myself, since entering the House of Representatives in 1969 I had kept my tax returns on file at my office, open to public examination.

Opinion polls showed Nixon doing poorly before his taxes came to light, with only 28 to 30 percent of the public saying they approved his handling of the presidency. Those low grades fell to about 20 or 21 percent after that, and he never recovered.

There are some who believe that it was Nixon's tax debacle more than anything else that led to the drive in Congress to impeach him. The reasoning is that while there may have been nuance in the Watergate scandals, there was none in Nixon's Form 1040 adventurism. It was clear, in-your-face arrogance that everyone could understand. As disclosures came pouring out at the end of 1973, the tax dereliction permanently hardened public opinion toward Nixon, putting pressure on Congress to move against him.

Nixon was forced to pay the additional $235,000. Along with the terrible publicity he suffered, that was adding injury to insult.

On August 8, 1974, a rainy day in Washington, DC, Nixon announced his resignation. That evening he made his last televised address to the American people. Outside the White House about two thousand people gathered, most of them cheering the news of his departure. The next morning he assembled his staff, made an emotional farewell statement, and shortly afterward left for California aboard *Air Force One*.

From this chain of events it may look as though I tried to hound Richard Nixon, or reveled in his departure from office. That was not the case. My role on the Watergate Committee wasn't to judge individual guilt or innocence of anyone, including Nixon. It was to bring to light the political, governmental, and constitutional abuses that threatened to undo two hundred years of democracy in America. That is what I tried to do. Richard Nixon ended up being a casualty in the righting of the Watergate scandal. Had he not been, then most certainly the casualties would have been the Constitution and democratic rule. As it happened, it was too close a call for comfort.

9

Saving the Oceans

I WANTED a positive outlet for my energies after Watergate, and I found one quickly. It came in the form of an invitation to observe marine scientists at work off the Bahamas. Little did I know that I was starting out on what was to become a main political interest and personal avocation for me.

I got involved in such diverse issues as saving the whale, protecting fisheries, helping bring along the infant aquaculture industry, setting guidelines for offshore oil development, and even writing environmental legislation governing the deep sea. In the past, the oceans and the scientists and fishermen who ply them generally had been ignored on Capitol Hill. I helped get the engine started.

I also became a saturation diver, or aquanaut, someone who stays under water for lengthy periods.* During the course of my senatorial career I made four saturation dives, for a total of ten days.

Through my interest in the sea and visits to the Caribbean, I came to spend time with Fidel Castro. As I shall describe, my experience convinced me that the sour nonrelations between Castro and a string of US presidents has hurt our country as well as his.

If I had to define in a word what our national policy toward the sea has been, the word I might choose is *nonexistent*. The oceans cover 70 percent of the earth's surface; if used properly they

---

* I was the only aquanaut in the Senate. Congressman Bill Alexander of Arkansas also was on this 1975 trip, and he later became the only aquanaut in the House of Representatives.

will help feed humanity forever and supply endless energy. But they are fragile and can be devastated, just as much of the planet's land cover has been.

What has been done in recent years is criminal, rapacious, and perilous to humankind. The old Soviet Union, we learned not long ago, regularly dumped barrels of low-level radioactive waste into the Arctic Ocean. When some barrels stayed on the surface, handlers riddled them with gunshots to make them sink! The Japanese have hunted down whales and engaged in massive, deliberate dolphin kills; the Soviets and the Japanese overfished extensively, almost exhausting supplies of some species. Our country has been no model of conservation, either, with oil firms guilty of defiling oil spills and hell-bent from time to time on precipitous offshore development.

For the longest time people dumped anything in the oceans, regardless of effect. The result today is that coral reefs are in decline, and in coastal areas in 1993 alone two thousand beaches were closed because of pollution. The toxic chemical PCB has been found in large quantities in the Arctic Ocean, which the Soviets polluted indiscriminately. Contaminated fish are a worldwide problem. More than a decade ago, a ship crossed the Atlantic sampling surface water continuously. Testers found Styrofoam in every bucket ladled, from one side of the ocean to the other.

There may be less environmental encroachment today than in the 1970s because of increased awareness and penalties. In part, that is due to legislation I helped write. But that is not to say things are going well. In the late 1980s and 1990s, we have had extremely misguided cutbacks in underwater research spending, especially considering the relatively small size of our oceanic programs and the abundance the oceans can provide.

I made my first dive in April 1975. I was invited to Freeport in the Bahamas because I was on a committee that had oversight responsibility for NOAA, the National Oceanic and Atmospheric Administration. Also on the trip were three members of the House, several committee staff aides, NOAA executives, and officials of the Ford administration.

We were there to look over some of the work in and around

the Hydro-Lab, a small underwater habitat. The goals of the project were to develop safety procedures for prolonged saturation diving, to learn more about ocean reefs and about the fish in the area, and to study the deep vertical wall off Grand Bahama. Aside from NOAA, a number of universities, foundations, commercial groups, and the governments of France and what was then West Germany sponsored and took part in the studies.

Our delegation went to Freeport for a three-day visit. Those who had diving experience were to go below the surface with scuba gear to get as good a view as they could of the underwater laboratory, submarines, and so on. Those of us with no experience were to see the facility with masks and snorkels.

No one told me in advance of this plan. Our teacher was a youngster, and I asked him to include me in the group that was going to get a firsthand look at Hydro-Lab. He consulted with his boss, a fellow named Bob Wicklund, and came back and said, "Mr. Wicklund says you can't go; those are the rules."

I told the kid as nicely as I could that there had been a misunderstanding, and asked if he could have Mr. Wicklund explain the rules to me. I later learned that Wicklund was one of the country's top divers. When he came by, I sized him up quickly: an outdoors type, probably someone who didn't have a great deal of respect for politicians. (You learn to sense that.) Wicklund was standing and I was sitting. Because I am so tall, we were eye-to-eye.

Our relationship didn't start off in the most friendly manner. Wicklund pointed his finger at me and asked if I was a certified scuba diver. He knew I wasn't. I said, can't we take care of that tomorrow? He said, that usually takes a few days or a week.

Wicklund said it was too dangerous for an inexperienced person to go out. I asked him not to point. I also said something to the effect that I hadn't come to the Bahamas as a tourist, that I wanted to see what was going on, and that I was interested in the oceans. I think I persuaded him that I was sincere.

Well, he said, under the circumstances, I guess we can at least get you in condition to go down some.

I spent the rest of that day and all of the next getting more scuba-diving instruction in a training pool. Following that, Wicklund and I went, alone, in a boat to where Hydro-Lab lay sixty-five feet beneath us. "I can see what's going on because the water is so clear," I told him, "but I certainly can't see as well as if we went below."

Wicklund was waiting for that cue. "Okay, out of the boat," he said. We dove about fifteen feet below the surface, where the view was just about perfect, and where I was quite comfortable.

At the bottom was the Hydro-Lab. Near it was a submarine. Sidling along the bottom were a couple of scientist—fish farmers, busily working with a schooling fish known as grunt. Grunt are about twelve inches long with yellow and white stripes. They school in great numbers and tend to stake out a territory and stay there, making them amenable to farming. There were thousands of them right below me. As I watched, I saw a couple of other people collecting samples of sediment and taking measurements of the current.

Hydro-Lab was the first underwater habitation of its kind. It was cylindrical, about eight feet in diameter and sixteen feet long, and had room for four people. The air inside came from above and was kept at the same pressure as the water outside. The longer a person stayed in Hydro-Lab, the more nitrogen he or she would take in. In about twelve hours, one's body would be totally saturated with it. When preparing to return to the surface, it takes about seventeen hours to decompress. Cutting corners on decompression leads to the bends on resurfacing. Rising to the top without decompressing, or with insufficient decompression, is fatal.

Structures like Hydro-Lab enable oceanic scientists to do their work without being influenced by the weather. Once saturated, they can stay down as long as needed. They are not subject to tides, ocean swells, wind, or rain. Their lives at the bottom of the sea are more similar to ours above the surface than most people would believe. Outside the chamber they wear a bathing suit and scuba gear; inside they dress informally. If they want to read a book, cook, or engage in other such above-water activities, they can.

The Hydro-Lab had two bunks, an air conditioner, a dehumidifier, electrical panels, a communications radio, an electric pot and pan, telephones, interior and exterior lights, a picture window four feet in diameter and six other ports, tables, emergency batteries, and a freshwater shower, with the water stored in a 250-gallon tank.

On that April day in 1975, Wicklund let me stay below the surface for about ten minutes. I was astounded and thrilled. He was watching me carefully, however, making sure I didn't overdo things.

I was very excited when we surfaced. Wicklund remembers that part better than I do. He says I started yelling, saying how fantastic the experience was. Wicklund is convinced that this dip below the surface was the genesis of my interest in the ocean. I agree.

Today I am glad that I acquired a certain curiosity about life under the sea, even if it came relatively late. Better late than never. As a boy, I spent a lot of time on Long Island Sound, one of the nation's large, beautiful marine environs. I sailed and motorboated long before I could drive a car. I loved the water and had much more experience with it than most people do. I was always in awe of the majesty, the mystery, the beauty, the tranquility, and the occasional fury of the waters. Yet my real appreciation didn't come until I was in my forties and found myself hovering fifteen feet below the surface.

More than half of all Americans live fifty miles or less from a seacoast. I'm sure that 99 percent look at the ocean the way I used to — as a good place for recreation, period.

The United States is almost surrounded by water; you'd think we would have a natural interest in what lies under the surface. We don't, not even in the coastal states. Connecticut is a good example. The nation has a sea-grant program for colleges that conduct marine studies, similar to the land-grant schools that study agriculture. By the 1980s, I had a leading role in overseeing congressional policy toward the oceans, so I urged state officials to bring the University of Connecticut into the sea-grant program. I couldn't believe their resistance, which seemed based entirely on logic that dictated, if we haven't joined until now, there must be a reason. I basically had to drag Connecticut kicking and screaming into the program.

And Connecticut is typical of all New England, a region whose history is built on the sea. With rare exceptions, attitudes toward the funding of exploration and development of the ocean are as backward in New England as in the Midwest, far from any ocean tides.

Only in the military has there been any major effort at maritime research and experimentation. In 1993, after the cold-war concern with Soviet submarines had ended, the US Navy turned its superb sound-detection facilities loose on a whale — one single whale, that is — and tracked its migration for fifteen hundred miles down the Atlantic Ocean's continental shelf. Also during 1993, Navy cameras took moving pictures at unbelievable depths in the Pacific, showing the effects of a series of deep-sea earthquakes.

By and large, though, military applications in the ocean are not easily transferable to peaceful ones. After all, once having shown that it can be done, what is the usefulness in tracking a whale from Cape Cod to Bermuda?

In the starkest terms, there may be a period when the fate of the world is determined by our ability to take food, energy, and minerals from the sea, but we are absolutely unprepared for that now. Our useful knowledge is terribly limited; it is as though we are infants. Underwater researchers, scholars, and explorers are marvelous people and make up a fine community, but a very tiny one. So tiny that I can, literally, count its leaders on my fingers: Bob Ballard. Jacques Cousteau. Sylvia Earl, Bob Wicklund, Bob Dill, Stan Waterman. A few others, perhaps.

I returned to the Bahamas and Hydro-Lab in August 1975, four months after my first visit. With me was Democratic congressman Bill Alexander of Arkansas, who also had been extremely impressed and awakened by what we saw in April. We both took full diving courses and did our first saturation dives. I spent three days in Hydro-Lab during this stay.

As I descended for the first time, I swam past two college students who were sitting on wooden stools on the sea bottom, scribbling notes on writing pads on their laps. Behind them a field of fake seaweed had been planted to create an inviting area for marine life out of an otherwise barren, desertlike environment.

My interest in the oceans kept growing, and as it did I was becoming better acquainted with Bob Wicklund, my instructor.

Wicklund was born in Brooklyn and grew up disliking crowds. For eight years he lived on an almost empty island in the Bahamas.

While associated with the National Oceanic and Atmospheric Administration in the Bahamas project, Wicklund did not work for NOAA. He was then and still is involved in private ventures dealing with the seas in one aspect or another.

Shortly after my first saturation dive, I got a letter from Wicklund asking for help because his company was about to lose its funding from NOAA. I wrote him back with a different idea. Drop your projects, I said, and come work for me in Washington. I need your expertise to help with legislation.

Wicklund joined my staff in 1976 and stayed for seven years. During that time we got substantial legislation enacted. One of our first achievements, in March 1977, was the Whale Preservation Act, which banned whaling within two hundred miles of the United States.

Shortly after New Year's Day in 1978, I made my second saturation dive, this time on the ocean floor at Salt River Canyon, about a mile north of Saint Croix in the US Virgin Islands, where Hydro-Lab had been relocated. I was stunned and thrilled at being in the midst of such brilliant colors and watching rhythms of life that were moved by wave and current, the unafraid grace of a million fish, the variety of a forest of coral, the quiet surrounding it all.

My stays in Hydro-Lab were humbling, moving experiences. On the ocean floor, one is easily prompted to recall the great natural beauty given by the Creator and to ponder the responsibility such a trust places on us. Humankind is ingenious; in Connecticut alone we have developed and make many things that are useful in modern life: aircraft engines, submarines, firearms, machine tools, insurance, silver utensils, ball bearings, bread, appliances. But at least as important as what we make, and a great deal more precious, are the things we were given — the forests, lakes, wildlife, rivers, air, wetlands.

I was now capable of doing deep dives. On my first one, with Wicklund accompanying me, I descended about 140 feet. As soon as we got there, Wicklund tapped me on the shoulder and pointed up, meaning we had to return to the surface. I resisted. He motioned toward my air tank. I could see that I was running low, so up we went. Being a big man, I have a large set of lungs and require substantially more air than most people. By the time we got to the top, I was out of air altogether.

Later on I invited Clive Cussler, the author of *Raise the Titanic* and other oceanic thrillers, to stay in the Hydro-Lab with me. Cussler is a neat, quiet guy, a good companion and good diver. We kept having one area of disagreement. Whenever it was time to eat, he wanted a beer. No way. After decompressing and popping to the surface, Clive made Jesse Owens look like a turtle in getting to the nearest bar. (With me close behind.)

These stays in the Hydro-Lab and the deep dives I sometimes made altered my perspective slightly, making me protective of the oceans, as though I were the one person in the US Senate who was responsible for them.

I believe that within our children's lifetimes or perhaps a little after that, humans will have to go to the oceans for energy and food. In preparation we must do our best to understand what we are dealing with before that period of urgency. If we don't, we will in a hundred years deplete a resource that should last a million years. I am talking about fish, plant life, energy sources, and rare minerals.

The ocean is rich with minerals, including cobalt, copper, nickel, and manganese, all of which make steel strong and without which gas turbines, turbo-superchargers, and jet engines won't work. Copper aside, we now import most of these minerals from nations we may not be able to rely on in the long term. In addition, there are vast supplies of oil and gas under the oceans, and uranium worth billions has been found in the Black Sea.

The seas have a very fragile ecosystem. Loud noise is jarring to underwater life. Temperature changes caused by practices on land, such as those of waste disposal plants, often have deleterious effects on the water. Resort development on any Caribbean island will let loose sediment and chemicals that may cover and kill coral reefs. Reefs are to the ocean as forests are to the land; destroy the reefs and you destroy the wildlife. Because of the ocean's fragility it is essential that we understand how our activities affect the sea.

We should have started exploration and analysis of this ecosystem in a major way before now, but we haven't. When we do, it probably will bring little initial productive return, but there will be enormous dividends later on.

Not a lot of people in Congress shared my interest in the sea, but some recognized that I was onto something worthwhile and encouraged my efforts.

One area in which I had little success, unfortunately, was aquaculture, or fish farming. In February 1978 I introduced an aquaculture bill aimed at stimulating fish farming in the United States. At the time stocks were being wiped out by massive overfishing. The legislation didn't get anywhere; no one listened. Today, a little late, everybody is looking toward aquaculture because continued overfishing has severely depleted many fish stocks.

Recently Canada, for example, announced that it would have to shut down many of its northeast fisheries because almost all the cod and haddock had been removed — all fished out — over the previous couple of years. Most of the damage had been done earlier by the Russians, Japanese, and Koreans, all of whom dragged the bottom with nets. This activity took place before 1977, when we enacted legislation preventing other nations from fishing within two hundred miles of the American coast. I was a sponsor of that legislation, but it came too late to do much good.

Aquaculture has started to take off as an industry. Some fish are already being farmed in cages off the coasts. Right now catfish are farmed in ponds, an easy, efficient method. There will be more such farming and eventually, because water resources near coastlines are limited, fish will be farmed in buildings, like chickens in coops. In fact, in one of the main chicken-growing areas, the Eastern Shore of Maryland, some chicken coops have been converted into fish cultures. Eventually all this will be computerized; little fish will go in one end and come out the other, in a carton ready for market.

In 1978 I helped create and Congress enacted the Outer Continental Shelf Lands Act, aimed at setting reasonable standards for offshore oil drilling. One segment of the bill mandated that there be safety studies for divers, and it is still the only legislation regarding diving safety. An amendment that I introduced set up a fishermen's contingency fund so that oil companies reimburse fishermen who damage their gear on underwater oil drilling equipment. As a result of that legislation, each time an oil company applies for a lease, it pays a certain amount into the fund.

In 1979 it came to my attention that some of the scientific research in the Caribbean was done by Cuban scientists. I also learned that Fidel Castro was interested in mutual oceanic studies. Castro had been trying for a long time to reopen relations with the United States in any way he could.

A joint US-Cuban venture seemed reasonable enough to me in principle, and in October 1979, having obtained the necessary permission, I went to Havana to discuss cooperative marine research with Castro.

Bob Wicklund went with me; so did an interpreter, my cousin Florence Weicker, who had grown up in Mexico. Also with us was an old friend, Shaw Mudge, a businessman from Greenwich, Connecticut. Mudge was the owner of the twin-engine propeller plane we flew.

We spent four days in Cuba. On arrival we were put up in an old, stuffy, formerly American hotel. We were there just a short while when an aide to Castro whisked us to the presidential palace. This was my first meeting with Castro and it lasted about an hour and a half. We talked marine research, since that was the purpose of the visit, and we both expressed the hope that our meeting would lead to joint scientific projects.

It wasn't only Cuba that would benefit by such research. Draw a circle around Cuba and you are marking off one big section of the Caribbean, a wide area that is off limits to US researchers. Among other things, we talked about fisheries and protecting turtles. We had a good dialogue in that first meeting; we didn't discuss politics at all.

The next two days my companions and I got to see agricultural facilities, educational projects, and a few other items on the tourist agenda. We visited what today is known as the Isle of Youth and was formerly the Isle of Pines. This is a large island off the coast that held a number of specialized high schools, each with six hundred students. Basic Communist philosophy is taught there, and those so inclined from throughout the world attend. Castro wisely exported education and health care as the come-on for communism, a lesson we should learn.

On our last day Wicklund and I and a few Cubans went on a diving trip from a fishing boat. We traveled about an hour offshore to the site. After the first dive a speedboat came toward us with a .50-caliber machine gun on its prow, attended by someone in military uniform. None of us, including the Cubans, knew what was going on. The boat circled us and left. A little while later, a large yacht — Castro's yacht — came along. He ended up spending the next ten hours with us.

Castro was very capable in the water. He didn't scuba dive; rather he just went under and held his breath, which in the argot is called a "breath-hold" dive. Castro was fifty-three years old then and I could see that he had been quite a good breath-hold diver in his day.

At lunchtime Castro said, "We are going to go out and get you some fresh lobster." He and his bodyguards, armed with Uzis and handguns, piled into a rubber boat. The group came back before long, and in a few minutes we sat down to dine on raw lobster, with a taste of lime. At that point Castro called to someone in the yacht's cabin, and out came his personal physician, scalpel in hand, to pick the lobsters clean.

For about three hours, Castro described his revolutionary campaign more than twenty years earlier, from his hiding out in the Sierra Maestras to his march into Havana, showing his route on a map. Listening to him was like sitting with Napoléon to hear of the conquest of Europe, or Eisenhower and the invasion of Normandy. In short it was history — live. Castro, of course, is notorious for talking endlessly. I guess I was a good listener, for after a while he said, in a very friendly manner, "Now, Lowell, what could I do for you?"

"I'll tell you exactly what you can do for me, Mr. President," I said. "If we normalize relations, I would like to have the professional baseball franchise for Havana."

"No, no, that belongs to us. The government takes that."

Well, it was worth mentioning — but not in a communist state.

I had hoped that my trip to Havana could serve as a kickoff to joint research that would transcend politics. I invited Castro to send

Cuban marine scientists to Hydro-Lab at Saint Croix, and five of them went.

Even that small gesture brought caused considerable ill will. When their visit was announced, I got major harassment from the Cuban community in Miami. They called my office every day and went on radio saying the Cubans had sent agents trained by the KGB to Saint Croix. Bob Wicklund pointed out to me, for what it was worth, that each Cuban had been cleared in advance, by name, by the State Department.

I had hoped to send a contingent of Americans to Cuban waters but that never happened. The Carter administration was not crazy about the idea; once Reagan took office there was no chance at all.

As for the complaining Miami Cubans, I couldn't care less what they thought. Somehow we have got to the point in this country where a few expatriates in Miami act as though they set US foreign policy toward the Caribbean, and a lot of politicians encourage that thinking. Instead of letting their hatred toward Castro determine our policy, it's worth remembering that he came to power by kicking out Fulgencio Batista, a very oppressive dictator — and that many who fled to Miami had ties to the Batista regime. And that under Batista, Cuba was largely illiterate and almost totally lacking in medical care for its people.

If you were rich or American and lived in Cuba before Castro took power, everything was okay. I might add that the Squibb pharmaceutical firm had a plant in Cuba in the pre-Castro days, which of course benefited the Weickers back then. But if you were an ordinary Cuban, everything was not okay, not by a long shot.

Today Cuba has one of the most literate populations in the world and one of the best health-care systems. Transportation is poor, housing so-so. It was Castro who brought these basics into the mainstream of Cuban existence.

By any Western standard, of course, Cubans are very unfortunate. The country, never prosperous, is sinking economically. Cuban life is so joyless that its people are discouraged as they look out on the rest of the world. Cubans are a warm, wonderful people. I truly look forward to the time when joy returns to their lives. But anyone who thinks most Cubans were better off under Batista has another guess coming.

I would say that US treatment of Cuba is probably the biggest, longest-lasting foreign policy blunder I can think of in the last thirty-five years. We embargoed Cuba, boycotted Cuba — use any phrase you want — and all we succeeded in doing was to remove US influence and replace it with a Soviet presence.

Our serious confrontation was with the Soviet Union, the superpower, not tiny Cuba. When I came back from my 1979 visit, I said in the Senate that "the daring and effective way to confront the Soviet Union isn't to heighten the controversy over Cuba but rather to take down the wall that has deliberately masked two crises and promises only more of the same in the future."

I recommended then that we have negotiations with Castro and that we "resume trade, lift the economic sanctions, establish diplomatic relations and give Castro the leverage and running room to end the indignity of ruling over a proud people totally dependent on handouts from Moscow." We were using Cuba to show how tough we could be toward the Soviets. How unfair, to the Cubans and to ourselves.

To me personally, it was obvious on my first trip to Cuba, and then on my second one in 1983, that Cubans had absolutely no affinity for the Russians whatsoever. It was oil and water. The thirteen thousand Soviets stayed segregated. On the other hand, Cubans feel warmly toward Americans, and Americans toward Cubans.

Any normal interplay of tourism and relations between the United States and Cuba from 1960 on would have eliminated the Soviet Union as a factor in Cuban life. Now that the Soviet Union has disintegrated, we are trying for the best of all possible relations with Russia, which is the correct thing to do. But with Cuba we have no dealings; we still maintain a hostile carryover from the past. This is more a sick joke than a coherent policy. Why does it persist? Well, in large part it is because of political leaders' apprehensions, or shall I say presidential candidates' apprehensions, regarding the Cubans in Miami.

Florida is the fourth-most-populous state in the union; the

candidate who wins the presidential primary there gains lots of delegates in the drive toward a party nomination. Cuban-Americans in Miami form a sophisticated, powerful voting bloc that occasionally can swing statewide elections, and they are not loath to advertise that power and use it. Every presidential candidate, whether Democratic or Republican, as the price of entering the Florida primary seems to feel it necessary to take the pledge that when it comes to Cuba, Castro is out and we are going to reestablish Cuban-Americans on Cuban soil. A return to the good old days, for them.

I don't blame the Cuban-Americans for exerting their power; that's what politics is about. But the candidates who bow to them are making a big mistake. To have eliminated all dialogue and commerce of just about any kind between the two countries is ridiculous. It doesn't do us any good; it doesn't do the average Cuban any good.

My criticism of our policy and our presidential candidates should not be interpreted as praise of Castro. He has always loved to nettle the United States, to provoke us, and when we would shake a finger at him, he would roar back at us. That has been purely unproductive for both sides.

However, in my two visits to Cuba, Castro sent strong signals that he wanted reconciliation with the United States; there was no question about that. In passing this on to the State Department, the message I got in return was to try again when Fidel got to his knees, as that would be the only satisfactory ending. Maybe that's what will happen. One way or the other, it is time to put an end to this expensive, long-running mistake.

It is not only Cuba where our policy comes up short. Our knowledge and relationships with almost all the Caribbean and South American countries are shortsighted, if not blind. We don't understand that part of the world, we make little or no effort there, and it is for good reason that we are often disliked. When we do play a role it is to get something for ourselves, not to do something for them. Thus we are losing the goodwill of people who by natural instinct are inclined to look at the United States in a favorable way. We turn them off; we have been turning them off for the better part of a century.

These views of mine toward Cuba and the Caribbean are not radical ones. They are shared by many in Washington, but few political leaders will voice them.

I hope the current US president or the next one proves me wrong, but until now the only time policy toward Cuba comes into play is during presidential primaries in Florida. Well, if I ever ran in a Florida primary I can assure you that about 99.9 percent of the Cuban-Americans would vote against me. Not for legitimate reasons, but because my views would be distorted beyond recognition. What I propose, after all, is to arrange free access back and forth with Cuba, and I'm sure many Cubans in Miami would love that. They're just not the ones that are so vocal.

In 1979 I became a member of the powerful Appropriations Committee, which writes the checks that have been authorized by other committees. Appropriations can and does hold back on spending if it wants, and it can find numerous ways to manipulate spending by adding or deleting funds.

Fritz Hollings, the South Carolina Democrat, was chairman of the appropriations subcommittee dealing with the oceanic programs and I was the senior Republican, or ranking member. Seeing my interest in the area, Hollings gave me a lot of leeway. In 1981, with the election of Ronald Reagan as president, Republicans held a majority in the Senate and I became chairman of the subcommittee, with Hollings and I changing places. (We switched once more when Democrats regained control of the Senate as a result of the 1986 elections.)

As chairman, you would think I'd be able to get more done than ever. Unfortunately, under Reagan, what had been a short-sighted oceans policy became a blind one. The administration had two interests when it came to the seas: to turn the areas off shore over to the oil firms, and to cut back on everything else. In the first instance, my efforts went to seeing that some sensible restraints were put on oil drilling. And in the second, my role was to see that worthwhile programs continued.

Before I was appointed to the Appropriations Committee, the focus of the National Oceanic and Atmospheric Administration was mostly on weather and only secondarily on the sea. I was able to help change that and greatly expand the underwater research program so that spending and personnel on the two areas were about equal. The original Hydro-Lab was refitted under government supervision to be more habitable; we then built another, Aquarius, that was four times larger and is in service off Florida now.

I also helped build the entire NOAA program while I was on the Appropriations Committee, to the point that it became the largest agency in the Department of Commerce.

These were the first, necessary steps. The only way we are going to understand the water bodies of the world is to have habitats all over the sea, larger and more sophisticated than we have now. Let me draw an analogy. Suppose there were a great cloud bank over the surface of the earth. Suppose also that you had never seen the planet, and you are flying above that cloud bank with a bucket, and every now and then you let down the bucket and scoop up some dirt. You would start to put together some sort of a mosaic of what Earth is. But obviously, that is no substitute for landing the plane under the clouds and getting out and walking around.

Similarly, the minor excursions we make on the surface of the ocean floor give us the briefest glimpses of what is going on beneath. Our knowledge does grow as we send robots under all parts of the sea and make worthwhile discoveries. But as in space, these unmanned ventures are not as good as manned ones.

After I left the Senate, national funding for oceanic research began to dwindle. The mistakes we made before have been repeated. Seventy percent of the fish Americans eat is imported even though the waters in our jurisdiction contain the richest fishing grounds in the world. In terms of dollars, fish imports account for the third-largest item in the US trade deficit, trailing only automobiles and electronic equipment.

Weather study now totally dominates NOAA's activities; underwater research has dwindled dramatically. Part of the reason may be that modern weather satellites are very expensive. Nevertheless, this to me is myopic. The waters are as important to the life and security of the world as are the heavens. Whoever masters the sea has a pretty good hold on the future.

I believe we must turn the narrow thinking of our government and identify manned undersea exploration as a national priority. The man on the street got behind the space program only because he was made part of its experience through TV programs and live broadcasts from the moon.

We must bring the oceans to the people in a similar manner. No one will get very excited about an inanimate probe lowered into the depths. But a person walking on the bottom, collecting, touching, describing his observations and experiences is a different story. The oceans are our heritage; they will provide our sustenance in the future. The United States can ill afford to overlook any aspect of our approach to understanding the oceans. The presence of men and women in the sea is extremely important, and must be made a national goal.

I had some initial success when I worked toward this end during my last twelve years in the US Senate. Now, though, because of our national inability to focus on long-term projects, we have fallen back. As might be expected, the Japanese have shown signs of moving to pick up the slack.

Sometimes I wish I were back in the Senate just to help develop and implement an intelligent policy toward the oceans. But the problem isn't so much that I'm not there; I know very well that no one is indispensable. The problem is that nobody in the executive branch and nobody on Capitol Hill is assuming responsibility. There's a vacancy.

All is not dim, however. In one very exciting project, the University of Connecticut is picking up where the federal government stopped. In November 1994 school officials announced plans for a major research center in Groton. Bob Ballard, a leading figure in oceanic study, was to relocate from the oceanic study facility in Woods Hole, Massachusetts, taking his important foundations with him. With Mystic Seaport, university research at Avery Point, and Ballard at the aquarium, it seems safe to say that Connecticut will become the world's foremost point of marine science, history, and exploration.

10

Protecting the Constitution

SCHOOL PRAYER, busing, and abortion aren't my favorite subjects, Lord knows, but some voters may have thought otherwise. I spent a lot of time, even filibustered, on them.

My main interest was in keeping far-right political interests from destroying the US Constitution. These phony conservatives wouldn't have hesitated to do that to get organized prayer in the schools and to strip the courts of their legitimate authority to rule on integration and abortion.

To me, the constitutional principles in each instance were more important than the issues themselves. The principles get into the bedrock foundation of our democracy.

I can't remember how many senators told me privately that they endorsed my battles with the far right, and that they would have joined with me — except they couldn't afford the backlash.

I'm sad to say, those senators knew what they were talking about. In any close election, lots of factors may be cited for the win or loss. There probably were very few voters in Connecticut who got ticked off at me for the time I spent on constitutional issues. Very few. Only enough so that when they stayed home or voted against me in 1988, I lost by 10,000 votes out of 1.37 million cast, less than 1 percent of the total.

I would still fight the New Right if I had it to do over, but I would try harder to help citizens understand the Constitution. It's a shortcoming in our educational system and among our people that so few appreciate or understand it.

The Constitution took effect in 1788. Under it, the United States has had more than two hundred years of stable government, which is almost a miracle. It is a living document that provides for its own change through the amendment process and through review by the Supreme Court, which has had no reluctance to interpret the Constitution or to overrule its own prior decisions.

In 1791 the first ten amendments, the Bill of Rights, became law. In 1865, the Thirteenth Amendment abolished slavery; in 1868 the Fourteenth Amendment gave citizens the same protection for their rights and privileges from state governments that the Bill of Rights gave from the federal government.

In 1913 the Sixteenth Amendment authorized Congress to levy income taxes. In 1920 the Nineteenth Amendment guaranteed women the right to vote.

As compared with the twenty-six amendments, the number of cases in which the Supreme Court has changed the Constitution is huge. As Oliver Wendell Holmes put it, "We are under a Constitution, but the Constitution is what the judges say it is."

It is an understatement to say the constitutional system has worked well. The fact is, it has been a thing of beauty, a piece of gold. But the Constitution is not self-enforcing. In every generation attempts have been made to overrun it, sometimes through legislative tactics called court stripping.

The phrase *court stripping* is widely used by some constitutional experts but appears rarely in the popular press. It refers to legislative attempts to remove authority from the courts. Court stripping has been at the center of the school prayer, busing, and abortion issues.

History is replete with attempts by Congress to "get at the Court's decision" or to "teach the Court a lesson." This tampering undermines the intent of our system of government, with its checks and balances assigning responsibilities to the three branches.

Congress is subject to popular elections and the pressures of countless interest groups; a neutral body it is not. We should not put the courts to a popularity test simply because some members of Congress are offended by judicial decisions. I am of the same school of thought as a distinguished judge from Connecticut, José

Cabranes, who once commented that "when the Supreme Court has acted in a role seen as activist, it is because the states failed in the task of protecting individual rights even as they failed for generations to meet other articulated needs in an industrial democracy."

We need to remember why the federal courts frequently go against the grain of popular sentiment. More often than not, they are doing what they alone among US institutions were designed to do: safeguard the fundamental rights of the individual against the potentially tyrannical attitudes of the majority, or, on occasion, against the tyrannical attitudes of the minority.

Even if we could assume that the states and the Congress could be trusted to safeguard individual rights, that assumption would not be sufficient to justify the Congress in limiting the role of the judiciary. To do so would be to overlook one of the strengths of our federal system — that it provides a two-tiered source of protection for our citizens, one state and one federal. Federalism is not served when the federal half of that protection is crippled. All three of its branches must be left intact.

The court is our barrier against tyranny. If that barrier is removed, we will have established a precedent for a series of amendments that would continue to undermine the independence of the judiciary.

The fight over these issues is a grinding one because the revisionists keep coming back. That is especially true in the issue of the separation of church and state.

No greater mischief can be created than to combine the power of religion with the power of government; history has shown us that time and time again. The union of the two is bad for religion and for government. It gives rise to tyrants and inquisitions, not just historically but at the present time as well, as evidenced by the "ethnic cleansing" (read genocide) by Serbs of Muslims in Bosnia.

On its surface, the most frequent attempt at church-state mixing in this country, prayer in the public schools, can be quite appealing. It summons up reassuring images of freckle-faced, Norman Rockwell children, heads bowed, hands clasped. But as inspiring as it sounds, prayer in school has the potential for doing damage to children and their families, to the cause of true religion, and to the ideal of separation of church and state our founders embraced.

In the Sermon on the Mount, Phillips translation, there is this passage: "And when you pray, don't be like the play actors. They love to stand and pray in the synagogues and street corners so that people may see them at it. Believe me, they have had all the reward they are going to get. But when you pray, go into your room, shut the door and pray to your Father privately. Your Father who sees all private things will reward you." That is a far more preferable method than the "religion on the sleeve" approach advocated by the Christian right.

History draws an ugly picture arising from the mixture of government and religion, not the simple, misleading Rockwell portrait.

Government-sponsored religion and religious suppression in Europe brought many immigrants to our shores. But there has been a lot of repression and misery caused by state-sanctioned religion in the United States, too. That is why clergy, lay people, and officeholders alike must fight radical rewrites of the First Amendment that masquerade as good, old-fashioned morality.

Until 1818 Connecticut was ruled by a fusion of government and the Congregational church. As the official religion of the state, even those Congregationalists who wished to form a new church in a new settlement were required first to petition the state legislature.

Throughout the colonies in the early days, the mix of church and state was dangerous for believers in the wrong religion. Quakers were beaten, exiled, even executed in Massachusetts. Presbyterians moving into Virginia were denied voting and other civil rights by the dominant Episcopalians. Later, adherents to the same faiths banded together to deny the same rights to other religions.

In Maryland, Catholics who were denounced in most colonies found peace, and the colony was called the "Free State" because of its religious tolerance. But in this "free state," Jews could not vote or hold office.

In 1871 there was a battle between Catholics and Protestants in which fifty-four persons were killed. The location was not Belfast, but Eighth Avenue in Manhattan.

We have taught our children the heroic story of the *May-flower* and Plymouth Rock. Those who visit Plymouth today can see for themselves, on a hill overlooking the sea, the names of the original English Calvinists inscribed on a monument. To these Puritans, persecuted for denying the ecclesiastical authority of the king, there is this dedication at Plymouth: "To the forefathers in recognition of their labors, sacrifices and sufferings for the cause of civil and religious liberty."

That was 1620. Before long, the persecuted became the persecutors. In 1692, for instance, entrenched Puritan hostility to freedom of thought and speech helped cause the deaths of nineteen men and women during the Salem witch trials.

Even after the Constitution and Bill of Rights were adopted, intolerance flourished. Perhaps no denomination has had a more bitter taste of homegrown, American religious intolerance than the Mormons. The founder, Joseph Smith, was driven out of New York; he and his brother eventually were killed by a lynch mob. The Mormon religion was literally driven across the nation by a mob.

In this century, radio preachers of the 1930s spewed messages of Protestant fundamentalism that warmly embraced the anti-Semitism of Hitler and Mussolini. Charles Lindbergh and Henry Ford drew large audiences with their anti-Jewish tirades. Both received medals from Hitler himself.

The message is clear that the mix of religion and politics is unhealthy and detrimental to government. It is also detrimental to religion.

We have heard much about a restoration of family values that prayer in the public schools would supposedly further. But we don't accomplish a strengthening of the family by imposing homogenized, government-dictated worship, particularly if such doctrine is alien to a family's own belief and tradition.

Anyone has a right to pray at any time anywhere in this nation. And the right not to pray. No legislation, no constitutional amendment is needed. But it is every bit as important that the potency of worship remain undiluted by government as it is that government be unfettered by shifting religious majorities.

Americans with faith in Jesus Christ rejoice in their religious beliefs, and they rejoice in a political union that also allows those

Forty thousand people massed at the capitol in Hartford in October 1991 to protest the new state income tax. I felt duty-bound to attend and was booed, cursed, spat at, and shoved by some agitators in the crowd.

Hanged in effigy at the October 1991 rally. Efforts to repeal the state income tax went nowhere, and the tax helped pull Connecticut out of a severe debt crisis.

My mother, born Mary Hastings Bickford, daughter of an English general and niece of an archbishop of Canterbury. In politics she became an unwavering Democrat.

My father, shown when he was deputy director of Air Force intelligence in Europe in World War II.

A Buckley School class gathering. At age thirteen, I am fifth from left, top row. The date was June 5, 1944, one day before D-Day.

In Greenwich with my first wife, Bunny, and our boys, Scot, Gray, and Brian.

This photo was taken during a benefit doubles match in which Jacob Javits and I beat Vice President Agnew and Peace Corps director Joseph Blatchford 6–1, 6–1. Notice the now-ancient wooden racket.

Yes, Nixon. In the Oval Office, August 1970.

At the Watergate hearings in 1973, with Senator Howard Baker, assistant counsel Terry Lenzer, assistant counsel Rufus Edmisten, and Senate Watergate Committee chairman Sam Ervin.

John Dean testifying at the Senate Watergate hearings, with his wife, Maureen, and his attorney Charles Shaffer at his side. Dean prepared me for attacks from the White House and suggested lines of inquiry for me and my Watergate investigative staff.

Below, left: H. R. (Bob) Haldeman, Nixon's chief of staff, talking to news reporters in June 1973, during the Watergate scandal. Haldeman was found guilty of perjury and was imprisoned.

John Ehrlichman, White House domestic policy adviser for Nixon, shown taking a break during testimony before the Senate Watergate Committee. Ehrlichman was sent to prison in connection with a burglary that preceded Watergate and set the stage for it.

The end of the trail for Nixon as president was captured on TV in August 1974, when he became the first president to resign from office.

I worked in the Senate to advance oceanic research and learned to scuba dive in the process. In the seventies, I spent ten days in a sea-bottom habitat.

On Fidel Castro's yacht in 1979. Castro caught lobsters for lunch; his personal physician picked them clean with a scalpel.

At a Washington reception with, *from left,* Jacob Javits, Mark Hatfield, and Gerald Ford. Javits and I were very close.

In the White House, 1985, with President Reagan and one of my favorite conservatives, Barry Goldwater.

With George Bush at a Republican rally at Fairfield University a few days before the 1988 election. I was booed; so was Bush when he mentioned my name.

Dennis Whitehead/Hartford Courant

Handcuffed and arrested in January 1985, for protesting apartheid at the South African embassy in Washington.

NEW HAVEN REGISTER

Best Wishes Bob Pich

For a time in the eighties I was able to hold my own against other Republicans, as this *New Haven Register* drawing depicts. Finally, I was forced out of the party—and made the old elephant even angrier by winning the governorship as an independent.

Stephen Dunn/Hartford Courant

Election night, 1988, with my wife, Claudia, and other family members. This was my only loss in a statewide election; defeat was toughest on the children.

Supreme Court Justice Lewis Powell, a family friend, presided at my inaugural as governor of Connecticut in 1991. Next to Powell is Claudia; at the top is my son Gray Weicker.

Official White House photo

Claudia and I at the White House with the Clintons, January 1994.

Some of the family: At left is my daughter-in-law Penne (wife of Gray Weicker), holding their daughter, Brooke. Next to me is Sonny; next to Claudia are Scot and Lisa Weicker, with Melissa. Up top are Tre, Amanda, Mason, and Andrew.

of faith in the Hindu spirit Brahma to worship freely and educate their children without fear.

John Kennedy was asked to comment after the Supreme Court in 1962 reaffirmed that government may not sponsor prayer. He said, "We have in this case a very easy remedy, and that is to pray ourselves. And I think it would be a welcome reminder to every American family that we can pray a good deal more at home, we can attend our churches with a good deal more fidelity, and we can make the true meaning of prayer much more important in the lives of all our children."

By striking down school prayer, the Supreme Court added new bricks and mortar to the constitutionally mandated wall between church and state. And so a generation of Americans — our children — have grown up in a nation much less given to bias and bigotry.

There are many, however, who would like to turn back the clock. As recently as March 1994, Senator Jesse Helms of North Carolina, supported by dozens of his colleagues, filibustered on behalf of his latest school-prayer amendment, which he had tacked on to a bill that laid out national educational goals. At one stage Helms came close to winning a majority vote.

In the eighties President Reagan frequently called for the return of "voluntary" school prayer. Let no one be fooled into thinking that school prayer was voluntary in the good old days when it was sanctioned. Those days were the ones when public school children were forced to recite the "Our Father" and read the King James Bible.

When I think about this issue, I can't help recalling Sir Thomas More as portrayed in *A Man for All Seasons*. The play concerns the conflict between Henry VIII and More, a devout Catholic, a leading lawyer, and a most respected citizen.

After More refuses to give a legal endorsement to the invalidation of Henry's marriage to Catherine, the king sends a spy to More's household. Upon discovering this, More's daughter tells her father to arrest the agent.

"Father," she says, "arrest him, that man is bad."

More replies, "There's no law against that."

More's son-in-law disagrees: "Yes, there is. God's law."

More replies, "Then God can arrest him."

At this point, More's daughter complains that while they are arguing, the spy is escaping. More tells her, "And so he should if he was the Devil himself, until he broke the law."

"So now you'd give the Devil benefit of the law," his son-in-law says mockingly.

"What would you do?" More asks. "Cut a great road through the law to get after the Devil?"

"Yes," was the response. "I'd cut down every law in England to do that."

That was when More had him. "Oh," he said, "and when the last law was down, and the Devil turned around on you — where would you hide, the laws all being flat? This country's planted thick with laws — man's laws, not God's — and if you cut them down, do you really think you could stand upright in the winds that would blow then?"

Once, on the floor of the Senate, Helms compared me to Humpty Dumpty. The wall I happened to be sitting on was that which separates church from state. The Senate was considering a Helms amendment to bar the Justice Department from using any of its appropriated funds to stop voluntary prayer or meditation in the public schools. I sought to add the word *constitutional* to the amendment, so that the Justice Department could not use any of its funds to prevent *constitutional* programs of voluntary prayer in the public schools.

Helms said I was trying to obfuscate the issue. He said I was like Humpty Dumpty, who said, "When *I* use a word, it means just what I choose it to mean — neither more nor less."

"What the Senator from Connecticut is doing," Helms went on, "is trying to use a word knowing that it will signal to the courts to keep on doing what they are doing, meddling in something that never was the court's business in the first place. It is just a code word."

To me it was a sign of the times that a senator should squirm at the mention of the word "Constitution" or "constitutional."

As senators, we take an oath to uphold that same Constitution. Uphold, not undermine. And if we or anyone else decides that some part of it no longer suits our purposes as a nation, we can amend it with the approval of three-fifths of the states.

But the fact is that Helms and his allies rarely try the constitutional-amendment route. They would prefer, with a simple majority of both Houses of Congress, to ban abortions and bring back school prayer and segregated schools, to take jurisdiction away from the courts and enforcement powers away from the Department of Justice.

My attempt to insert the word *constitutional* into the school-prayer amendment failed. I then offered another amendment with this qualifier: "Except that nothing in this Act shall be interpreted as the establishment of religion, or prohibiting the free exercise thereof." That, of course, is the wording of the First Amendment. Three senators disapproved the recommendation but reversed their vote when told what they were disapproving.

Helms suggested on the Senate floor that he would like to paint the school-prayer debate as a pitched battle between God's elect and the forces of darkness. He said he had met with Bill Murray, son of the atheist Madalyn Murray O'Hair, and that Murray said that while his mother was fighting school prayer, a number of Communist functionaries had visited their home. My response was, so what? You don't have to be a Communist or atheist to oppose school prayer. One senator who joined with me in speaking against the Helms amendment was John Danforth of Missouri, an ordained Episcopal minister.

My job as a senator was to make certain that every person is free to practice the articles of his or her faith, whatever they may be, without fear of reprisal. It was not my job to take up on Monday on the floor of the Senate where the rabbi left off on Saturday or the priest or minister on Sunday.

Mark Twain's Connecticut Yankee, propelled backward through time to King Arthur's court, decided that he should start a system of public schools. "I confined public religious teaching to the churches and the Sunday schools," said the Connecticut Yankee, "permitting nothing of it in my other educational buildings. I could have given my own sect preference and made everybody a Presbyterian without any trouble, but that would have been to affront a law of human nature ... and besides, I was afraid of a united Church; it makes a mighty power, the mightiest conceivable and then when it by and by gets into selfish hands, as it is always bound to do, it means death to human liberty, and paralysis to human thought."

We must all do what we can to keep standing the wall that separates church from state. For if it ever falls, we may never be able to put it back together again.

One of my strongest supporters in the fights against Helms was Senator Barry Goldwater, a genuine conservative who appreciated as much as I did the importance of the principle at stake. Goldwater quoted Alexander Hamilton as having written in *The Federalist*, "There is no liberty if the power of judging be not separate from the legislative and executive powers."

During my years in the Senate, there were numerous attempts at court stripping, most of them led by Helms. Helms was a clever parliamentarian who came to the Senate two years after I did. On some occasions, he and his allies did seek constitutional amendments. In 1984 they came up thirteen votes shy of a two-thirds majority needed to submit to the states an amendment calling for organized prayer in public schools. After it failed, school-prayer proponents resorted to highly questionable tactics that threatened to undermine not just the First Amendment but the separation of powers as well.

At one point the Senate spent a full day debating a prayer bill. "I don't want my child to be taught any innocuous prayer," I said. "Maybe you can find some language that is unobjectionable in a political sense or a parliamentary sense, but it's going to be extremely objectionable in an ecclesiastical sense to anybody who really cares about his faith."

Any school prayer acceptable to all factions would be so bland and watered down as to be demeaning to children who want to pray.

Nevertheless, such a radical rewrite of the Constitution was put forward as good, old-fashioned morality. How can a little prayer hurt? we were asked. In the 1984 arguments, I cited an eight-year-old, Justin Ross, for the answer. Justin had sent a letter to the White House about his experiences at a school in Canada.

"In my school," the boy wrote, "we had to say a prayer. Some of the children stood in the hall instead of saying the prayer. Everybody thought they were bad. One boy told me that I was going to Hell. Please don't make people hate me because I am Jewish. I do not hate you because you are not Jewish. It made me feel terrible to say the prayer."

The child wrote with the voice of authority. When I was growing up, Protestantism was de facto the official religion in the United States. To be a Roman Catholic or a Jew or anything but some mainline Protestant denomination meant you were different, and by the definition of the times, discriminated against.

Over the years, Helms repeatedly tried to legislate constitutional change. Almost invariably, his chief opponent in the Senate ended up being yours truly. He won some and I won some. We went round and round so much that a *New Haven Register* article once said, "It is so predictable, you might just want to call it the 'Weicker and Helms show.' "

In 1985 Helms offered a bill to block federal court challenges to prayer in the public schools. Under the legislation, wherever local school boards enacted prayer laws, the courts could not outlaw them.

I pointed out that the proposal stood for total infringement by Congress on the courts. I noted that support seemed to be waning for Helms and the fundamentalist Christian ministers who tried to link religion more closely to public life. "The more they try to bring the government into religion, the more people object to it," I said, pointing out that fifty-four senators supported Helms on school prayer earlier but that he was headed for certain defeat this time.

Other opponents said that if Helms succeeded, the school-prayer bill would be followed by proposals prohibiting the courts from considering school desegregation, abortion, and church-state relations in general.

In this instance, Helms's legislation was smashed in a 62-to-36 vote. Thirty-six votes is more than this kind of bill ever should get, but it's far from a winning number. True to earlier form, Barry Goldwater said Helms should have been ashamed of the bill, and asked him, "Did you really write that bill?" Such comments never seemed to bother Helms.

The recent merging of Christian fundamentalism with a so-called political conservatism has been branded one of the most potent political forces in the nation. Potent, yes. Conservative, no. For if the goal of this movement is to Christianize America, then it must be seen for what it is: a form of radical extremism which we all — liberal and conservative, Christian and non-Christian alike — must resist.

I don't fault the fundamentalists on what they choose to believe or how they interpret the Bible; it's their interpretation of the Constitution that bothers me. And I fault them for attempting to foist that interpretation off on the rest of us in our public schools.

People who practice fundamentalist politics and have school prayer at the top of their legislative agenda talk of a return to "traditional values." I say to them that here in the United States there is no value more traditional, more central to our way of life, than that of separation of church and state. It is our great gift to the world.

For my continuing opposition to school prayer, I once got a telegram postmarked Elmhurst, Illinois. It said: "You're doing a great job, keep up the good work. Have room for you and yours." It was signed, "Your pal, Satan."

Later on, I got one saying, "Do not be misled by fallen angels from Elmhurst, Illinois. You *are* doing a great job." It also was from Illinois, but the return address was marked "Heaven."

The fact is, my constant opposition to organized school prayer is an effort to retain religious freedom. Separation of church and state protects the church as well as the state.

In 1902 Pope Leo XIII applauded the separation of church and state in the United States by writing to American bishops, "The state of your churches in their flourishing youthfulness cheers our heart and fills it with delight. True, you are shown no special favor by the law of the land, but on the other hand, your lawgivers are certainly entitled to praise for the fact that they do nothing to restrain you in your liberty."

At one point around the time of Leo XIII, my family had a personal involvement in the mixing of church and state because, as I mentioned earlier, my mother's uncle, Randall Thomas Davidson, was the sixty-ninth archbishop of Canterbury. Nevertheless, I have come to believe along with Mark Twain that established religion "means death to human liberty, and paralysis to human thought."

My first conflict in the Senate over the Constitution came in 1972, on the subject of busing students for integration. Personally, I felt busing fell short as a means of achieving educational equality. Busing is jarring, especially for small children. But at the same time, antibusing politics was a charade, aimed at vote-getting pure and simple.

President Nixon was attempting to circumvent the Supreme Court's busing decisions. He came up with a bill called the Equal Educational Opportunities Act, which would have prohibited school busing in the future and reopened all previous cases of court-ordered busing.

In the Senate, I stated my opposition. "I have a deep belief in the sanctity of our courts," I said. "Under no circumstance would I see that sanctity violated, even in the smallest way for the shortest period of time."

I gave serious consideration to filibustering. "In years past," I said, "many availed themselves of the right of unlimited debate on the Senate floor to slow the process of desegregation in this nation. Should the occasion arise, I would hope my colleagues would avail themselves of the same right to slow the reintroduction of the separate but equal philosophy into the enactments of this body.

"What I am saying is that for those who think we are going to get the hot busing issue over the election year hump by a little moratorium on the courts, I suspect they are going to see the Senator from Connecticut and others still arguing the propriety of such a method right up to Election Day. And during that time the courts will continue to operate without presidential or congressional back seat driving."

Nixon's proposals sought to erode constitutional power and block the courts' right to decide on the legality of busing. I pointed out that the "function of Congress should not be to collaborate in such talks but to see to the business of legislative rather than judicial or executive solutions to America's problems."

In late September 1972 I was one of three Republican and four Democratic senators to pursue this issue. We got nearly five hundred law school professors to join in opposition to Nixon's anti-busing, court-stripping act.

The professors said the bill would place the legislative and judicial branches in conflict and would remove a remedy for the vindication of constitutional rights, even when that remedy is constitutionally required. They said the bill would "impair the Supreme Court's role of final arbiter of constitutional matters."

The seven senators, Jacob Javits, Hubert Humphrey, Edward Brooke, Ted Kennedy, Philip Hart, Walter Mondale, and I, said in joint statement:

> We are deeply troubled at the prospect that this complex and controversial measure — which would have an incalculable impact on the future of our nation's schools — might be acted upon hastily by the Senate, in the closing days of a busy session, under the pressure of election politics and without any consideration by a Senate committee. . . .

Separately, I made a point that holds today:

> As Americans who live under the protection of the Constitution, it is essential that we don't nibble away at the judicial and legislative branches of government. I am unalterably opposed to any legislation which would limit the scope of judicial review and remedy. If we can legislatively limit the courts' authority over busing in 1972, we could do the same with habeas corpus in the year 2000.

That flap over busing made me alert to the issue of court stripping ever afterward.

In 1980 language was inserted in an appropriation bill to prohibit the Justice Department from "bringing any sort of action to require directly or indirectly the transportation of any student to a school other than the school nearest the student's home."

Jimmy Carter was president then. In late September that year, the Senate voted 49 to 42 in favor of this antibusing position, which earlier had been approved by the House.

On September 26 I offered an amendment modifying the language to say that the Justice Department would not be prevented from securing remedies for violations of the Fifth or Fourteenth amendments to the Constitution. The idea had been worked up by an aide of mine, Stan Twardy, and the change, of course, would have nullified the antibusing stipulations.

A motion to table my amendment failed in a 27-to-54 vote. At that point, Jesse Helms of North Carolina and Strom Thurmond of South Carolina threatened to filibuster the appropriations bill. The bill was then laid aside until after the presidential election.

One day around this time, I took my child Sonny, then two years old, to Children's Hospital in Washington for a minor ear operation. Stan Twardy went with me. In a large waiting area we noticed a small boy who had one leg that was enormously wide, wider than his thighs and stomach. The problem was cancer and he was about to have his leg removed. He was from Connecticut, it turned out, and he and his parents talked with me for a while. This boy, four-and-a-half years old, was the picture of courage.

I reflected to Stan after the child was taken to the operating room that scenes like this underscore the real problems in life. And the thought came to me that the function of a US senator should be to help unfortunate children like that boy as much as possible, not to work against them. What a waste it was for people in positions of power to labor for months and years to keep all kids from getting equal educational opportunities.

On November 4 Ronald Reagan defeated Jimmy Carter. Nine days later the Senate, bending obsequiously in Reagan's direction, adopted by a 42-to-38 vote a Helms amendment exempting busing from the remedies available in cases the Justice Department could initiate or participate in.

It was clear to me that the amendment was an unconstitutional encroachment by Congress into the judicial branch. On November 19 I telephoned President Carter, at that point a lame duck, and asked him to veto the appropriations bill. I had a very good personal relationship with Carter, based in part on my early support for the Panama Canal treaty.

At the beginning of December, Carter said he would veto the appropriations bill. I then introduced a new amendment eliminating the antibusing language, and it was approved by the Senate.

After so much hassle, this was a victory for the Constitution. But it was a short-lived one.

The busing issue did not disappear. The following year, it was me — not Helms and Thurmond — who took the filibuster route. With Reagan as president we now had a court-stripper in the White House. He was sympathetic when, almost right away, a new antibusing bill was introduced.

The filibuster procedure has become more dignified since the time when Jimmy Stewart collapsed from the effort, hoarse and worn out, in the movie *Mr. Smith Comes to Washington*. Today there is no need for continuous control of the Senate floor. But despite the changes, filibustering is not exactly a relaxing experience.

I led one filibuster to block congressional court-stripping regarding busing that lasted almost eight months, from June 16, 1981, to February 2, 1982. There were seven cloture votes (attempts to limit debate), forty-seven roll calls, and twenty-five days on the floor.

Six months earlier, when Helms attached an amendment to the Department of Justice authorization bill to bar use of funds for desegregation that might lead to busing, I countered with an amendment that said: "Except that nothing in this Act shall be interpreted as barring the Department of Justice from enforcing the Constitution of the United States." My amendment was beaten down by a sizable margin; so much for the Constitution.

At the end of February 1982, my colleagues and I lost the fight over court stripping, unable to carry it any further.

The difference between the busing and school-prayer issues was that while the Justice Department had school desegregation cases pending, there was no current litigation over school prayer. It was Senator Helms who was trying to send a message, encouraging the public schools to embark on their own particular programs of prayer.

There are always a number of House and Senate members who, like Helms, would scrap the Constitution to win passage of their so-called social agenda. I consider it an antisocial agenda. They describe themselves as proprayer protectors of the American family and its neighborhood schools. On the matter of abortion, they say they are prolife. Who is it, I'd like to know, who is antiprayer and antilife? Certainly not me. But I am also for a child's equal protection under the law and a pregnant woman's right to privacy.

The issue of abortion, or choice, as many refer to it nowadays, has come back time and again as one of the most divisive problems in the United States. Helms and others tried to change the Constitution through amendment. At that time, Terence Cardinal Cooke of New York testified before the Senate Judiciary subcommittee on the Constitution in support of such an amendment.

Cooke said there is "a situation of lawlessness in our country," which he attributed to our "abortion mentality." I agree with him on the first point, then and now. There is a lawlessness pervading the politics of our country. But it did not begin with the Supreme Court's 1973 *Roe v. Wade* ruling that abortion was legal.

In the abortion debate, the lawlessness comes mainly from those who have sought, like Cardinal Cooke, to alter our constitutionally mandated system of checks and balances in favor of one particular system of religious belief.

Senator Orrin Hatch, who chaired the subcommittee and introduced the constitutional amendment, criticized Supreme Court justices "who impose their personal standards on 230 million Americans." In 1981, when Hatch made this statement, very few judges could be said to have imposed their personal standards on the public. That change came later, under President Reagan.

No constitutional amendment went out from Congress on abortion; the move fell eleven votes short. The following year, 1982, Helms came up with a proposal to make permanent numerous prohibitions on the use of federal money for abortions, and to declare, as a finding by Congress, that "the life of each human being begins at conception."

Again I filibustered, this time with Senator Bob Packwood of Oregon and three or four others. "No matter what the law states," I pointed out, "each year more than a million women will choose to have abortions. They will do so no matter what Mrs. Jones next door or Rev. Smith down the block says. They will do so no matter what this Senate says, whether we pass this bill or not. They will do so because they feel they must, and that, Mr. President, is not going to change."

On this occasion and others, majority leader Howard Baker could have closed down my filibusters but he never did. After our shaky start on Watergate, I came to have the utmost respect for Baker. His tenure as majority leader ended in 1987 when the Democrats regained control, and much of the civility and effectiveness in the Senate left at the same time.

There can be no compromising on the Constitution. Once it is compromised where one group of Americans is concerned, it loses its strength and no one's rights are safe.

Every generation of Americans has had to fight to reaffirm the country's commitment to the Bill of Rights as not just a museum piece but a living set of principles guaranteeing quality of life for all our citizens. That is because in every generation, there have been — and will continue to be, no doubt — those who would take us back to a medieval mind-set wherein the rights of the individual are neither recognized nor respected by those in positions of power.

What we have witnessed in the Senate of the United States and society at large in the past fifteen years is a mentality that says for every problem, real or perceived, there is a simple solution: revise the Constitution. Young people aren't listening to their parents? Well then, let's ban a few books they might be reading. Church attendance is declining? Well, then let's do away with the First Amendment's separation of church and state. Minority Americans getting a little too close for comfort? Well then, let's do away with court-ordered remedies and grant tax exemptions to segregated schools.

Again and again, the Constitution is asked to pay for our own shortcomings. When we've solved problems and met challenges in the past, it has been because we have applied our ideals, our ingenuity, and our resources to the task.

The problem then as now was only partly that a few people in high places were intent on making a mockery of our constitutional freedoms. The main problem was that the great majority of Americans allowed it to happen. The problem then, as now, was not peculiar to any one politician, or any one party, or any one philosophy. It was said in the early 1960s that the failure to pass civil-rights legislation was the fault of a few southern senators who were filibustering the bills. That was a superficial view. It was not just a few southern senators blocking that legislation; it was the people of the United States.

The problem is never one of the few, but of the many, and their ignorance of the origins of our greatness. This is not a recent development. In their own lifetimes, when the ink was still wet on the Bill of Rights, Madison and Jefferson were forced to speak out against the establishment of religion, against official censorship of the press, against the entire spectrum of the abuse of power. So must we speak out.

If there is a difference between then and now, it is perhaps the level of cynicism among the politically aware. Cynicism is not to be found in the writings of the Founding Fathers or in their deeds. They led by selfless example.

Two hundred years later, cynics are the stars of the Washington social circuit. Sophistication precludes ideals, making everything open to negotiation. And so we lose sight of what could be achieved if we had ideals and stuck to them. Everybody knows that there is really no such thing as representative government; consensus by the establishment has replaced it. The Constitution is a quaint but primitive document to which we pay lip service and nothing more. Automatic pilots more and more are expected to replace individual initiative.

Where have we come to when this nation can go to war and leave the press corps behind? Yet that is what it did in Grenada in 1983, in Panama in 1990, and, basically, in the Persian Gulf in 1991. And why isn't the press clamoring more about the problem?

Where have we come to as a country if the membership of the ACLU, the American Civil Liberties Union, can be characterized as something less than loyal, when in fact a more patriotic organization, in the true sense of the word, cannot be found anywhere on these shores.

When it comes to elections, when it comes to governing this country, the American people are couch potatoes who complain about the results, never having availed themselves of opportunities to shape the results.

They must be brought back into the mainstream of political life, by example and by every means of encouragement we have at our disposal. The best defense for our civil liberties is a good offense, and by that I mean a broadly based effort to educate people about the issues and about the Constitution itself. All too often what we learn in our civics classes is forgotten by graduation day. Or perhaps it is that the principles learned there are not taught in such a way that they can be easily applied to everyday life.

And so we find ourselves in a position where a majority of church leaders and organizational spokespersons oppose mandatory school prayer while a majority of their parishioners, as interviewed by the pollsters, support it.

The greatness, the practicality, of our Constitution isn't being communicated to the American people. Yet if we are to survive as a nation committed to the same goals as the founders, it must be communicated — by the press, by teachers and community leaders, and by people elected to public office.

These days the politicians who *are* getting people fired up about government tend, for the most part, to be those who would have it dismantled or reconstructed in such a way as to pit some Americans against others. McCarthyism was one variant of this sort of politics. We see many others at work. The cure is not hate for hate, or ill will repaid in kind. The cure is positive politics — activism on behalf of the Bill of Rights, however unpopular that may make us.

The attack on the First Amendment has been bipartisan in nature. So must its defense be bipartisan. And not simply bipartisan, but composed of people of all faiths and no faith at all. What we are fighting for is the freedom to interpret life and the world around us as each of us chooses.

Our purpose in banding together as a nation is not to promote Catholicism or Judaism or Buddhism or the faith of Islam but to ensure that as individuals we are free to find our own way to God.

The Statue of Liberty holds up a lamp for all the world to see —
not a cross but a lamp. And it is by the light of religious liberty that
we must continue to make our journey.

Who knows, maybe the one true faith is yet to be revealed. I
want to make sure that it can flourish in the United States, if nowhere else in the world.

11

Slowing Reagan Down

ALONG WITH Ronald Reagan's presidential victory in 1980 came an unexpected majority status for the Republicans in the US Senate. It meant committee chairmanships and other cachets for senior members, but for some of us there was a new concern. Our party was in control, yes. But we were more at odds with our own right wing than we had been with the Democrats.

In my sphere of interest, it was clear that Reagan and his supporters wanted to slash or eliminate major federal initiatives in health, education, and human services. One day toward the end of 1980, before Reagan took office, I got a call from Robert Stafford, the moderate Vermont Republican senator. He asked that I take on an additional assignment, a seat on the Labor and Human Resources Committee.

I already sat on a full complement of two major committees, one minor committee, and several subcommittees, so I had plenty to do. Stafford reasoned that without someone like me on it, the Labor Committee and its new chairman, conservative Orrin Hatch of Utah, would have eight conservatives matched against a total of eight moderates and liberals. With me on board, Stafford would have an ally and, when teamed with former chairman Ted Kennedy and six other Democrats, the committee could be controlled by an effective moderate majority.

His request presented problems. I already had begun the very substantial and unfamiliar steps of organizing the Small Business Committee, which I was to chair. That committee, through my efforts and those of majority leader Howard Baker and minority leader Robert Byrd, was undergoing a change in status from that of a select committee to that of a standing committee. The change was more than symbolic; as chairman of a full committee, I participated in the weekly meetings that set the legislative agenda.

I also wanted to maintain my commitment to undersea research and other programs in the jurisdiction of the Energy and Natural Resources Committee. Another assignment would mean a nightmarish schedule of concurrent meetings and floor votes. In addition, I would be running for reelection in 1982, so I would soon need time for fund-raising and campaigning.

I weighed these factors against the service I might perform with Stafford. The Labor Committee would decide what future, if any, there was for biomedical research, college loans and grants, disability education and job training, community-health and mental-health centers, and countless other human-service programs. I knew my presence could make a difference, so I said yes to Stafford.

I soon was named chairman of the subcommittee on the handicapped. To help run it, I recruited staff leaders from among people I knew well, mostly from Connecticut. With little time for committee and subcommittee assignments, I had to rely more heavily than usual on staff fact-finding and homework.

The first year of the Reagan presidency, 1981, was extremely contentious for me and set the stage for what was to follow. I was in a continual tug-of-war with those who were advancing the so-called Reagan revolution.

On issues I cared about, such as advances for the disabled, *tug-of-war* is exactly the correct term. Everywhere — except in the White House, it seems — attitudes had changed for the better. The physically disabled no longer were assumed to be mentally deficient. It was widely recognized that ninety-seven of every hundred mentally retarded children could, with help, become useful members of society. A person's IQ no longer was considered predetermined at birth. Environment and early life experience were known to exert a strong influence on ability to function. Early diagnosis could stem the damaging effects of disabilities.

President Reagan himself proclaimed 1981 the International

Year of the Handicapped in the United States. He said there "are thirty-five million disabled Americans who represent one of our most under-utilized national resources. Their will, their spirit and their heart are not impaired, despite their limitations. All of us stand to gain when those who are disabled share in American's opportunities."

Those were fine-sounding words. Unfortunately, Reagan's actions spoken louder, and delivered a much different message. That message was, let's get the federal government out of the business of helping the handicapped. In 1981 the Reagan administration did more to undermine than to promote the international year of the disabled, and there was no change in future years. It was a battle from beginning to end.

Reagan had gotten 51 percent of the vote to 41 percent for Jimmy Carter and less than 8 percent for independent John Anderson. Because of the ten-point margin over Carter, some Reagan supporters were claiming he had won in a landslide and that he had a public mandate for massive change.

As the winner, Reagan was entitled to lead, and he certainly knew how to do that. But the mandate claims were a crock. He took actions totally out of line with what Americans, including many of his voters, wanted.

Did the people who voted for Reagan want the Defense Department to get a blank check for unspecified new weapons systems as well as the resurrection of several tired old battleships and aircraft carriers? Did they decide that we should favor a racist government in South Africa over majority governments in black Africa? I don't think so. The election of 1980 contained a million different messages and not any monolithic mandate.

My intention from the start was to examine the administration's budget proposals in the light of as many of these voter messages as I could determine — and not in terms of a nonexistent mandate. That approach meant continuing conflict.

Reagan was shot and badly wounded in an assassination attempt on March 31, 1981, little more than two months after he took office. One predictable effect of that terrible incident was a burst of sympathy, as evidenced by a sudden, sharp boost in his popularity ratings in public-opinion polls.

In such a moment, most politicians, nervous Nellies that they are, wouldn't be caught dead criticizing Reagan's policies no matter how much they objected to them. Well, I'm careful but not that careful.

At the time of the assassination attempt, Reagan's budgetary goals were before Congress. On April 2, 1981, two days after the shooting, I issued a strong critique of them.* In hindsight, I think the critique holds up well as a sad but accurate commentary on all of Reagan's eight years in office.

> Social and scientific programs are forced to bite the budget-balancing bullet even as we hand defense a blank check. I tell you now that what we are going to wind up with is less security, not more. Hardware will never make us secure. Only superior technology can. Technology is a product of education — education that is shredded in this resolution.
>
> Similarly, we will not have a strong economy if our cities crumble, if we default on our commitment to energy independence and mass transit. Our poor cannot be productive if they have no housing and are without medical care.
>
> . . . I urge my colleagues to join me in voting against a resolution so lacking in substance and common sense. This is a mean-spirited venture by a great nation.

And later that month I made these remarks:

> This Administration preaches self-reliance even as it promotes profligate energy use that robs the world of its resources. It seeks military solutions to what are essentially social problems. Instead of weapons, we should be exporting education and economic know-how. . . . What we need is individualism with a human face, not survival of the fittest.

* There was nothing personal in this; indeed, I sent Reagan a note wishing a speedy recovery, and a month later he sent me back a warm reply. Later, when Reagan was hospitalized briefly in 1985, I sent him a note saying, "My prayers (in church, not school) have been with you. . . . After all, I need someone to fight with and you're the best." He responded that time with a message saying, "News of your church-going has brightened my day considerably."

As Reagan recuperated from the shooting, he went in his own, opposite direction. Citing the alleged mandate, his budget blueprint called for repeal of many Labor Committee programs in favor of loosely constructed block grants to the states. Each block grant meant a 25 percent reduction in federal funding. Block grants were described by their proponents as a start of a "new federalism" between the government in Washington and the states. In actuality, they were a means of repealing numerous worthwhile programs and abandoning federal government responsibility for them.

Block grants, according to Reagan, were to spur a renaissance in charity. Increased charitable giving would be a natural consequence once government made necessary program cuts.

Reagan's glib reasoning was like that of the woman who ran the orphans' workhouse in Dickens's *Oliver Twist*. Her philosophy was that the government's seven pence halfpenny's worth a week was "quite enough to overload a child's stomach and make it uncomfortable. So she appropriated the greatest part of the weekly stipend to her own use."

Dickens compared her to "another experimental philosopher who had a great theory about a horse being able to live without eating, and who demonstrated it so well, that he had got his own horse down to a straw a day," and would have reduced his feed to nothing at all, if the horse had not died.

Those were my views on block grants. They were meant to pare away at social programs and make people suffer. Charitable donations would have had to double or triple to balance the proposed Reagan budget and tax cuts. How farfetched. It wouldn't be the supply-side philosophers who suffered, either, for by the time they were proved wrong, they would have retired from government to some corporate board or teaching post. The elderly, the poor, the handicapped — the people those programs served — may have been harmed for life.

Orrin Hatch came to me, as he did to other members, to try to gain approval for these block grants. Hatch was too smart to take the approach with me that there was a public mandate for Reagan's cuts. Instead, he pleaded that, as chairman, he himself needed to be supported. He knew which strings to pull, for I was a true believer in the Senate's seniority system. Some people have long recalled me as a maverick, but the fact is I was a traditionalist who believed in the system. And in 1981, after twelve years as part of it, I myself stood to gain by having a good bit of seniority.

Even as Hatch was seeking my support, I was being lobbied by the Democrats. Late one afternoon I got a call from Ted Kennedy's office to ask if he could come by to discuss a legislative matter. This was a first for me. I was accustomed to making similar calls myself and trekking to Kennedy's office when he was in the majority. An aide, John Doyle, staff director of the subcommittee on the handicapped, and I met Kennedy at the door and ushered him in. After the meeting, Doyle expressed surprise that Kennedy knew the details of the issue at hand so well. "Don't act so surprised," I told Doyle. "Ted Kennedy is one of the brightest and most persuasive people in the Senate." As for Kennedy, I told him I would support his position.

By the time of that meeting I had worked out a strategy. I would generally go along with Hatch, but I would help Stafford maintain the moderate majority and cut the best deal possible in committee on the most important programs. The basic aim was to keep the full Senate, with its conservative majority, from trampling on Labor Committee decisions. My position was a risky one. Working with Hatch on the one side and Stafford and Kennedy on the other could backfire at any time, leaving me in the middle.

Reagan's budgetary goal was to boost defense spending by $100 billion, cut taxes by $280 billion and, according to his pronouncements, balance the budget by the year 1984. The balancing would come through the slashing of social programs, including education, to the bone. The whole plan was absurd.

Among other things, I was concerned over what would happen to science education. Most of the world, including what was then the Soviet Union, lived in awe of American scientific achievement. Every year, almost without exception, American researchers won a handful of Nobel Prizes that did as much for our prestige abroad as anything I can think of. Yet under Reagan, support for research in nondefense areas played second fiddle. The administration proposed $40 billion in research-and-development expenditures in fiscal 1982, with more than half going to defense in the form of a hefty increase and most other research programs getting reductions of varying magnitude.

By mid-April 1981 the die for Reagan's first four years had been cast. That year 37 percent of the budget was to go to so-called safety net programs, including Social Security, Medicare, aid to dependent children, and the like. Twenty-four percent was to go to the Defense Department. The plan was to increase the defense share to 32 percent by 1984 and leave the safety net programs pretty much standing in place, making a gain of up to 4 percentage points.

Something had to give if there were to be huge defense-spending increases and no decline in the safety net items. That something was a category craftily called "all other." Pity "all other." Its share of the pie was 29 percent in 1981 and was to be 18 percent in 1984.

And what exactly was "all other," with a name that hinted at obscure expenditures related to upkeep and such? Well, "all other" included education. It included science and technology. It included urban-development action grants and low-income energy assistance to the needy who couldn't afford to heat their homes. It included mass transit, public housing, vocational training.

I didn't blame Reagan and his budget director, David Stockman, a former congressman, for bundling these items into a group called "all other." If they had sketched in the microscopic slices of the pie given the school kids and the handicapped and the cities vis-à-vis those served up to the generals and the admirals, the budget story would have been better illustrated. We would have needed a magnifying glass to read it, but the picture would have been clearer nonetheless. They didn't want that.

I favored increases in defense spending, but Reagan clearly was overdoing it. We were asked to approve $3 billion for an MX missile without knowing if it was to be based on a racetrack in a desert or on submarines in coastal waters. Some basing modes were better than others and we should have been told what the administration had in mind before being asked to commit money, not afterward when it might be too late to change.

The administration failed to define the roles and missions of its weapons systems but asked for billions more even as we were to cut billions from the advancement of humanity. Had I gone to the Appropriations Committee with no plan but asked for billions for education or housing or transportation, I'd have been laughed out of the committee room, and rightfully so.

We were being asked to throw dollars at defense just as we threw money at social programs in the 1960s. It was equally inefficient both times.

It was natural for the president to lobby hard for his program, to try to get as much of it as he could unscathed. It would have been equally natural, within the realm of checks and balances, for Congress to give that program the once over, scrutinize its every facet, close up the loopholes, clean up the inequities, and reorder priorities if necessary. That is what should have occurred.

Instead, we were being asked to dispense with the details, to sign on the dotted line without reading the fine print. So that the country could pull itself out of its economic mess, we were asked to give Reagan carte blanche. That way, his lobbyists argued, his program's impact would be more intense and more immediate.

In the second week of May I laid out publicly what was wrong with the Reagan program. In retrospect, I couldn't have been more on the money about Reaganomics. I wish I had been wrong, but I wasn't.

"I disagree with the distribution of budget cuts and I believe the huge tax cut will be destructive of our economy," I said on the floor of the Senate on May 11, 1981.

> On the spending side, I support the bottom-line figure of roughly $40 billion in cuts, but the mix is all wrong. Defense spending is projected to grow at an annual rate of 17 percent over the next four years. By 1985 the four-year net increase will exceed the absolute level for 1978. Nothing is more important than national security. But that does not mean you throw money blindly at it.
>
> With respect to the tax cut, I am opposed to a 30-percent across the board cut in personal income taxes. Within three years that tax cut will cost the treasury $240 billion. . . . Anyone who says you can start out with a $63 billion deficit in 1981 and by 1984 increase defense spending by $87 billion, cut

personal and business taxes by $302 billion, and still balance
the budget is just deluding himself, and it is high time someone stood up and said so.

My call to arms landed with a thud, and before long, my
"work both ends" strategy was tested. In committee, some Republicans huffed and puffed about the need to support Reagan's mandate (the phony mandate). Nevertheless, Stafford and I were able
to manage it so that when the votes were taken, we were recommending increases in spending on programs for the handicapped
and other top-priority areas. Then the squeeze came.

Led by budget director Stockman, the administration seized
on the so-called reconciliation process, a feature of the congressional budget law, to allow Reagan to make all his cuts in one fell
swoop. Simply put, all programs in the Labor Committee's jurisdiction were to be considered together by the committee as to
whether they would remain as law or be repealed and block-
granted to the states, less, of course, the 25 percent reduction in
funding.

Stafford and I resisted, and were supported by Kennedy and
the other Democrats. Hatch avoided a markup session to adopt
final language for the bill because he knew he would lose when a
vote was taken. The two sides were at a stalemate.

Stafford and I had our aides assemble a package of the most
critical education, disability, and health programs. The time was
late June 1981. By now most Senate committees had finished their
reconciliation work, and not one of them had won concessions
from the White House. Reagan's landmark budget package was
almost ready for floor debate, except for the more than $50 billion
worth of programs under Labor Committee jurisdiction. Stafford
and I refused to let the budget out of committee until we had
restored at least some key funding.

I was in Connecticut, about to board a plane back to Washington one morning, when I got a call from John Doyle. Senate
majority leader Howard Baker wanted to meet that afternoon with
me, Stafford, Hatch, and Stockman to reach agreement. I asked
Doyle to work up the best compromise plan he could with
Stafford's people. On the flight back I drew up my own list. Doyle

met me at National Airport and went over what they had developed as we drove to the Capitol. The casualties included abandonment of several smaller programs and funding cuts in others. Stafford could live with the compromise, Doyle told me. I thought we might be giving away more than we had to.

The principals and a bunch of aides were waiting for us at Baker's office. There were no niceties, just business. Baker throughout was urging that a compromise be struck but he didn't push Stafford or me to accept demands we didn't like. With my own list as an outline, I ticked off what I wanted, stopping here and there to say why a particular health or disability program was so important. I said I would give my support only if my conditions were met.

Stockman and his aides briefly retreated to an adjacent room. When they came back, Stockman asked Stafford and me, "If you agree with this compromise, will you support the entire package through committee and floor debate?"

We all knew there would be numerous recorded votes, forced by the Democrats, on the lesser items to be cut or eliminated, aimed at embarrassing us before various constituencies. The political fallout for me could be heavy in the 1982 election, but I had held out for everything I thought I could get. When we reached a tentative agreement, I asked Stockman if he personally and the rest of the Reagan administration could be counted on to support the compromise throughout debate on the floor. When he said yes, the deal was cut.

The upshot was that we saved the bulk of the programs under the committee's jurisdiction. Health centers would remain open; vocational education would remain; disabled youngsters and adults would continue to receive special education, job training, and legal help; college students would continue to get loans and grants. Programs for disadvantaged youth would continue. So would certain maternal and child health-care programs.

Stafford and I had done the best we could in slowing down Reagan. Publicly, the Democrats on the committee criticized the features of the reconciliation bill but in private, some of them congratulated me for what we had been able to retain.

On the House side, there were many more Democrats than

Republicans. Theoretically, therefore, the House version of a reconciliation bill should have retained more important programs
than the Senate's. But much of the Democratic edge was only
nominal. Dozens of House Democrats voted with the Republicans,
and the result was that the House caved in to Reagan more than
the Senate had. That made the Stafford/Weicker compromise even
more important, for its tougher features almost always prevailed in
the ensuing House-Senate conference.

Within weeks the Reagan administration tried to renege on
our deal. In October 1981, a $900-million program for rehabilitation
services for the handicapped turned out to be missing from the
president's budget. Stockman's Office of Management and Budget
informed the Education Department that it could have the program back — but not the money. I wrote to Stockman, reminding
him of our meeting in Senator Baker's office. Not only had he
agreed in general that programs for the handicapped would be re-
authorized in their current categorical form, but we had singled
out the very vocational rehabilitation program that was missing for
protection and continuation.

The funds were partially restored, then built up further in
later years.

Ironically, when the 1982 Senate election campaign got under
way in Connecticut, the very first press release that my opponent
issued was a report from the Children's Defense Fund, an activist
group, saying that Weicker was against children. The release cited
my votes against Democratic statements of goals that pretended to
aim at revising the reconciliation package but in reality were done
only for show.

The developments in 1981 — the massive cuts proposed by Reagan,
my personal reaction to them, and, independent of that, my growing advancement of programs for people unable to help
themselves — radically altered my role as a US senator for the re-
mainder of my career in Washington.

No longer was I a high-visibility Watergate interrogator. Instead, drawing substantial notice from special constituencies but
little from the general public, I became ensconced in years of
struggle to improve conditions for groups that had been on the

verge of abandonment in our society: the physically disabled, persons with mental retardation, the poor, and, in sum, mostly all of those who were disadvantaged in one way or another. When AIDS became a scourge, I was one of the first in public life to address it.

On occasion these activities drew flurries of news media coverage, but much of the time they did not. Often, when reporters did focus on me, it was because of a clash I may have had — with Secretary of Education William Bennett over lack of funding, with President Reagan over his militaristic foreign policies and abominable domestic cuts, and so on. Generally, I got little press attention for the work I cared about the most, which was improving the lot of those in our society who, through no fault of their own, had the door to opportunity shut in their face. William Bennett was a special fraud. As secretary of education he spent all his time trying to choke off funds and programs for his own agency, while at the same time pleading the case for the Department of Defense.

The falloff in publicity never bothered me personally; I had won enough notice to last a lifetime. But a press that found abundant room for coverage of wrongdoing, or for soft Reagan "great communicator" features, was missing the boat in conveying to Americans an important fact of life in Washington. Despite its weaknesses, despite a cast that included some blowhards and cowards, the Congress of the United States did honest, conscientious business regularly, day after day, week after week. Important things got done.

The main news organizations have done a disservice by focusing their reporting of Congress as much as they do on confrontation, error, personality, and silliness. Fine, cover those aspects. But somewhere along the line, put the same effort into showing that government, and Congress in particular, can and does work.

Those who ridicule Congress are only looking at part of the story. In my main area of interest, advances for the disabled, we as Americans have witnessed a success story almost without parallel in history. It began before 1980 but continued throughout the Reagan years despite his opposition.

A key element was the enactment of Public Law 94–142, in 1975, which transformed educational opportunity for handicapped children from a distant hope to a basic right. In PL 94–142,

Congress recognized that the retarded have the potential for learn-
ing and a right to the kind of training to develop that potential.

For millions of the disabled, PL 94–142 was a marvelous opportunity to move toward the mainstream. For Reagan and his
public-relations planners, it was also a marvelous opportunity — a
marvelous photo opportunity. His administration was big on dis-
plays of partnership with handicapped children. But its real partnership was with the past, when the disabled were locked into
institutions and out of the nation's schools and workplaces.

In addition to Congress, the Justice Department under Jimmy
Carter investigated allegations of abuse of mentally retarded persons in institutions for a good while and established a reputation
for affirming and defending these rights. In 1980 Congress enacted
civil-rights legislation giving the Justice Department the necessary
mandate to continue critical intervention on behalf of the institu-
tionalized handicapped.

Under Reagan, the Justice Department retreated from this
role, and the White House tried to block advances. The successes
were enormous anyway. Millions of youngsters, once confined to
the outskirts of society because of their disabilities, joined the
ranks of their nondisabled peers. No longer were they hidden in
distant institutions with their minds, bodies, and talents left to
wither.

Because of programs I helped enact, millions of these courageous kids, eager and capable, now sport the bright faces of self-
worth. They tend to live at home and go to public schools, and —
most important of all — grow to their potential. Many share in the
credit for this success story. Loving, caring parents who give gener-
ously of their time and other resources; dedicated providers of education and related services who devote their careers to making
special education work. The largest share of the credit goes to the
priceless children themselves. They have made us see them as
people — not disabled people — but young people more than willing and able to overcome their handicaps.

Congress also deserves praise. Congress maintained, funded,
and extended the life of legislation for the handicapped despite
attempts by Reagan and his helpers to eviscerate it.

The only proposals from the Reagan administration were

ones to gut and slash. Reagan asked Congress to repeal PL 94–142; when that failed he asked to cut its funding by 25 percent, then another 8 percent, and, failing that, an even 30 percent. Reagan sent bills to Congress repealing portions of the act, and Congress rejected them all.

When Reagan couldn't get Congress to slash aid to the handicapped with legislation, he tried to do the same thing by rewriting regulations. That didn't get by, either.

In 1983 I assumed chairmanship of the Senate Appropriations Subcommittee on Labor, Health and Human Services, and Education.

Standing alone, the $100 billion in spending overseen by this subcommittee was more than the annual budgets for all but two nations. For fiscal year 1984 it included $4.3 billion for the National Institutes of Health, which supported nearly half of all the nation's health research and development and provided two-thirds of the federal funds for it. The mission of NIH — to combat and, if possible, prevent the major killing and disabling diseases of our time — is surely among the most difficult in government.

In the 1980s NIH's mission became greatly imperiled when the Reagan administration tried to achieve budgetary savings by cutting back on biomedical research and reversing decades of progress.

From 1960 to 1980, the share of private-sector and government research-and-development funds that went into health grew steadily, despite the Vietnam War and Great Society domestic programs. After 1980, a decline in private-sector spending on health research set in, paralleled by Reagan's attempts to slash programs.

The decline amounted to a few percentage points but it was dangerous nonetheless. And it was especially difficult to deal with because, although we were cutting back in scientific studies, our researchers and doctors were reaping rewards such as Nobel Prizes for work they had done earlier. Outward appearances, therefore, suggested that the United States was strong in biomedical research just when we were beginning to lag.

In conversations with researchers and administrators at NIH and elsewhere in 1983, I was told that we probably were at the start of a good-news cycle with regard to medical breakthroughs. New products and processes stood to be coming on stream. But what people would fail to grasp was that any good news was the result of funding decisions made ten to fifteen years earlier by individuals with vision. And the corners we would have to cut by going along with Reagan economics would not show themselves for years.

Aside from my social-services subcommittee, I also sat on the defense-appropriations subcommittee, where I constantly had the importance of lead time hammered into my head. We won't have a strong defense tomorrow unless we invest in a strong program of research and development today, we were constantly told. It was true, of course. But those quick to make that argument with regard to the Pentagon budget were frequently the same individuals who voted against increases in funding for NIH.

The original Office of Management and Budget proposals for fiscal year 1984 called for a total increase of $7 billion in research-and-development obligations. Nearly 97 percent was to go for military spending. NIH was to receive a mere 2 percent over fiscal year 1983.

What NIH ended up with, after our subcommittee went to work on the recommendations, was actually a 12 percent boost over the previous year's budget, enough to fund five thousand new and competing research grants, pay full indirect costs on grant awards, and keep all its research centers open. Included were funds that were made available for new initiatives against Alzheimer's disease. Arguably, recent breakthroughs in the understanding of Alzheimer's would not yet have been made had Congress accepted the Reagan-Stockman budget proposals. Ten million dollars was earmarked for a Jacob Javits neuroscience-research award program. Money was made available for a 20 percent increase over the previous year for augmented research activities by the National Institute on Aging.

Also in 1983, the administration tried to cut $2 billion in spending on education. Among programs that were to be axed were vocational education and the so-called Pell grants to financially needy undergraduates.* Severe cuts were contemplated in funding

* Reagan first went after the Pell grants in 1981, as soon as he took office. At that time he requested cuts in individual grants and stricter eligibility requirements that would have removed 150,000 needy students from the program.

for disadvantaged elementary and secondary students, and on education for the handicapped.

The bill we eventually reported out not only prevented the program eliminations, it restored over $1.7 billion of the cuts and included more money for education overall than the bill from the Democrat-controlled House. When Reagan signed the 1983 bill into law, it marked the first time in five years that a Labor–Health and Human Services–Education appropriations bill had stood on its own feet instead of being lumped into a continuing resolution. That meant that instead of funding only existing programs, the new law was able to update spending priorities and target money for important new initiatives. Part of the reason for that was purely political, having to do with the presidential election upcoming in 1984. But in part what we got was the result of our standing up to Reagan.

The task that fell to those of us in Congress carrying on the fight in the eighties was dictated by the political dynamic of our day, one construed by many in the Reagan administration to be a time for tearing down. Thus, we who worked for the handicapped were preservationists first, trying to hold the line, and pioneers second. Well, we held, all right. And we also made solid gains through a wide array of initiatives.

I would be hard-pressed to name another group within the human-services spectrum that not only survived the policies of the Reagan administration but also defeated them as consistently and as convincingly as did the disabled community.

In some Republican quarters, the ability to thwart Reagan was looked on with admiration, as I discovered one day in 1984 when I got a call asking me to come to New York Senator Alphonse D'Amato's office. D'Amato, successor to Javits, was meeting with a few other first-term senators; I remember that Paula Hawkins of Florida and Bob Kasten of Wisconsin were there.

The question put to me, asked in all seriousness, was pretty funny. They wanted to know how they could vote against Reagan's budget reconciliation bill for 1985. "That's easy," I told them. "Go to the floor, vote, go back to your office, and don't answer the phone."

Throughout Reagan's two terms, the battle remained nasty.

Reagan never lost a fight, only rounds in a fight, because he and his minions always came back for more, sometimes long after others thought the match was over.

One person who prepared and encouraged me for the continuous battle in the Senate was my mentor, Javits. In May 1984, on the occasion of his eightieth birthday, a badly ailing Javits, attached to a respirator, prodded me on in a stunning, highly emotional scene that made me cry like a baby.

The occasion was a birthday party for Javits, held at the "21" club in Manhattan. About eighty family members and friends were there. Javits had spent twenty-four years in the Senate, but I was the only senator present, and only one other, Ted Kennedy, had been invited. The mayor of New York, Ed Koch, attended; so did Barbara Walters, Douglas Fairbanks, Jr., and a number of other well-known and not-so-well-known friends of Javits's. Marion Javits, his wife, spoke lovingly of him, as did other family members and some friends.

When Javits responded, he could speak only haltingly, his phrases interrupted by deep gasps for breath. He briefly thanked his family and friends for their kind words and attendance, and then went on to say: "I want to tell all of you that the US Senate is a very cold place. No one knows that more than Lowell Weicker. It is difficult to be different within the Senate, hard to bring a conscience to it." He complimented me for standing up for the underprivileged, said I was playing a very important role.

When he was done, my wife, Claudia, whispered that all Javits's comments were directed at me. One would have thought it was my party, not his.

Later that year, just before Christmas, Claudia and I met with Javits once more and we were strongly reminded of how forward-looking a presence he always was. This time Javits was a patient at New York Hospital. We took him a gingerbread house and sat with him for a while. He was still on a respirator but had papers piled up everywhere.

Again speaking in short gasps, he said, "Lowell, the most important issues facing American families today are day care and child care."

While he was talking, we had a bad scare. Javits was lying

with his head down, and suddenly his face began getting redder and redder. Claudia ran out and came back with a nurse who took one look and said, "Oh, damn!" She got a roll of Scotch tape and taped a loose tube back to the respirator. If not for that, Jack might have died right then. How's that for a commentary on the high-tech world we inhabit: fly to the moon, be incredibly inventive with computers and everything else — but better not forget the Scotch tape!

As it was, Jack Javits lived about one more year. We had always been close but I nevertheless felt it extraordinary to have been treated so kindly by him in his later, ailing years, to have him so attentive to my work. Javits, himself the conscience of the Senate for so many years, had never served at a time when the Republicans had a majority. He left just as Ronald Reagan won, bringing in a GOP Senate majority from 1981 through 1986. Javits may have looked at me not only as his successor, but as someone who had a better chance than he did to create and enact important legislation.

On a personal level, I was close to a few senators aside from Javits, but not many. I enjoyed good professional relations, even admired many of my colleagues, including ones whose policies and beliefs often were distasteful to me. In that vein, I got along very well with Alan Simpson, Bob Dole, Orrin Hatch, John Tower, Barry Goldwater, and some others. Seldom did I ever agree with any of them on issues, but I respected them and I think the feeling was mutual.

Ones who come to mind as personal friends are Ted Kennedy, Chris Dodd, John Warner, Dale Bumpers, Tom Harkin, Fritz Hollings, Thad Cochran, Abe Ribicoff, Mark Hatfield. These friendships sprang from common interests and beliefs but were not consummated in the usual socializing sense. Instead, they grew into a bond continually forged on the floor of the Senate, where we faced up to many of the most unpopular issues of the day.

12

"To Hell with the Begrudgers"

ONE LESSON of Watergate was the value of good, solid investigative reporting. In 1984 I read about the death of a mental patient at Creedmore, a New York State institution. If the horrible
conditions described existed in a progressive state like New York,
they might be found anywhere, I conjectured.

So, as chairman of an appropriations subcommittee dealing
with the handicapped, I sent five staff members across the country
looking into conditions at various state-run mental institutions.
They went to thirty-one facilities in twelve states, sometimes making official visits, sometimes dropping in unexpectedly. In one institution in Massachusetts where we had bad reports, an aide got a
job as a staff person and worked there for three weeks.

After six hundred interviews in six months, they came back to
Washington with one horror story after another, and in the beginning of April 1985 I held televised committee hearings to underscore some of the problems.

Witnesses included former residents, parents of residents, facility employees, administrators, rights advocates. We subpoenaed
some, put all of them under oath in testimony. They told of physical abuse, ill-trained doctors and staff, overmedication, excessive
paperwork. The investigators documented inadequacies in systems
for reporting abuse, so that terrible conditions almost certainly
would go undiscovered. We found hundreds, perhaps thousands of
individuals who had no access to legal representation or advocacy.

These hearings were very dramatic. On one or two days they

led the evening news on network TV. A main message that was issued was, here are people whose lives could be restored — let's end the neglect and abuse.

Later in April 1985, I sponsored the Protection and Advocacy for the Mentally Ill Act to ensure the rights of those confined to mental institutions. The legislation, enacted a year later, created agencies with the authority to receive and investigate complaints of abuse and neglect, and to pursue administrative and legal remedies where abuse was found. Thirty million dollars — not a lot of money, but enough for a good start — was authorized for the program in its first three years, with the National Institute of Mental Health in charge of disbursement.

Also in 1985, I found myself in the peculiar position of siding with my perennial foe, Jesse Helms, on a matter of principle. What happened was that Charles Percy of Illinois had been defeated in 1984, leaving open the chairmanship of the Senate Foreign Relations Committee. According to seniority, the position should have gone to Helms. At first it was uncertain whether he wanted the job, and Richard Lugar of Indiana put himself in the running.

Helms then said he did want to be chairman, and a nasty battle ensued. Lugar far more than Helms fulfilled my concept and philosophy of a foreign-policy chairman. Helms and I could not have been further apart. There was not a single issue on which we agreed and we fought each other endlessly on the floor of the Senate.

But when Helms expressed his choice, I was duty-bound to support him. The one unemotional, dispassionate arbiter of committee chairmanships was seniority. It was an accepted tradition that worked to everyone's advantage. If the rule could be broken in Helms's case, it could be broken in mine as well. As a minority in my own party, I might not be able to achieve the things that were due to me.

I could not see in any set of circumstances why the system should not prevail on Helms's behalf. Furthermore, despite our opposing each other throughout our careers, I have no doubt that Helms would have fought for me had the situation been reversed. As it happened, Lugar got the job.

*   *   *

Like many Americans, I became concerned about the AIDS epidemic in the early-to-middle eighties. Unlike most, I was in a position to be of some help. From the moment I got involved, AIDS for me became a test of how well the government in Washington could work to assist people.

In 1984 I visited Hawaii and while there stopped at the Hansen's disease, or leprosy, settlement at Kalaupapa on the island of Molokai. It was a beautiful place, a quiet place. But as I stood there overlooking the Molokai channel, I was aware that 120 years earlier, lepers in wooden crates were thrown into that channel, to make it to Kalawao Beach or not depending on waves, rocks, and sharks.

Once ashore, theirs was the tragic existence of being in a living graveyard. No care, no food, no shelter. Indeed, the cry of the inhabitants as new patients arrived was, "In this place there is no law." One man changed that hell. Father Damien Deveuster, a Belgian Roman Catholic priest.

At first, and all by himself, he brought dignity, comfort, and additional years of life to the hurt. He had no public-opinion polls or wonder drugs to support what was to be a life commitment. Most of his clerical colleagues would not accompany him on his rounds of mercy. Just Damien himself brought a world from out of the darkness of cruelty and despair toward the light of understanding and hope.

Kalaupapa is now a national park. Beautiful Saint Philomena Church, built by Father Damien and his patients, is a historic monument. The history it recalls is one in which seven thousand ostracized victims who lived and died at Kalaupapa dwindled to a few dozen who presently populate the settlement.

In the 1980s we were presented a new Damien's challenge, AIDS. It too traveled in the company of fear born of ignorance.

Once again as a nation, we had the choice when it came to those afflicted with AIDS: was it to be "over the side," or "into our hearts"? As time passes, the answer to that question, more than the transmissibility of an AIDS virus, will determine the life and death of this nation. The issue is not yet settled. But in Congress in the 1980s, we made a fair, intelligent start on it.

In 1984 President Reagan requested $33.8 million in AIDS

funding; Congress appropriated $61.4 million. In 1985 Reagan asked for $60 million and Congress appropriated $108.6 million. In 1986 he asked for $128 million and Congress appropriated $244 million. In 1987 Reagan asked for $213 million and we appropriated $413 million. Each time, we roughly doubled the amount Reagan had requested. Our response was timely and productive. From time to time, it was even speedy.

At the end of April 1986, for example, Democrat Bill Proxmire of Ohio and I had come to agreement on the next year's funding for health programs under the appropriations subcommittee that I chaired. Proxmire was the ranking Democratic member, and we were to present the budget to the full subcommittee the next morning.

That afternoon an aide told me that two AIDS activists wanted to see me about an urgent matter. We met, and they described the drug AZT to me. AZT was providing hope to AIDS sufferers, but it was expensive. They asked me to include $46 million dollars in the budget for clinical trials of AZT. I explained that it was too late, the legislation was complete.

When they left I had an assistant, Maureen Byrnes, call Dr. Tony Fauci at the National Institutes of Health and ask him about the effectiveness of AZT, which was sold under the name Retrovir by the Burroughs Wellcome pharmaceutical company.

Fauci told Byrnes, "Yes, we think AZT can do something; it's our only hope at this time."

I found Proxmire on the floor of the Senate the first thing the next morning. We agreed on an additional $30 million, which was then included in the supplemental 1987 budget with bipartisan support. Later we got additional funds to provide AZT to those who couldn't afford it.

The funding legislation was signed into law by Reagan, but not without a great deal of concern expressed about the cost of covering AIDS drugs, and indeed, the cost of caring for a person with AIDS.

I found it ironic that with the threat posed by AIDS to the safety of the nation, the Reagan administration could be so divided, getting into discussions of philosophy when the need for treatment was so urgent.

In my view, it was no time for discussing homosexuality. We in Congress were not philosophers. Our job wasn't to sit in judgment on AIDS victims, it was to pay heed to what scientists were recommending in dealing with this scourge. The threat of AIDS was the most severe crisis to be posed to this country in the lifetime of all of us. That includes armed conflicts.

AIDS has proved a stubborn, vicious enemy. The drug AZT, while useful, has not been a panacea. None has been found. Nevertheless, we should take pride in the rapidity of the discovery, isolation, and cloning of the AIDS virus. What ordinarily would have taken a decade was done in a very short time. Why? Because, over the objections of those who felt government has a small role to play in our lives, this country, led by Congress, year by year made more of a commitment to basic biomedical research, and more of a commitment to the National Institutes of Health. We were in a position to confront the enemy very quickly, and we did.

I worked hard to help ensure these accomplishments, but I'm not looking for any special credit for that. The point I want to get across is totally different. It is that Congress can and does respond to people's needs. Sure, some said AIDS was a homosexual disease, let the gays take care of themselves. But that decidedly was not the sentiment of Congress as a whole, which acted quickly and properly.

On top of Reagan's attempts at cutting programs, Congress was hamstrung by the Gramm-Rudman-Hollings provisions of the 1985 debt-ceiling bill, which imposed a limit on all spending outlays. Gramm-Rudman-Hollings created a painful, unconscionable, arbitrary standard for across-the-board cuts. It forced legislators to look at numbers, not programs and people.

Reagan's second term was as miserable as his first in terms of hypocrisy and attempts to slash social programs. Hardly anything could be more hypocritical than Reagan's treatment of small business, a vital force in American life and a core of Reagan's political constituency from the moment he entered politics.

Today the government's Small Business Administration is a principal vehicle for economic development. Its programs are responsible for $9 billion in loans, with more banks than at any time in the past providing long-term capital. But back in the mid-eighties, while I was chairman of the Senate Small Business Committee, Reagan tried to kill it outright.

My position as Small Business chairman came to me almost totally by accident. I joined the committee in 1975 at Jack Javits's request. Led at the time by Democrat Gaylord Nelson of Wisconsin, it had little authority or consequence and was the third or fourth committee assignment for most of its nine members.

I would have left in 1977 except for circumstances that catapulted me into being the senior Republican, with a staff of five people. I brought in Bob Dotchin, my legislative director, to head up the operation.

With Jimmy Carter as president, more government focus began to be placed on small business. The size of the committee jumped from nine to seventeen members to accommodate requests from senators wanting to join. Small business, responsible for 43 percent of the domestic product and 50 percent of private employment, was getting increased recognition.

When I became chairman in 1981, I hired half a dozen more staff members, including one person, Kim Elliott, who was to be my chief aide through the rest of the decade, and who has handled special assignments for me since then. In 1981 we held five comprehensive hearings on the workings of the Small Business Administration, which at the time was riddled with fraud and abuse and crying out for strong oversight. The following year I got an important ally in efforts to revitalize the SBA when Jim Sanders was brought on as its administrator.

At one point late in 1983, Reagan taped a video, to be shown at a small-business conference, in which he extolled government's relations with small business. Things seemed to be going very decently, until the president did an about-face.

Early in 1985, in preparing the fiscal 1986 budget, Reagan instructed budget director Stockman to end government-backed loans to small businesses and eliminate the Small Business Administration entirely.

On February 28, 1985, Stockman appeared before my Small Business Committee. I asked him if we were supposed to believe the Reagan in the video or the one trying to kill off SBA.

Stockman's tongue-in-cheek answer was that people in the White House had regrets over a number of movies Reagan had made.

As was always the case with Reagan, multiple programs, not just one, were on the chopping block. It was difficult to round up colleagues to help save SBA because they were busy working to stave off cuts elsewhere. For example, the Small Business Committee chairman in the House, Parren Mitchell, was a natural ally. But Mitchell, a leader of the Black Caucus, was deeply concerned about cuts in human-resources programs, and had to spend his political capital trying to save them.

Luckily, Reagan was having extreme difficulty getting his budget through the Senate, and I was able to negotiate with Stockman for my vote, just as I had in 1981 over social programs. This time one of my requests was that SBA be maintained as an independent agency. It was, and I voted for the budget, which passed the Senate by a razor-thin 50-to-49 vote.

Reagan never stopped his reckless attempts at slashes in social programs. One of his next steps was to propose that, for fiscal 1987, funding for special education and vocational rehabilitation be reduced to 1985 levels. His Education Department budget stated that the increases approved by Congress for fiscal 1986 "should not be maintained, and the department proposes that they be rescinded."

At the same time, a Louis Harris survey showed that disabled Americans had far less education than the nondisabled, that the disabled were much poorer, and that two-thirds of the disabled between the ages of sixteen and sixty-four were not working, though they wanted to work.

Even as Reagan was proposing cuts in spending for the handicapped in 1986, preparations were under way at 1600 Pennsylvania Avenue for a celebration of ten years of progress in educating the nation's handicapped children under Public Law 94–142.

What shabbiness. One day the White House took credit for social advances; in the following weeks the administration was to send its officials, one by one, to testify before me and others in the Appropriations Committee, going through the motions of defending a proposed cut of $108 million in the program whose success they were celebrating.

In 1986 Congress again deflected Reagan's proposed cuts in aid for the handicapped. Instead of cuts, there were modest increases in funding, based on a better understanding of needs. Under a new law, which I helped enact, Congress created what were called "early intervention" state grants to provide comprehensive services to handicapped infants from birth to age two. Fifty million dollars to carry out the program was provided in fiscal 1987, with incentives given to states that offered the services to handicapped preschool children up to age five. An additional $180 million was provided so that at the end of five years, early intervention would consist of aid from birth through age five in all states.

In January 1987 Secretary of Education William Bennett proposed cutting almost 30 percent of his department's budget — $5.5 billion from a current spending level of $19.5 billion. In testimony before the Labor and Human Resources Committee, Bennett said that "total national spending for education has climbed steadily," and that "American education has improved on this Administration's watch."

I pointed out to him that he could put up a chart and show how education spending had increased, but that if he put up another chart listing what Reagan had requested over the years, that one would show decreasing support. It was congressional rejection of Reagan administration budgets that accounted for the increases in spending, not his advocacy of cuts. Mr. Bennett had a very facile if not truthful mindset.

Overall, in four years as chairman and two as ranking Republican member of the Appropriations Subcommittee on Labor, Health and Human Services, and Education, I helped deliver almost $25 billion more for education than the Reagan administration had requested. Almost every year, Stafford and I, despite the cries for slashes from Reagan and his supporters while we worked in a slash-minded Republican-controlled Senate, allotted more funds for education than did the House, which, was, of course, overwhelmingly Democratic.

It is my firm belief that by finding room in the budget for programs that Reagan had consigned to the ash heap, we helped provide a healthier future for all Americans. Charles Kettering, the industrialist and philanthropist, once said, "We should all be concerned about the future because we will have to spend the rest of our lives there." I think that understates matters. The fact is, initiatives begun today may not pay off until long after the politicians who voted for them have disappeared from the scene. It is because the founders of this nation acted in the interest of future generations that we were able to become, in so many ways, a model for the world.

We as a society will be judged not by how well we lived, not by the number of possessions we accumulated and consumed, but by what we did to improve the condition of humanity. Which peoples do we revere? The Huns for their brute strength? The Romans for their capacity for conquest? No, it is the Greeks and their pursuit of wisdom and beauty that we study and pay tribute to even today.

On April 28, 1988, I introduced legislation that was to become the landmark Americans with Disabilities Act. Enacted in 1990, after I left the Senate, it was the jewel in the crown for me, the culmination of years of effort.

The aim of the act was to establish a broad prohibition of discrimination against people with disabilities and to spell out specific methods by which such discrimination was to be eliminated. It prohibited discrimination against the handicapped in housing, transportation, communications, state and local government, construction, and by employers with more than fifteen workers.

The history of the disabilities act goes back at least as far as 1978, when Congress established the National Council on the Handicapped as part of the Department of Health, Education, and Welfare. In 1984 the council was made an independent federal agency, and in 1986 it proposed forty-five legislative recommendations, with the Americans with Disabilities Act heading the list. I had worked with the council in each step of its development, and its leaders asked me to introduce the legislation in the Senate.

In doing so, I cited some of psychologist Kenneth Clark's testimony in the *Brown v. Board of Education* school desegregation case in 1954, repeating his observation that "segregation is the way in which a society tells a group of human beings that they are inferior to other groups of human beings in the society."

"On a number of prior occasions," I said, "I have stood in this chamber and quoted various authorities' conclusions that the history of society's formal methods for dealing with people with disabilities can be summed up in two words: segregation and inequality. As a society we have treated people with disabilities as inferiors and have made them unwelcome in many activities and opportunities generally available to other Americans."

The disabled, I noted, had experienced workplace discrimination, denial of educational opportunities, lack of access to public buildings and public bathrooms, the absence of accessible transportation, and other forms of social ostracism. In one survey, a quarter of the disabled interviewed said they personally had encountered job discrimination. In another survey, nearly two-thirds of individuals with disabilities said they did not go to a single movie in the past year — about three times the proportion of the general population that did not go to the movies. The disabled were three times more likely to say they never eat in restaurants.

Many disabled Americans were isolated, due in major measure to discrimination. Two-thirds of the disabled of working age did not have jobs, and among them, two-thirds wanted to work.

I noted that the costs associated with the requirements of the Americans with Disabilities Act were a small price to pay for opening up our society. "We cannot afford not to require that discrimination on the basis of handicap be eliminated. . . . We cannot afford to have people subjected to discrimination when they seek to find jobs. We cannot afford to have two-thirds of people with disabilities not working when two-thirds of those without jobs say they want to be working. We cannot afford to pay for the institutionalization of individuals who could live independently if they were not confronted with discriminatory practices that make it impossible to find appropriate housing in the community. We cannot afford to have our transportation systems unusable by people with disabilities. . . .

"The costs to our society of discrimination are much greater than the costs of eliminating such discrimination," I said.

Around the time I introduced this legislation, disabled people were making an incredible imprint. Two very different handicapped authors could be found on the best-seller lists in the

Sunday *New York Times*. The number-two book on the nonfiction list was *A Brief History of Time*, by Stephen W. Hawking. The book was a comprehensive look at great thinkers from Aristotle to Einstein and beyond, and their efforts to arrive at a unified theory of the universe. Hawking was considered by many the most brilliant theoretical physicist alive. But when he wrote, he had been confined for twenty years to a wheelchair by Lou Gehrig's disease. He was unable to hold a pencil, and he worked out the complex details of his theorems and formulas in his head.

Number thirteen on the nonfiction list was *Under the Eye of the Clock,* the autobiography of a twenty-one-year-old Irishman named Christopher Nolan. Nolan's first book, which he wrote at the age of sixteen, got him rave reviews and comparisons to James Joyce. Nolan had cerebral palsy and was paralyzed, spastic, and speechless since birth.

We can talk about mainstreaming special children until we are blue in the face and not have half the force of Nolan's first-person testimony. In a passage from *Eye of the Clock,* the narrator, whom Nolan calls Joseph Meehan, is about to graduate from Mount Temple, where he had been mainstreamed. He is sad about leaving, excited about prospects of attending Trinity College. Nolan changed the boy's name, but the story is his own.

> Was that the clock striking, mused the boy, as he drove along the avenue to Mount Temple? Now the voyage of discovery was at an end. It was his last day in the noble school. His eye glanced gamely over the lovely-spired building, glanced up into the just and watching clock, and voicing loneliness for his merry days here, weathering gang warfare and loud laughter, his had been the fun, his the beauty-packed life. Never assessed as anything but normal by his class-clanned friends, he experienced things which he would never tell, saw things which he would never describe, snared life that would last him to the grave, and all because a school said to hell with the begrudgers, we'll welcome Joseph Meehan into our midst.

It was to take a little longer for our society to do the same where Americans with disabilities were concerned. I introduced the landmark act during the 100th session of Congress, but it wasn't acted on then.

I myself never made it to the 101st Congress. Iowa Democratic senator Tom Harkin did, and he took charge of the disabilities act. The bill was revised and introduced in both houses in May 1989, and enacted in 1990 while George Bush was president.

The legislation was changed substantially after I left the Senate, but nevertheless, no bill ever had more of my stamp — or more of my heart in it — than the Americans with Disabilities Act.

Much of my work in the 1980s consisted of seeing to it that the Reagan administration not be allowed to destroy what had gone on before. Reagan proposed massive cuts in labor, biomedical research, family planning, alcohol and drug abuse, mental health, health professions training, and doctors and nurses for the underserved communities across the country. As chairman of an important appropriations subcommittee at the moment when Reagan was most successful elsewhere, I, along with a few others, blocked most of his cuts in the field of health.

In some areas, we went beyond simply blocking the cuts. You know the street sign "Don't even think about parking here"? Well, every sign posted by the Reagan administration in the years 1983 to 1986, said, "Don't even think about new social programs." Fine. No new programs. But there were ways around that, too.

One way was to incorporate new programs into existing ones. That is what we did when we provided scientists money for immediate study of AIDS, for example. In that manner, working with the National Institutes of Health, I and a few others helped thwart a good deal of the Reagan cuts. Here and there, despite the taboo, we even drew up and enacted new legislation.

In fact, all or almost all of whatever new social programs came into being during the two Reagan terms were in the fields of health care and aid for the physically and mentally handicapped. I am proud of what I did to help that along, but I am especially proud of having been associated with the disabilities act, because it outdid the others in reach.

I was delighted, therefore, when I was invited to a ceremony at the White House Rose Garden in 1989 to mark the installation of a new chairman of the President's Committee on Employment for

Persons with Disabilities. By then George Bush was president. I went with Kim Elliott, my assistant. We never got past the kiosk at the White House gate. "Sorry, your name has been scratched off the list," a guard said.

I had had my ups and downs with Bush, but I didn't think he was that petty. John Sununu, his chief of staff, was. One person in the White House, the vice president, Dan Quayle, was horrified by this deliberate poke in the eye. He had the grace to be on the telephone apologizing even before I got back to my office, saying that he was mortified.

But that incident, along with numerous others, helped push me further and further from the Republican party. The following year about three thousand people were invited to the White House for the signing of the Americans with Disabilities Act. Everyone involved knew my role in creating that legislation and a number of people submitted my name for the invitation list. No invitation came. Again, how petty.

At one point after my 1988 election loss, George Bush asked me to the White House and brought up the possibility of a presidential appointment. A specific job was mentioned. But that was it; I never heard about it again. It wasn't as though I had asked Bush for a job; he had initiated the discussion. It seems to me that Republicans get a certain unseemly pleasure from punishing their own.

It was true, of course, that over a period of many years I had taken positions opposed to those of the Republican leadership. Nevertheless, I always considered myself a good party man, a team player. It is not "Republican" to be corrupt as Nixon was or to drive the country into the ground with pie-in-the-sky budgets and policies that ranged from sheer meanness to absurdity, as Reagan did. They are the ones who were untrue to their party's principles.

I think these conclusions are obvious, fair ones. More and more, however, because I wouldn't fall in with the crowd, the word *maverick* was used to describe me. *Maverick*, after Samuel Maverick, a nineteenth-century rancher who wouldn't brand his cattle. When some of them strayed, no one could tell to whom they belonged. Some mavericks are thought of simply as lost from their herd; others, as being strongly independent.

I saw my job in the Senate as one in which I spoke for the disadvantaged, bringing their voices to the rooms of power they could not reach by themselves. It is fine to say, okay, I'm not black, I'm not poor. But then one morning you wake up as I did to find you have a handicapped child. Then, suddenly, you are a minority and you better hope there is someone to represent you, someone to speak out for you and see that your voice is heard.

Mine was an attempt to have the political process accord to science, medicine, and education the same patriotic tribute it bestows upon arms, ritual, and narrow morality. I never thought of these efforts, or my other work in the Senate, as that of a maverick in the sense of being lost from the herd. But on occasion — as when colleagues said they would vote and speak out as I did, except for fear of a backlash — I sometimes did see myself as a maverick. Independent, unafraid, an oddity: a loner on issues, a loner in politics.

Just after I lost my Senate seat in 1988, I was given an award for being of service to those who couldn't help themselves. At the presentation, a reporter asked what I regarded as my greatest disappointment, and I responded with this story:

Several weeks earlier a young mother from Indiana testifying before the Senate subcommittee on the handicapped recounted a tale of discrimination as practiced upon her. She had contracted AIDS from blood transfusions when she had a stroke during childbirth. After describing a town turned against her and her children, she spoke these haunting words: "Senator, America is *not* a very good place if you are different or if you are ill."

I told the reporter that I was disappointed not with the previous Tuesday's political events; officeholders must be prepared to lose elections. What disappointed me was that too many Americans, given the opportunity to petition their government, would reiterate the testimony of that young lady from Indiana.

Another reporter asked what I liked best about public life. I didn't have to hesitate; I had known since I was a child why I wanted to be in politics: "The opportunity to exercise power. That's what it's all about. Power. The opportunity to use it on behalf of those who are in need.

"Let's face it," I said, "there is very little I can do here for my friends in Greenwich. There is a great deal I can do in the towns and cities in our state on behalf of the homeless, those who are suffering from AIDS, the elderly in need of health care, the disabled, minorities, and those seeking a better education. That's the big thrill in life, bringing everything this nation has to offer to those types of people."

13

Republicans — the "Against" Party

THE 1988 ELECTION campaign was my last as a Republican. The party had squeezed me out little by little. The last straw was the race for Senate against Joseph Lieberman. I lost by a razor-thin margin, seven-tenths of one percentage point. I did well enough among Democrats and independents, but crossover Republicans, taking their cue from state party leaders, did me in.

I had discovered the extent of pettiness and spitefulness among Republicans much earlier in my career, at the 1964 convention in San Francisco. When Barry Goldwater won the presidential nomination, I was very concerned, as was he, at the reaction. Instead of joy, many Goldwater supporters spewed hate and bitterness at everyone in reach. Their elation, it seemed, was not so much that Goldwater had won, but that his opponents had lost. That meanness hasn't gone away.

The Republicans were the party of Lincoln, the party born in the fire of national conflict over whether all people were created equal. The party that stood for the rights of the individual, for equal opportunity for the individual, for private initiative, private enterprise. But what has been the Republican position on minorities, on labor, on cities, on taxes, on abortion? Often it is to see what the Democrats do, and then to say — regardless of the worth of the Democrats' position — "We're against it."

From time to time, Republicans have spoken a good game about getting blacks into the party. They have even put a few blacks in the window to make it appear that Republicans are tolerant, reaching out. But I don't recall a single program that ever integrated black interests in the party.

I counted some in the Connecticut GOP as friends, but there was an element that from 1973 on sought to punish me for Watergate. These were diehards who convinced themselves that Weicker was to blame for Nixon's fall, and they would have liked nothing better than to cut me down. I was accused also of being a maverick, and too liberal.

For a long time, opponents in the party and I wrestled to a frustrating standoff. Their problem was that I had become the strongest Republican candidate for statewide office. Not only the strongest, but the only one to win statewide after 1970. My dilemma was that, while popular with voters, I was vulnerable to the whims of extreme, unprincipled partisans in my own party.

From my start in politics I wanted to build a Republican majority; I didn't like the idea of waiting to win on a twenty-year cycle — that is, for a person like Eisenhower to come along or for a negative vote like the one that elected Nixon in 1968. The party had to be more inclusive. But the Republicans had a way of chopping off everyone — labor, blacks, young people — everyone except for a small, exclusive group.

Yes, I was critical of the party. But a Republican who wasn't critical was the one who deserved raised eyebrows, not the critic who wanted the party to succeed. It was clear that Republicans had to change, that they were unpopular — why else were so few of them elected in this country?

After Watergate, opinion polls showed that I was the most popular politician in the state, Democrat or Republican. That was at a time when Republicans nationally were reeling because of the Nixon scandal. Everywhere, it seemed, the party was losing elections, unable to find decent candidates. The contrast between Connecticut and the rest of the country was absurd: Outside Connecticut, Republicans couldn't find strong contenders; in Connecticut, where they had a strong contender, many in the party were looking to ditch him.

In 1974 I was a scheduled speaker at a state Republican convention but the party chairman canceled my appearance. Just another slap in the face. A magazine writer, Alexander Burnam, wrote in 1976 that he had interviewed Republicans in the party structure who expressed "their vehement dislike — even hatred — of Lowell Weicker and his Watergate performance."

At the state convention that year, when I was running for reelection to the Senate, my Watergate Committee colleague Howard Baker addressed the gathering. "I don't know who is trying to destroy the two-party system," Baker started saying, when he was interrupted by shouts of "Weicker! Weicker!"

The Democrats ran a very popular candidate, second-term secretary of state Gloria Schaffer, against me in 1976. The only woman in the nation seeking election to the Senate that year (how times change), she had won her previous election by an enormous margin. Part of Mrs. Schaffer's strategy was to get into nasty personal exchanges. She tried to bait me continually, but that never was my style of politics. To her attacks on me, the strategy my camp and I developed was to respond by saying, "We know what Weicker's record is, but what is her record?"

Despite the behind-the-scenes Republican sniping, I was in a very strong position with the electorate in 1976 and won in one of the biggest landslides in the history of Connecticut. (Later, as governor, I made Mrs. Schaffer commissioner of consumer affairs in my cabinet.)

My easy victory did nothing to help my relations with the state Republican party, however. I got no money from it, no support in the sense of any accolades. I had no party position. Opponents said I was some sort of naive idealist. Naive? I had spent six years in the state legislature, four as first selectman of Greenwich, two in the House of Representatives, and at the time Watergate hit, two in the US Senate. Naive I wasn't.

I understood when I took a hard-nosed approach to the problems caused by Watergate, rather than a partisan approach, that I was going to lose party support. On the other hand, I also felt, from the Republican party's point of view, that the best thing would be for a Republican, not a Democrat, to expose the facts. The facts were there; the facts were known by others. It was really a matter of who was going to tell the story. Strictly in a political sense, I thought it would be far better to have the Republicans clean up their own house.

When I ran for Senate again, in 1982, a new factor, Ronald Reagan, entered the equation. My difficulties with the state Republican hierarchy were exacerbated by my frequent lacing into Reagan and the New Right. Many Republicans would have liked nothing better than to knock me off, and they almost got the chance when Vice President George Bush's older brother, Prescott Bush, Jr., challenged me for the Republican nomination. Prescott Bush saw an opportunity in that he was the vice president's brother on the one hand and in that there was discontent in the Connecticut Republican party on the other.

He got about 35 percent of the delegates at the Republican state convention and was ahead of me in several preprimary voter polls. Bush was helped when high Reagan officials in Washington made phone calls to obscure delegates, urging them to support him.

Confusing things for some delegates, I imagine, was a fluke "photo opportunity," shown on every Connecticut TV station, in which Reagan congratulated me in the White House Rose Garden for a job well done. What happened was that Warren Rudman, the New Hampshire Republican at the time, had asked for a Rose Garden ceremony to note his first major bill to become law, a piece of small-business legislation. Because I was chairman of the Small Business Committee, the White House had to invite me, too.

One high Reagan official who made calls to delegates on behalf of Prescott Bush was the late Malcolm (Mac) Baldrige, who was then the secretary of commerce. That was payback for a recent spat. At Commerce, Baldrige was in charge of NOAA, the National Oceanic and Atmospheric Administration. Going along with the Reagan philosophy of cut-cut-cut in 1981, Baldrige first tried to eliminate NOAA. When that failed, he worked up legislation to strip NOAA of its ships. Great; we were to have seagoing scientific research with no ships!

My response, in the same item of legislation, was to remove all the payroll funds for Baldrige's staff, expenses for his autos, and so on. That's the way the game is played sometimes. In the end, I got my ships, he got his staff. Mac was a decent man. His problem — too many people's problem — was toadying to Reagan's cuts.

(Some years later Mac Baldrige was trampled in a freak rodeo-type accident and died. I got a phone call saying the biggest NOAA research vessel was going to be named the *Malcolm Baldrige*, and would I give the speech, please. Baldrige and I had reached a certain rapprochement toward the end, so I said I would. This, as I remember it, was my first truly hypocritical act in politics. People had tears rolling down their faces as I spoke. But I felt like an ass, extolling the man who tried to scuttle the ship being named for him.)

Baldrige's attempts and those of others to keep me from getting the 1982 Republican Senate nomination were very upsetting to me. Not Prescott Bush's actions; he was entitled to run. But I was a two-term incumbent senator with a very broad constituency, and it was clear that many Republican-party chiefs and functionaries, state and national, really didn't care about that at all.

I was slated to get $250,000 from a fund for Republican senators seeking reelection, but a scheme was worked up in the White House to keep the money from me. Luckily, it was blocked by a party official in Washington. Acting just in time, she wired the entire $250,000 in the middle of the night to Pete McSpadden, who handled my political advertising.

Such incidents led me to do a little thinking out loud about running as an independent right then, but that turned out to be counterproductive. As my campaign manager, Tom D'Amore, pointed out, it was hard to corral Republican delegates for a candidate who was talking about running as an independent.

In the midst of Prescott Bush's efforts, calmer heads began to prevail. Fifty-one of the sixty-nine Republicans in the state legislature endorsed me, saying I was the only Republican who could win in the fall. That view — a correct one, in my judgment — took hold, and some state and national party leaders exerted pressure on Bush to drop out.

Bush did well enough that he could have forced a primary. For a while it looked like he would, but instead he suddenly quit the race. To this day, I am not sure why. Some people have told me his brother persuaded him to avoid a bitter fight within Republican ranks.

My Democratic opponent that year was a liberal congressman, Toby Moffett. On reflection, Moffett might have won had he moved to the right and run an all-out attack campaign, as Joe Lieberman did in 1988.

Moffett, however, was a liberal who ran as a liberal. It was a close contest, physically and mentally the toughest campaign of my career. Moffett was a worthy opponent. He articulated his beliefs well and was totally honest intellectually. He did not do the chameleon job that Lieberman did six years later of becoming a conservative Democrat. Lieberman was just as much a liberal in the course of his career as Moffett; the difference was that Moffett remained true to himself.

Many Republicans had trouble voting for me, but hell, there was no way they would vote for Moffett. Let me put it this way: There were some Neanderthal Republicans in Connecticut who viewed Lowell Weicker as a socialist. But if I was a socialist to them, well, Moffett was a Communist.

Moffett was a vigorous campaigner and a good debater. Pushed by him, I myself performed as well as I ever did in the debate format. In one debate, in Waterbury, Moffett left me an opening that, I believe, turned the election. He had been bashing me for some votes in which I sided with President Reagan despite having held a contradictory position. Some of these were procedural votes, taken in loyalty to one's political party and because there was absolutely nothing to be gained by voting the other way. Procedural votes may look hypocritical but almost every member engages in them from time to time. Others were trade-off votes, for having gotten Reagan's aides to back away from cutting the frail elements of society off at the knees.

My staff discovered that for every procedural vote I had made, Moffett had made one himself. I used that at the Waterbury debate, turning the tables on him. I don't think he was prepared for it, and it showed.

I won with 50 percent of the vote to 46 percent for Moffett, with a third candidate, a conservative, Lucien deFazio, drawing minimal support.

Internal sniping at me by Republicans continued as long as I stayed in the party; on my end, I kept attempting to make the GOP more inclusive. After the victory over Moffett, my drawing power had to be recognized and my influence in the state Republican party grew, at least for a spell. I helped install Tom D'Amore as state chairman. With a lot of sweating and lifting, we then got the party to permit independents to vote in Republican primaries. I figured what have we got to lose: if we get the public interested in us in the primaries, they may stay with us for the general election. And that was a huge number of voters out there: blacks, Hispanics, women — you scoop up everybody.

The state of Connecticut, using taxpayer funds, sued over the issue and the case went to the Supreme Court. Except for some of its more ultraconservative members such as Justice Scalia, the Court said you are darned right, this is the essence of the right of association, and upheld the right of the GOP to set the rules as to what association would mean.

In March 1988 I made my case for a broad-based GOP at a hearing on discussion of the national party platform for the up-coming presidential race.

"We must win more than the White House if we are to become America's majority party," I said.

> That won't happen until Republicans return to their roots as the party of the Constitution and the party of fiscal responsibility. This means putting aside the philosophical agenda favored by the single-interest groups and taking up the issues of importance to all Americans.
>
> Farm failures, factory closings, diseases for which we have no cures, a budget deficit that defies our imaginations, the spiraling costs of health care, illiteracy and underemployment, diminished opportunities for small businesses to thrive and grow: these are matters that make a difference in our quality of life. They are the business of life and as such the legitimate business of government. . . .
>
> Instead of presiding over the systematic dismantlement of civil rights enforcement and the abandonment of our commitment to equal justice under law, the Republican party

should — as the historical party of individual rights — lead
the fight to break down the barriers to opportunity and equality which still exist in our society.

It was like talking to a wall.

The 1988 election loss to Joseph Lieberman was my first defeat
since taking local office in the early 1960s. I still have very mixed
feelings about this campaign. Did I work as hard in the Lieberman
campaign as in the Moffett campaign? No, I think I was weary. My
Senate work had been intense, with filibusters and other fights.
Also, I must admit to a certain smugness: I felt I had established an
extremely worthwhile record in terms of advancement of the National Institutes of Health, legislation on handicapped issues,
health, education issues, and so on. I was winding up what I considered the six most productive years of my career, and lurking
inside me was the thought that I deserved everything from the
state of Connecticut.

I ended up running a sloppy, lazy campaign. It wasn't the
intellectual or the debate side — there were three debates — that
cost me the election. No, what I did was to violate my original
rules. I didn't campaign physically. I disregarded the one-on-one
style that had been so successful.

In the past I also had covered my flank by courting activist
Republicans. I was forced to do that in 1976 and 1982 because of
the threat of opposition in the party to my renomination for the
Senate. There was no such threat in 1988, and I made the mistake
of not shoring myself up within the party. Given the difficult relations I had with the hierarchy in Connecticut, it was an under-
standable error. But it was a costly one.

The right wing of the Republican party had made a conscious
decision not to primary me; instead it hid in the weeds and nailed
me in the general election. I didn't lose in terms of the Democratic
vote; I lost because of the Republicans. In town after town, they
either stayed home or went in alarming numbers for Lieberman.

I had simply been too cocky; I thought the voters owed me
something. Early opinion polls also made me relax; a survey at the

end of April showed me with 51 percent, Lieberman with 27 percent. At one point I was asked the "why" question by a reporter. "Why run again?" I allowed as to how my duty station in the fight for constitutional ideals would be left uncovered were I not to run. My special role, I said, had been to give voice and strength to those on the outs. At some time or other, that has meant just about everyone and everything.

In 1988 that was not a winning message, as D'Amore warned early on. D'Amore had helped run my campaign in 1982 but advised me not to run in '88. He said the electorate had changed, that there was a self-centeredness among voters brought on by the presidency of Ronald Reagan.

D'Amore was right, of course. Reagan as president told the biggest group of Americans, the middle class, that they could have it all and not pay for it. The young people, the new immigrants, blacks, and others might suffer, but that was brushed under the rug. With that self-centeredness, a spreading Me-ism, the last thing voters wanted to hear was Lowell Weicker talking about AIDS, about civil rights, about the Constitution.

Throughout his political career, Joe Lieberman had been about as liberal as Toby Moffett. His strategy was to move to the right, and to run a very negative campaign as well. Lieberman, an Orthodox Jew, called for lowering the wall that separated church and state and attacked me for my staunch opposition to any such lowering. Specifically, he came out in behalf of moments of silence for meditation or prayer in the schools. I was astounded by this tactic. The principal beneficiaries of church-state separation have always been religious minorities. Some of the strongest, most eloquent supporters of church-state separation have been Jewish. I don't know how Lieberman reconciled his religious beliefs with his political actions in this instance, or if he even tried. If he wasn't denying his faith by criticizing me on separation of church and state, he certainly wasn't far from it.

An editorial writer at the Bristol, Connecticut, newspaper was among those who saw Lieberman's move for what it was. The writer noted that Lieberman had "hit on a real crowd pleaser" after having "a tough time selling himself as a middle-of-the-road kind of guy." The journalist concluded that "Lieberman has stepped from his traditional progressive viewpoint past the middle of the road." Which was just what Lieberman wanted.

Lieberman also charged that I missed important votes. This was a sham issue but a somewhat effective one. Absenteeism was never a problem of mine. Given the long days and weekends I spent on filibusters, in fact, I believe I put in more time on the Senate floor than any other member in the years preceding the 1988 election.

Lieberman ran an extensive, nasty ad campaign against me, in line with the current view that a negative campaign is the only way to go. In response, toward the end my advertising team came up with an ad mocking Lieberman, showing his head getting smaller and smaller as he mouthed hypocritical and conflicting statements. The ad may have run once. I pulled it; it just was not my style. Given the closeness of the race, that ad might have made the difference. But I knew that at the time, and I said then that I would rather lose reelection than run it.

The 1988 campaign was the first in which I got broad labor union support, endorsed by the AFL-CIO and every major union. But the Republican party in Connecticut wasn't interested in labor, a constituency that had never before come their way.

In the politics I played there was an unwritten set of rules. I would hit as hard as the hardest hitter, but I wouldn't close out the debate in a cheap, uncalled-for manner. You win with substance, not tricks.

Looking back, I guess I was behind the times: the rules were changing but I wasn't changing with them.

Aside from the ads, there was some old-fashioned pragmatic politics at play. In the presidential race early in the year, Bob Dole won the Iowa caucuses and looked as though he would win the GOP nomination if he could get by George Bush in New Hampshire. The Dole people wanted my endorsement, feeling it would be useful in the New England state. I had been helpful to Dole earlier, especially in the Watergate year of 1974 when he was engaged in a close, hard-fought reelection contest, a rarity for him. As Republican-party chairman at the beginning of the scandal, Dole was being linked with Richard Nixon by a tough opponent. I campaigned for him in Kansas and, I believe, helped him win.

In 1988 I decided to support Bush, not Dole, in part because of Bush's ties to Connecticut. For me and all other Republican candidates in Connecticut, there was more to gain with Bush at the top of the ticket. I supported Bush and he supported me. If that seems cold and calculated, so be it. The flip side is that in politics one works with people despite disagreement on issues.

There must have been dozens in the Senate whose views clashed repeatedly with mine. There was no way I could get along with them on policy. But I enjoyed and admired each of them as colleagues.

Being on a ticket with George Bush wasn't enough to help me among Republicans in 1988. My old associate Hank Harper said he could measure the erosion by invitations to Lincoln Day dinners, the annual Republican-party events. Harper's wife's birthday was February 12, the same as Lincoln's. In all the years Hank worked with me, what he did on her birthday was to attend a Lincoln Day dinner. Except in 1987 and 1988, when he got no invitations.

Dole supporters among Connecticut Republicans tended to be more right-wing than Bush supporters, and they held key positions in the state. As my 1988 campaign progressed, this group, which had no love for me to begin with, actively worked against me. One such leader, Dick Bozzuto, publicly endorsed Lieberman, a stunning act of disloyalty to the Republican party, in my judgment. It hurt personally, too, in that in 1980 I supported Bozzuto over James Buckley in a run he made for the Republican US Senate nomination.

Also working against me was Buckley's brother, the haughty columnist William Buckley, the debate opponent from Yale days. He created a "BuckPac" for fund-raising against me and did his best to taunt me whenever he could. Clever and vicious, Buckley resented my working against his brother in 1980, and my blocking James Buckley's appointment to a federal judgeship in Connecticut later on.

In late October 1988, Bush and I campaigned before a Republican gathering at Fairfield University. It was Bush's last big rally before Election Day, and the arrangement was for him to speak and then introduce me. As I was proceeding toward a holding room, I heard some loud, raucous booing. What in the world is going on, I wondered — until I realized that some in the audience had caught a glimpse of me, and I was the object of their Bronx cheers. A short while later, Bush introduced me. That brought a new round of boos. To my recollection, this was the first time that rank-and-file Republicans in Connecticut gave me such treatment.

I lost to Lieberman by ten thousand votes, 50 to 49 percent. The toughest part was being with my children as the results came in. They were broken up and teary-eyed. It was much worse for them than for me; I wasn't happy but at least I could find a little humor in the situation, as when Claudia and I finally were alone for the first time that night, around three AM. I put my arm around her and said, "Well, Claudia, this never happened with my first two wives."

After the election, control of the state Republican party reverted to the conservatives. They eliminated the inclusion of independents as voters in party primaries. Republican primaries in Connecticut once again are limited to party members.

Right-wingers got their wish by ousting me, but almost immediately, the law of unintended consequences came to play. In Washington, President Bush nominated John Tower as secretary of defense. As far as I am concerned, Tower was a person who always played by the same rules I did. Our views were different, but he would have had my vote. And with it, he would have been confirmed.

14

Independent and Unfettered

REMOVED FROM OFFICE in 1989, I took a position as head of Research! America, a company in Alexandria, Virginia, that raised funds for medical and scientific study. From my office I could see the Capitol dome across the Potomac.

I also taught a constitutional-law class at the George Washington University law school. The first-semester class was a seminar-size group of third-year students; on day one I showed a tape of *A Man for All Seasons* so they could see what it meant to be a nation of laws, not men. I brought Orrin Hatch and others in to talk to the students. The second semester I dealt with health policy. Shades of things to come!

I enjoyed teaching and think the students enjoyed me. Occasionally I would end up telling the class what political behavior was right, what was wrong. And when I did, I'd ask myself why was I teaching, why wasn't I in the ring? I felt I still had a lot to contribute.

The 1988 loss grated. I am a large man with a large appetite, and, I guess, an outsize ego when it comes to competition. I didn't like getting shoved off the field, and that's how I viewed the race with Lieberman. My vision always had been that I would depart on my own, walking off under my own power, on my own schedule.

To friends, these feelings must have been transparent. Some began bringing up the subject of reentry. The post they had in mind was the Connecticut governorship.

The first to push hard in this direction were old Senate staff colleagues John Doyle and Bob Dotchin, at dinner in my home in Old Town, Alexandria. Claudia and I had just bought our house and hadn't even unpacked. I am talking now about the late fall and early winter of 1989.

The political situation was this: The incumbent governor, Democrat William O'Neill, was not expected to run again. The two most likely candidates were John Rowland the Republican and Bruce Morrison the Democrat. Both were members of the House of Representatives in Washington.

Rowland was the youngest person in Congress, age twenty-seven, when first elected in 1984. A Reagan loyalist, he had been a constant critic of my record in the Senate. He was one of those in the party who worked hard for my defeat in 1988.

In October 1989 Rowland asked to meet with me and we had dinner at the City Club in Washington. He asked if I was going to run. The bottom line, I told him, was that I had not made up my mind. Later, when he tried to shore up his Republican support, Rowland said I agreed to support him. A total falsehood.

A week later I met with Morrison, at his request. He asked for my support. I said I would back him if Rowland got the GOP nomination, but I also told him that people had been importuning me to run, and that I had not made up my mind.

Dotchin and Doyle had done a lot of plotting before sounding me out. When they first broached the matter, I said I wasn't interested. They didn't believe me (I always did recruit bright people), and they pushed a little harder in several cocktail-hour sessions at a hotel in Old Town. Doyle said I *had* to get back in politics, that I was a fish out of water otherwise.

They and some other friends had commissioned a voter poll in which I emerged as a strong contender for the governorship. Not surprisingly, I did well with Democrats and independents, not so well with Republicans. We all agreed that seeking the Republican nomination was the riskiest part of the exercise.

The situation remained static into February 1990. Both Morrison and Rowland announced their candidacies and, as days and weeks passed, some Republicans began asking what my plans were. The more I said I wasn't sure, the more convinced they were that I would be seeking the party nomination. Some asked my close associate Tom D'Amore what I was doing, and he said he didn't know. To which the response from Republicans was, "You're as big a liar as Weicker is."

About this time, one person in the Republican hierarchy sized up the situation and told John Doyle that it was impossible, totally out of the question, for Weicker to run as a Republican. If I was going to run, this operative said, it would have to be as an independent, so I might as well drop any idea I had of seeking the governorship. Doyle agreed with everything this man said, except the part about dropping the idea. Thus it was Doyle, a strong Republican himself, who first raised with me the thought of running on a third-party banner.

I had toyed with third-party possibilities for years, ever since the Republicans started ostracizing me. This time I began sounding people out. Chris Dodd, for one, said the landscape had greatly changed since 1970 when his father ran against me as an independent. Dodd thought it entirely likely that an independent would win in Connecticut. Some others had the same sense of things, but for every one of them there was another person who thought a third-party candidacy would be futile.

I then set up a meeting with Tom D'Amore, without going into any of the details in advance. I wanted him managing my campaign if I ran, as he had in 1982. D'Amore knew I wanted to discuss running for governor. He had concluded that my only winning chances were as a Republican, and he, like my other friends, wouldn't ask me to run that gauntlet. He was prepared to tell me to forget electoral politics.

I told Tom I had this one last idea: "What if I run as an independent — are you with me?" Of course he was, despite the skepticism.

Claudia and I then went to have dinner with two men who were longtime friends and major campaign contributors. They were furious when I broke the news to them — not because they held the two-party system sacred, but because they thought reentry into politics would bring me a lot of anguish. They yelled at me for hours; we ended up drinking too much and not going to dinner at all. In the final analysis, we both were right. Politics is great anguish. Also great joy.

Within weeks, Bob Dotchin set up a $250-a-plate dinner for me in Washington. The nation's capital is not much of a place for gubernatorial fund-raising under any circumstances; for an independent gubernatorial candidate, the thought of raising money in Washington is bizarre. My case was a little different. Old friends like Marion Javits, Tom Harkin, Paul Laxalt, Ed Brooke, Bill Proxmire, and a lot of others showed up. The affair raised $50,000, and we were off and running.

The main people in my campaign were ones who had worked with me for years. Some were enthusiastic; some felt I had poor chances of winning. All agreed with Doyle that I had been a fish out of water, and were glad that I was back in politics. Most tried to make it appear that they were signing on because of their warm feelings for me. In part that was true. But over the years we had become like a family, and I know they missed the action as much as I did.

As we got going in this uncharted territory of independent campaigning, some of the smart money would approach people like D'Amore and ask, "What do we get out of this if Weicker wins?" The reply would be, "Nothing." They would wink and say, "Yeah, okay, we get you." But as we went along it was clear that we weren't going to be beholden to anyone. Campaigning outside the two parties was indeed liberating.

Connecticut was hurting in March 1990 when I entered the governor's race. Its cities were dying, its infrastructure, public and private, was in shambles, its defense industry in decline, the insurance industry ensnared in bad real estate loans, and the government balance sheet ready to fly apart after decades of political chicanery.

Masking the internal rot were the statistics of a state with the highest income per capita in the nation.

Through most of the election campaign, officials in Hartford anticipated a budget deficit of $50 million to $100 million. That was a disappointing but manageable gap, and I saw no need to alter any of my positions as a candidate because of it.

John Rowland, the Republican, announced his candidacy early. He had good chances of winning, the best of any Republican since Thomas Meskill in 1970. Good chances, that is, until I got in the race.

Bruce Morrison, the Democratic candidate, also announced early, angering the incumbent, William O'Neill, by saying he would run even if O'Neill stood for reelection.

Morrison got the Democratic nomination after beating a state representative, William J. Cibes, Jr., of New London, in a party primary. Cibes did poorly in votes but very well in terms of intellect and integrity. As things worked out, he was to play a more important role for Connecticut than either Morrison or Rowland over the next four years.

As a candidate, Bill Cibes made the establishment of a statewide income tax the cornerstone of his platform, a bold but self-defeating action. It may seem strange that as late as 1990, Connecticut, so progressive in its social policies, was one of only ten states in the nation that did not tax wages. Not only was there no income tax as such, but just mouthing the word "tax" after the word "income" was deemed suicide for a candidate or officeholder. There was a tax on unearned income, including interest, dividends, and capital gains, but most of the state's revenues came via an 8 percent sales tax, the highest in the country, and through corporate taxes that also were the highest. Businesses were leaving Connecticut long before the national recession because of the state's punishing taxes.

Connecticut had flirted with an income tax for a brief period in 1971. The General Assembly had been in special session, deadlocked over how to deal with a budget deficit. With no public hearings and little warning, the Senate adopted an income tax plan in a postmidnight session and then disbanded. The outcry was so great that another special session had to be called and six weeks later the tax was repealed.

I took note of Bill Cibes for three reasons. Number one, he ran a forthright campaign; number two, he was extremely knowledgeable when it came to state finances; and number three, his defeat showed how hopeless it was to campaign for an income tax in Connecticut, even if such a tax, as Cibes described it, was a fairer and more reliable source of revenue than existing levies.

I myself opposed a state income tax. I knew how unsettling

the concept was to voters, and I also felt the current tax structure was sufficient to handle the anticipated deficit of $50 million to $100 million, and future budgets as well. At the same time, I wouldn't rule out an income tax or any other revenue measure. Who knew what the future would bring? I felt it stupid for a candidate to eliminate options, so my position, repeated time after time, was that "everything is on the table."

I emphasized broadening the tax base as my way to get more revenue. I also wanted to provide greater incentives to the private sector to grow and expand, and I advocated cuts in spending. I didn't spend much time discussing new revenues; you don't emphasize taxes in a political campaign. I thought it was bold enough just to say that "everything is on the table." If people asked does that mean increased taxes, the answer was yes. Everything meant everything.

The other candidates were not for an income tax either. Rowland said flatly that he was "taking the pledge," i.e., read his lips. Morrison devolved a strategy saying new taxes should be put to referendum. For Morrison, I think that was a fatal flaw, causing him to come in a distant third in November. As much as people don't like taxes or cuts in services, they dislike indecision more. The idea of saying "I'm going to take tough issues and put them to referendum" diminishes a candidate in the eyes of voters, raising questions about the capacity to lead.

Rowland kept one-noting, "Read my lips," but it wasn't doing him any good. I was the front-runner from the day I announced my candidacy in March. Soon afterward our polls showed me with a bit over 40 percent and Morrison in the high teens and Rowland in the twenties. It stayed that way into October. I was much better known than my opponents, so running as an independent was not proving to be the drawback it might have been for a newcomer.

Failing to make any gains, with time passing and no real issues to promote, Rowland kept experimenting with variations of "Read my lips." On a Tuesday in mid-October, he ran a TV ad that finally clicked. He charged that my "everything is on the table" and Morrison's referendum meant that in reality we both favored instituting an income tax. He hammered the point home in additional ads and in speaking appearances over the next few days. I was for an income tax. Morrison was for an income tax. The message was a total lie, but it began taking hold.

Working for me in the polling and strategic end of the campaign were Peter Gold, my campaign cochairman, and Charles (Chip) Ward, a computer maestro. Starting in April, Gold and Ward did tracking polls of potential voters, conducting five-minute interviews with 150 people almost every evening. By the end of the campaign they had 10,000 interviews, far surpassing any normal political research for a state like Connecticut. They would call me almost every night about nine-thirty, with that day's results.

On Friday night, October 19, I was with the other cochairman, Tom D'Amore, when Gold and Ward phoned to say that we had to respond to Rowland and dispel the notion that I favored an income tax. From Tuesday on, they said, Rowland had cut into our lead, and Friday's numbers showed an extreme tumble for us.

"What else can I say?" I asked. "I've said, 'Everything is on the table.' And I'm certainly not signing on to the pledge."

I pointed out that the national recession had started to hit Connecticut harder now than in any previous time and that I had a highly focused message on issues that really mattered to voters. My main theme, for the dual purposes of employment and broadening the tax base, was jobs. I was saying jobs, jobs, jobs and hammering at the need to keep and create them. Did I have to stray from that message? And if I did respond to this lie by Rowland, how was I going to leave myself the flexibility needed to govern?

Gold said we had given Rowland too much leeway already, that political assertions, like other advertising, become public beliefs if they are not rebutted quickly. Let a candidate air a charge four times with no rebuttal, and the charge tends to sink in as a fact.

I had learned this bitter lesson at the hands of Lieberman in 1988. His negative ad campaign was a disgrace, but a winner. "Once shame on you, twice shame on me" was the old adage that finally got me off the dime as to this tax charge.

About twelve hours later, on Saturday morning, we were in a studio at Hartford's Channel 3 preparing our own ad. "Don't speak for me, John Rowland," I said in the ad. "Stop distorting facts and scaring people with misquotes and half-truths. Long before your negative ads, I was opposed to a state income tax. The people of Connecticut and I know it would be like pouring gasoline on the fires of recession. And nobody's for that."

The fact is, I did not want an income tax, I was set against it, and the ad made that very clear. But I still felt it would be wrong to rule it out entirely, and I didn't. Gold and Ward moved quickly, so the ad made its first showing during *Star Trek* that afternoon.

The ad ran frequently all across Connecticut except in the Fourth Congressional District, the well-to-do New York City suburbs that include Greenwich and Fairfield County, my home base, where it did not run at all. Ads shown there had to be placed on New York City TV stations, with sky-high advertising rates. We passed for lack of cash.

Without intending it, my two strategists had set up a textbook, controlled situation through which they could measure just how powerful the income tax was as an issue, how effective my response was, and, at the same time, how important TV is in elections.

Before Rowland made his income tax charges, there was no difference in the projected vote region by region. Similarly, from the Tuesday to the Friday after the charge was made, my support fell and his climbed in an almost lockstep pattern all across the state.

Then came our rebuttal ad. I made gains immediately, and after a few days our polling showed me climbing back toward my earlier lead and Rowland moving steadily down — except in the New York suburbs.

Where my ad was shown, my lead over Rowland was about five or six points above the pre–October 15 level. But in the Fourth Congressional District, my support was down about ten points, and it continued to sink through Election Day. I won in most of the state, but lost to Rowland by about four points in the New York suburbs. So much for unanswered attacks. Statewide, I ended up with 41 percent of the vote, beating Rowland by a bare three percentage points.

For a while I jerked the chain of Ward and Gold about how they left a flank uncovered and almost lost an election. Their response (true, of course) was that we didn't have the money.

By the time I was elected, the state deficit was projected at a startling $250 million to $260 million. Added to the problem of failed budget gimmicks was the national recession, which was snowballing in 1990. People were curtailing spending and businesses were leaving; that, in turn, meant lower sales-tax receipts and sharply dwindling state revenues.

In the days and weeks following, still before I took office, Connecticut's annual deficit hit the stratosphere. It rose to $963 million out of a total budget of $7 billion. That was bad enough but not nearly as serious as what lay ahead. Without an increase in revenues we would face a $2.4-billion deficit in one year's time, a debt equal to 35 percent of the entire program for state spending. Connecticut had fewer than 3.3 million people. Proportionally, its deficit was the worst in the nation. What irony: I ran for governor in one of the wealthiest states in the country and was elected in one of the most insolvent.

An old tenet is that if you have tough duty that needs doing, get it behind you early. Don't let it bite you in the ass two or three years down the road. As governor-elect I was facing the worst fiscal crisis in Connecticut since the Great Depression.

I knew I would need help, big time. And by help I meant brains, not politicians. Peter Gold agreed to serve as chief of my transition; Chip Ward remained as a consultant to help prepare the state budget. I named two former associates of mine, Stan Twardy and Tom D'Amore, as chiefs of staff. Twardy, who had been US attorney in Stamford, became chief for legislative affairs. D'Amore was in charge of making law out of policy, or, as he put it, "cooking the macaroni."

D'Amore had gone to the Democratic primary campaign debates between Bruce Morrison and William Cibes. "If we win, Cibes is the guy we want to get hold of," D'Amore told me. "He knows this government better than anybody I've seen out there."

A few days after the election, I offered Cibes the job of budget chief, in charge of the Office of Policy and Management, the second-most-powerful position in the state. Cibes was a lifelong Democrat and none of us knew him well. To a great extent I was putting my political career in the hands of a stranger.

When he was in the legislature, Cibes had a nickname, Magic

Billy, for his sleight of hand in creating "one-shots," the gimmicks that kept the state's budget in balance, at least technically. Of course, these one-shots helped cause the disaster we were facing. I joked at the time that no person was better equipped to understand the problems of the state than Bill Cibes, as he had created so many of them himself.

Some political opponents charged immediately that by appointing Cibes I was showing my hand and that a state income tax would be the next step. That was simply false. I told Cibes that he was not being brought on board to set up an income tax, but rather because he better than anyone knew what had to be changed in the system. During our first interview he asked if I would listen to his plans for an income tax. I said, yes, but that was to be a last resort.

It was at this point that Connecticut's deficit began bursting upward. With the blessing of Governor O'Neill, I met with the state's lame-duck agency heads, asking them to avert further disaster by preparing extensive cuts in the budgets for fiscal 1992.

Our next step was to try to increase revenues mainly by eliminating or reducing the number of exemptions in the sales tax. People knew that food, drugs, medical care were exempt. What they didn't know was that because of lobbying in the legislature over the years, many other items were also exempt. But eliminating such exemptions didn't work either. The problem was that even if we could clear up the deficit for the current fiscal year, there would be a bigger hole in the next one.

Every day we would walk into room 410 in the state capitol and I would add a new twist, asking Chip Ward to run additional sets of numbers. Nothing worked. The crisis was unyielding.

At this point I was still holding out and I said once more to Cibes, "There will be no income tax."

Bill Cibes is a huge man, 350 pounds or more. Forty-seven years old at the time, he had a doctorate in political science from Princeton and had taught political science at Connecticut College in his hometown of New London. He had tried his best and failed. He knew before any of us that my assignment to him was futile. He was just about in tears. "One more thing," I reminded him and the others: "No fiscal sleight of hand. We all know that's what brought us into our predicament."

A week later the situation remained the same despite continued concoctions.

At a meeting with just a few of us in the room, I finally told Cibes that his chance had come. "Okay, Bill, I failed," I said. "You take over. It's your turn." This time Cibes's eyes did well up with tears. For those of us there, after so many days of fruitless struggle, it was an oddly warm moment.

When Cibes made his presentation, I asked him in tough questions, why an income tax? As he explained it, it was no contest, no contest at all. The income tax was a no-brainer. I could resist all I wanted but in the end there was no other honest option.

A year and a half later there was no multibillion-dollar deficit in Connecticut; in fact, there was no deficit at all — the state was in the black. For fiscal year 1992, a $110-million surplus. We were in the black again in fiscal 1993 and 1994. The turnaround was as swift and dramatic as any in the history of the nation. It was due in large part to the efforts of a few dedicated staff members who understood finance and eschewed politics, and to a number of courageous legislators who gambled their careers on the truth, and to a handful of agency heads who ran the ship of state even while repairs were going on in the engine room.

The toughest part of my first budget was not the call for an income tax but rather the cuts in services that I had to propose. I had spent an entire career in Washington helping the disabled, building the National Institutes of Health, creating programs for children. Now everything I stood for had to be put on hold, or worse, cut. It would be the repudiation of a life's work spent at the side of the frailest elements of society.

I knew that if I were perceived as playing favorites, the whole budget would be jeopardized. This was especially true of the disabled. Having been one of the authors of the Americans with Disabilities Act and as the father of a Down's child, I knew my detractors were waiting to catch me in a tilt. In all, I was preparing to recommend cuts of $1.2 billion, a gigantic reversal in a state where no governor in memory had ever actually tried to reduce dollar spending from one year to the next. Fairness in the hardship had to prevail.

I had come up chair by chair in the profession of politics, Greenwich first selectman, state representative, congressman, US senator, governor. In these positions you touch upon lives in very direct ways.

As chairman of health and human-services appropriations in the US Senate, you literally have the power of life and death over many of your fellow citizens by what gets money and what doesn't, what becomes a policy and what doesn't. You never want to cut where there is legitimate need. But government, like a family, must live within its means or pay for it dearly later.

Intellectually and emotionally, therefore, the cuts were much more difficult than the request for a state income tax. Politically, though, it was a different story. My staff and I felt we would have problems with individual constituencies regarding the cuts, but we knew we would have a bruising battle, both with a recalcitrant legislature and statewide public opinion, over the income tax.

I was installed as governor on January 9, 1991. An icy rain fell on the outdoor ceremony on the capitol grounds. My mother, then eighty-three, was there, sitting in a wheelchair, wrapped in lap robes but beaming and not at all concerned about the weather. Also present were close associates from twenty years in Washington, including a few who had taken it very hard when I lost my Senate seat in 1988. For each of us, this was a moment of happy return.

As former Supreme Court justice Lewis Powell, my father's old friend and mine, delivered the oath of office, it was hard not to be eternally grateful to all those who had made the moment possible. Little did I know that such gratitude was to be short-lived, and that soon I would long for the free, family-oriented lifestyle that had marked my forced retirement from politics two years earlier.

Economically, things in Connecticut continued to go from bad to worse every day. We had a serious crisis among almost all of the companies in the insurance capital of Hartford. A banking ca-tastrophe was in play, with two dozen or more state banks in jeop-ardy, overextended because of bad real estate loans. Defense contracts were the main source of income in the state, and the end of the cold war, welcome as it was, was causing substantial job losses. In all, ten thousand jobs a month were being lost. There was even concern that the state's dairy industry was going to collapse because of plummeting milk prices.

I was about to call for early retirement and layoffs of thousands of state employees, knowing I would have bitter opposition from labor unions, a group that had always been among my strongest supporters. (Before long there were union bumper stickers saying, "Layoff Weicker.")

In the larger picture, the United States was on a war footing in the Persian Gulf, with 300,000 troops encamped in Saudi Arabian deserts and President Bush getting ready to start the bombing of Iraq, which had invaded and taken control of Kuwait months earlier. At such moments of international tension, the FBI and other security organizations take special precautions across the country, so there were ramifications even for a small state like Connecticut. For me, it meant briefings regarding Connecticut's substantial nuclear facilities and defense installations. The historic state capitol itself took on a different character, included as it was in a list of possible terrorist targets.

It was not the most auspicious moment for a new administration. Perhaps the situation was best summed up by a simple incident at the governor's mansion, Claudia's and my new home. Located on several acres in a luxurious residential section, the mansion was impressive from the outside but falling apart within. One of our first guests was my former US Senate colleague Daniel Inouye of Hawaii. We were in the large, formal dining room when a chunk of plaster fell from the ceiling, narrowly missing him. Inouye told me that the Royal Palace in Hawaii was 150 years old and in considerably better shape.

The residence thus was symptomatic of the state's problems: a gorgeous asset, fallen into neglect, now rotting.

From time to time one aide or another suggested that I unload on the previous management — Governor O'Neill and the Democrats who controlled the legislature — for letting state finances come to such a poor pass. I chose not to. Pointing a finger would have served no good purpose. As for Bill O'Neill, whether he led poorly or well, he did serve, which is something to his credit in an age of too many spectators. And after all, no one made me take this job, I fought hard to get it.

Politics is more than adopting good positions and explaining them; tactics and strategy weigh heavily. As we worked up the final details of our budget now that I was in office, I cautioned my staff not to let a word of it become public. No leaks. None, and especially none about the income tax. I wanted the budget made public and explained in toto, not by way of daily leaks.

During this period, statehouse reporters were desperate to uncover budget details. Day by day, working out of the pressroom on the fourth floor, they were becoming more and more frustrated. Some had reached a point, one of my aides said, where they would do almost anything to get a story. Then a thought came to that aide: Why not let them get their hands on an entire tax portion of a fake budget?

Bill Cibes and his colleagues had worked up three complete proposals, two with no income tax included and one with an income tax. They had given them code names: aardvark, wildebeest, and camel, with camel standing for the income tax budget. On a weekday afternoon, the aide with the brainstorm walked up a capitol stairwell toward the pressroom area and carefully dropped a copy of the aardvark budget close to the upper landing. It was a fat document, and it landed standing up, tucked against the top step.

I wasn't told about this in advance. I had long-standing relationships of trust with members of the press, and this wasn't the way to start off as governor. As it happened, the ploy worked to perfection. An Associated Press reporter got hold of the document. He proceeded to call around, ask questions, and write a story saying Weicker was going to ask for a substantial increase in the sales tax. The decoy couldn't have been more effective; my real plan, camel, called for a 50 percent cut in the sales tax.

Most news organizations in the state either ran the AP item or produced ones of their own like it. Connecticut's main paper, the *Hartford Courant,* held off because its reporters were unable to confirm the account and, to their credit, because reporters and editors distrusted it. But the next day, with the news all over the state, the *Courant* made mention of the item, citing the AP and handling it with some skepticism.

I was embarrassed by this ploy. Though conceived in jest, it was deceptive. On the other hand, I have to admit that I still get a little perverse pleasure just hearing or seeing the word *aardvark*.

Two days after the AP story, on February 13, 1991, I unveiled my budget proposal in a statewide address. It came as a total surprise to legislators, the news media, and the citizens. I asked for a 6 percent tax on personal income, the 50 percent cut in the sales tax, and elimination of a corporate tax surcharge. I said I would accept any plan with or without an income tax as long as it balanced the budget (which was required by law), did not rely on gimmicks or excessive borrowing, and encouraged economic development by lowering business taxes. I laid out my proposals for spending cuts.

Thus began more than six months of bitter fighting. The Speaker of the House, Democrat Richard Balducci, had opposed an income tax in the past and was not for it at the outset. Before long, however, Balducci came over and worked closely with us for passage. But Balducci's counterpart in the Senate, President Pro Tem John Larson, and his assistant, majority leader Cornelius O'Leary, were staunch opponents. They became the focal point of conservative Democrats who opposed the income tax.

As for Republicans, their leaders felt they had been handed a grand opportunity to retake power in the legislature and bury me. They had one eye on New Jersey, where the political result of tax increases instituted by a Democratic governor, James Florio, was an electoral rout that gave Republicans control of both houses of the legislature.

In addition, Republican leaders were looking to punish me for winning the governorship. Some great acts of courage were to come from a few rank-and-file Republicans, but as a party, the Republicans were unequivocally opposed to the income tax purely for reasons of self-interest.

In one of the most extraordinary instances of nonleadership that I have ever seen, John Larson, rather than attempt to work out a Democratic-party resolution of the problem, threw in with the Republicans. His action effectively stripped the Democrats of their power as the majority party. Balducci could deliver the Democrats in the House, albeit narrowly. But with his Senate colleague and fellow party member on the opposite side, the natural leadership group on this issue — the governor and the Democrats — was sundered.

I had far more Democratic than Republican allies in the General Assembly. We faced a serious financial crisis, and any legislative action was going to be unpalatable to the electorate. Had Larson, O'Leary, and other Democrats followed Balducci's lead, we could have put the state on decent footing quickly and gone on to other issues. It would have been easy for them, as they could have blamed me, the independent, third-party governor, for this bitter medicine.

I was perfectly willing to accept the blame. I was saying, look, dump it on me, but at least help me deal honestly with what in the past has been given a lick, a promise, and a retreat. I'll give you the cover of my office. "I'm your escape hatch" was the message I put to Democrats. "Use the governor's office and your majorities in the House and Senate to do the right thing by the people of Connecticut."

House Speaker Balducci didn't ask for cover; he went along because he knew it was the right thing to do. The exact opposite was true of Larson in the Senate. He wanted to play politics, whether for reelection or greater ambitions. He proceeded to create an unholy alliance with Republican leaders, aimed only at sabotaging me and the state. He could see the damage to Connecticut, but it made no difference.

One incident, uncovered by the press, shows how well a third party, like my group, "A Connecticut Party," can serve as an honest broker, and how the two-party system, through collusion, can end up being nothing more than a corrupt, impenetrable political monopoly.

As I mentioned, legislators, prodded by Republican leadership in the House and Senate and Democratic leadership in the Senate, came up with three budget proposals of their own. "Coalition budgets," they were called, and none of them was balanced. Everyone in the General Assembly knew these proposals were shams, but there was a big push for them nevertheless.

To encourage support, legislators were promised they would

have no opposition from the other party in their next election campaign. As reported by the *Hartford Courant,* this deal was put together by Republican leaders in both chambers, and by Democratic leaders in the Senate.

The coalition budgets never got through because there were too few votes to override my vetoes. In part, that was because enough legislators were convinced, like me, that the income tax was a no-brainer. And in part it also was because we were able to show the massive defects of each proposal. Whenever the legislature presented a coalition budget, I would have Bill Cibes and Chip Ward go over the documents as though they were our own. None of the coalition budgets could withstand such scrutiny.

In the meantime, D'Amore and Balducci spent more and more time together trying to put our budget over. We made extensive compromises, reducing the proposed income tax to 4.5 percent from 6 percent, agreeing to raise the sales tax to 6 percent from 4 percent.

We held many meetings, in groups small and large. Once we had a budget summit conference of about forty people at the governor's residence, trying to develop a compromise proposal. That day the residence was picketed by state union employees over reports that Claudia and I were putting a full-time cook on the state payroll. The accounts were false; Claudia did all our cooking then and still does, except for occasions when I am the chef.

The union workers outside were shouting, "Dump the cook! Fire the cook!" Inside, Claudia, who was getting sandwiches for forty, said, "I wish they would."

During lunch at that meeting, Bill Cibes was sitting on a couch with the proposed budget document, the size of three or four telephone books put together, on his lap. My Down's child, Sonny, happened to come by, and he asked Bill what that was on his lap. Bill said it was the budget.

Sonny was then twelve. To him "budget" was a bad word because it was keeping his father away from him. He picked up the document, took a look at it, and announced in stentorian tones to the whole room, "This is bullshit!" All I could think was, I'm with you, kid.

The politics of these months was frustrating. I authorized

D'Amore to make any deals needed to push our program through. Still we remained short by about ten votes in the House and sixteen in the Senate. Time and again legislators would say to him, "I know you and the governor are right, I know we have to do this, we have to fix it, but shit, I won't get reelected." D'Amore would reply, "What good is it to be reelected if you know damn well that by voting the way you are you are guaranteeing yourself a failure?"

These conversations were much like ones I myself had frequently in the well of the US Senate, when I would vote one way and so many of my friends another. Often they would come up to me and say, "Lowell, I know you are right but it's political dynamite."

A good part of the frustration came from the unreliability of some legislators. To colleagues, all a legislator really has to offer is his or her word. Thirty years ago, in the Connecticut General Assembly and bodies like it across the country, trust prevailed. You could disagree, fight hard, ask for a lot, but once you said you were going to do something, you damned well did it. Not anymore.

A Republican who was the head of an important committee had agreed to support our budget. One day he told D'Amore he was breaking his commitment. That's it, just breaking it.

Another Republican, a freshman, volunteered to vote for the income tax after hearing the first debate because he knew it was the right thing to do. As the vote approached, Republican caucus members told him to renege. He asked a colleague for advice. "This is a measure of who you are," the colleague said. "You can either vote as you agreed to and take your medicine, or you can break your word and vote against it, or you can go to the governor and ask to be released from your pledge."

The legislator, in tears, went to D'Amore. "I don't want to do this anymore; you have got to release me." D'Amore refused, saying, "I can't do that. If I knew I had the vote margin, I would, because I don't like to see you in such agony. But look at it like this: If you roll over that easily for the bad guys in your caucus, your career here is finished anyway. People will know you by the fact that you back out of deals," D'Amore told him, "and nobody will treat you as a serious player. The only lesson for you is, next time, don't give your word so quickly."

D'Amore then brought this legislator, still in agony, to see me. I told him he had to live with himself, that lots of little things like this happen in a political career. He ended up voting for my proposal, and when it didn't pass that round, he voted for it again on reconsideration.

For the most part, individuals who agreed to switch their vote and support our budget did so in return for small favors for their constituents. "I need funding for a firehouse" is the kind of request D'Amore would hear. Hardly anyone was dealing for himself or herself in terms of money or jobs. One exception was a Democrat who offered to trade his vote for a position in state government. He said he would cast his vote, then resign from the General Assembly and move right in to his new job. D'Amore told him that such an arrangement was a little too venal for us, and illegal, as well.

After the first vote, when we got some support but not nearly enough, we became more aggressive. D'Amore would approach legislators and say, "Tell me what you need." The response would be, "My constituents don't want this income tax. To vote for it I have to get something. It's not enough to say that it would be better for the state, I can't come home empty-handed."

Tom didn't predicate any deals on passage of the income tax but rather simply on a legislator's onetime vote. So when we lost the early showdowns, we told legislators that no, they didn't have to vote for the income tax again, although it would be nice if they did. We put no pressure on them. Things like that, I feel, built credibility.

Throughout, two institutions were helpful in this extended battle. First, the editorial writers in the state, almost to a one, supported the budget as we presented it, including the income tax. The average citizen may not read editorials but politicians do, and what the papers were saying was not lost on them. It was an important force on our side.

Number two, we were getting backing from business organizations. Normally business as an institution would be against further taxes, and antigovernment as well. But most businesses in Connecticut either remained neutral or actively came out on behalf of my budget, including the income tax. That took a tough player off the field in terms of a moneyed group that could have advertised against us.

My old friend and senatorial colleague, the former governor Abe Ribicoff, who was a longtime opponent of the income tax, made a moving, nostalgic return to the state capitol to speak in favor of my proposals. This personal act of courage contrasts with Connecticut's two sitting US senators, Dodd and Lieberman, who opined gratuitously from their aerie in Washington, DC, that the income tax was not for them. Neither was any form of fiscal reality for the rest of Congress — ergo, four trillion dollars of national debt.

The real break came when two Republican senators, William Nickerson of Greenwich and Larry Bettencourt of Waterford, agreed to support the income tax budget. Nickerson was a key player in the process and was my hometown senator. We were long associated in politics. Bettencourt took untold abuse at home for his courageous stance and afterward retired from public service in disgust. Waterford lost a helluva public servant.

Then, on a weekend in the middle of August, at a meeting during the Volvo tennis tournament in New Haven, three Democratic senators also agreed to change their vote. We were almost home, but not quite.

The following Wednesday, August 21, the Senate began discussing the budget in an evening session that ended with a vote at three AM. The result was a tie, 18 to 18. Lieutenant Governor Eunice Groark was presiding; she used her vote to break the tie and gaveled the meeting closed.

A few hours later, about eight-thirty, House members conducted their own vote after lengthy debate. Some were sure the income tax would pass, others sure it wouldn't. It failed by a count of 81 to 69, meaning that we were seven votes short. Claudia and Eunice were in the governor's office with me, and we heard the vote over the public address system. It was one of the lowest moments in my public life.

As they say, though, things are not always what they seem. In actuality we were two votes short. Several members who supported the budget had been convinced it was going down to defeat, and they voted against it to be in a position where they could demand a new vote. Under House rules, only a lawmaker on the prevailing side can move for such reconsideration.

We moved as quickly as we could to repair the situation. The logical place to look for help was the among the Republicans, because that's where the votes were, and, additionally, we knew that some GOP leaders finally wanted to cut a deal.

D'Amore was sitting in my office at one point talking to House Speaker Balducci on one phone and the Republican minority leader, Edward Krawiecki, Jr., on another. The Republican leaders truly wanted to have their cake and eat it: they were willing to bring the impasse to an end, but they wanted to embarrass me in the process.

The games they played were petty. Having been burned earlier by a poor vote count, we were determined not to go ahead until we were sure we would win this time. But we never could be sure, for just as we would approach the point at which we were within one vote or so of victory, the Republican leaders would pull two yes votes back.

Republican-party chairman Dick Foley told D'Amore he wanted to meet with me. D'Amore brought him in, along with Krawiecki. Foley, one of my most vicious critics, was completely untrustworthy and corrupt. (In 1994 Foley was sentenced to forty months in prison for wrongdoing involving influencing state legislature votes five years earlier.) D'Amore felt Krawiecki's presence would make the meeting appear more proper, and also, that if a deal was cut, Krawiecki would make the Republicans stick to it.

As the meeting began, D'Amore could barely contain his anger, convinced as he was that Foley's main aim was to nail me. Tom told them we didn't care how they got the votes, just to get them.

They made two requests. One was that, in the appointing of judges, I follow a practice of naming Republicans as well as Democrats. I was flabbergasted, since I had been adhering to a longstanding gentleman's agreement that the governor do just that. The second request was also inane, having to do with certain endorsements that my independent group, A Connecticut Party, might make. That was it. No difficult, costly trade was sought. D'Amore and I kept waiting for one — D'Amore thought originally they would be asking for the gold leaf off the capitol dome — but there was no other demand. We reached agreement and the meeting broke up.

Foley and Krawiecki didn't tell us how they were going to swing the vote and we didn't ask. But no sooner did they leave the room than the fun began. D'Amore called Balducci to say we were ready for a vote. Balducci said, I don't want to hear about your deal making; I'll do whatever is necessary to make this happen, trust me. That was after almost seven months of saying "trust me" and always delivering.

So now, for the first time, the Republican and Democratic House leaders were pledged to support the income tax budget in a vote to be held immediately. But, lo and behold . . . no vote was taking place. The leaders were holding off. Having counted, they knew they didn't have enough Republican votes.

Foley had blown it. The moment he left my office, I found out, he stopped the first person he saw, a lobbyist, and boasted, "I got him — I cut a deal with the governor."

That news spread like wildfire in the chamber. By the time Foley and Krawiecki got there, the legislators whose votes they wanted to manipulate objected to being toyed with. Foley had out-slimed himself.

Foley called D'Amore and blamed us for leaking the deal. Tom told Foley, "Go fuck yourself, and put Krawiecki on the phone." He told Krawiecki, "Eddie, I don't know what's happened or why; I do know you people were in here and made a commitment, and you must do whatever you have to do to honor it."

Finally, the vote came. Three Republicans switched from no to yes; two others who had voted no left the building and did not vote at all. That carried us over in the House, 75 to 73. Between the House and Senate, we got twelve votes from Republicans.

The budget had passed, but there was a lot of blood on the ground, much of it mine. My popularity rating in public-opinion polls sank to the levels of Nixon's after Watergate. Conditions were even worse for the legislators who supported my program. I had state police and secretaries to answer my telephones when they rang; living in the governor's mansion, I also had some security. These legislators had no such insulation. They and their families were threatened by telephone and in person. One had a gun fired into her home. Others couldn't go to their own churches without being harassed. Perhaps worst of all, of the few brave Republican legislators who supported me, several were ostracized by their party leaders, forced out of important positions, and, in one case, eventually gerrymandered out of the legislature altogether.

As soon as the new budget was enacted, a small group began a repeal effort. One of the leaders was Thomas Scott, a political lowlife whose career was at a crossroads. He had quit the state senate in 1990 to seek the Third District congressional seat and lost.

It was Scott, with a few others, who called for the repeal rally in October 1991 and turned it into a hate-Weicker event. There was no low behavior Scott wouldn't engage in as he tried to position himself for a comeback.

For my part, I knew there was a lot of educating and politicking to be done. We just couldn't let this new tax hang out there; I had to sell it, to finish the picture in a political and communications sense. I began working to help legislators who had supported me; all were on the endangered list.

Early on I used the talk shows as much as possible. I also attended meetings all over the state, explaining things as best I could to the general public. D'Amore said I was a bore who wouldn't let a small boy and a dog pass without explaining to them that Connecticut was no longer in danger of losing our good bond rating, that we were actually getting $300 million back from the federal government, that the budget was balanced, and so on.

Sometimes I found myself at meetings where I would repeat myself three or four times to get the message across. I was not going to let anti–income tax know-nothingism triumph if there was anything I could do to stop it. Connecticut was not going down on my watch. Like the Republicans who wanted to do me in, I had my eye on New Jersey, where one of Jim Florio's problems was that the new tax structure had not been adequately explained.

Even as I went about defending and explaining, my opponents continued to try to tear the income tax down. Scott, among others, made stabs at repeal in the legislature but got nowhere. He and a few others promised to make legislators who had supported the new tax pay dearly at election time in 1992. But their message didn't take because at no time did they have an alternative to the budget or to the hard times.

Understandably, Connecticut residents had become preoccupied with worsening economic conditions. That hurt Scott because citizens were looking to government for a response to their troubles, and they realized that if the state went bankrupt there wasn't much it could do to help them.

As the 1992 political campaign began, I made it a point to appear on the scene as much as I could when there was a factory saved or a factory opening or an expansion. "Listen," I would say on these occasions, "a year ago I couldn't be here helping anything. Now I am here because we have the money to invest in you."

I made one visit to the O. Z. Gedney Company, a manufacturing firm in the Naugatuck Valley, an area that had been the bedrock of opposition to the income tax. I was there to announce that the state was saving the company, which otherwise would have gone out of business. The crowd was blue-collar, and as I rose to speak there was almost dead silence, little of the polite applause that elected leaders often get.

I took the tack that because of their sacrifice and the sacrifice of residents throughout the state, Connecticut was getting back on its feet fiscally. The state was using its new taxes to save their jobs. That's what legislators had voted for, saving jobs, not an income tax just to have an income tax. And the jobs were not government jobs but their jobs. That's how the state was reinvesting their hard-earned money.

When I was done I got a standing ovation. For these workers it was a breakthrough: what they had opposed as a matter of philosophy and perception had undergone a complete turnabout. Their union steward came up to me and said, "I want you to know I led my people in opposition to you on the lawn of the capitol a year ago. We were just wrong."

As we got closer to the election of 1992, I could feel the momentum. As happens in a free society, the violence and threats against state legislators boomeranged. Perhaps people like to hate a governor, he's only one guy, and in my case a pretty big target to

shoot at. But there were too many stories coming out about legislators whose lives were threatened, whose wives and children had
been abused, who were getting obscene phone calls. Connecticut
is a decent state. People said, nuts to this. Hate is not the business
we're in.

Election night, 1992, was a great moment for me. No, A Connecticut Party did not win any legislative seats, even though we contested a good many. But we did help elect a lot of cross-endorsed
candidates to the General Assembly and to the US Congress.
When you look at what happened, it was somewhat spectacular.

We endorsed Democrat Chris Dodd for reelection to the US
Senate (tax opposition aside), which meant that on voting ma-
chines his name appeared on our line on the ballot as well as on
the Democratic line. Dodd won by more than two to one, with a
total of 1.3 million votes cast for him. Of that number, 320,000 were
on A Connecticut Party's line. Dodd's supporters could have voted
for him only on the Democratic line; why did so many of them
make the effort not to? I think it was a way of saying thank you to A
Connecticut Party.

In one congressional race, incumbent Democrat Samuel Gej-
denson of the Second District in eastern Connecticut would have
lost if only Democratic and Republican votes were counted; it was
the votes cast for him on A Connecticut Party's line that put him
over. The same was true for about twenty-five state legislators.

As for the vendetta against legislative supporters of the income tax, well, it struck out. The people of Connecticut — not the
media, not Weicker, not the legislators, but the people of
Connecticut — passed their judgment. They could have passed a
judgment that would have made those two years and all the sacrifice worthless. Instead they accorded it one hell of a vote of affir-
mation. I have never been as proud of the state of Connecticut as I
was that night.

We had gone through the entire American constitutional process: from an idea in 1991 to committee action to legislative action
to law to election in 1992.

Throughout the entire election process, primary and general,
Republican and Democrat, only four income tax supporters were

defeated. Democrats retained control of both the Senate and the House. Connecticut voted for common sense, courage, and the truth.

Thomas Scott, the main enemy of the income tax and the most persistent Weicker critic, ran once more for the Third District congressional seat, having come very close to winning in 1990. This time he was trounced, 65 to 35 percent.

Connecticut, like most of the states, is not yet whole economically. But if not for the strong medicine, it would be bankrupt, with programmatic decisions forced on it by courts or creditors. Instead, we were able to establish our own priorities and have funds available to create jobs in a recession, revive the cities from poverty, and care for our children at a time of abandonment.

My job rating improved, declined, improved, declined. I don't blame people for being grumpy in a recession as severe as the one we were having.

Except for vastness of scale, the economic problems we faced in Connecticut from 1991 through 1994 were the same as those that have been confronting the nation for more than a decade. The government in Washington has built an incredible debt, spending enormous amounts of money it did not have during the 1980s. The simplest explanation is that Ronald Reagan never counted defense spending as spending. In other words, the guns portion of the budget was not to be paid for while he and George Bush were in office. As a result, unpalatable cuts and tax increases are now necessary.

Out of every federal tax dollar today, seventeen cents goes simply to pay interest on the debt — more than all the discretionary money for direct services. As a country, we are broke. In 1993 Washington began cutting spending to a degree and adding new taxes, but it didn't do enough. The program set by President Clinton and Congress left the nation with enormous annual deficits and did not reduce the national debt, now headed toward $5 trillion, by one red cent.

Washington must come up with further cuts and tax increases — ones that are tough and, above all else, fair. Getting the budget in balance becomes more painful each year, and at some point it will be impossible without chaos. We may have reached that point already. So let's get on with it. The process will take a decade, not the one year allotted Connecticut.

A main impediment is that too many members of Congress, like some in the Connecticut General Assembly, are more interested in soft landings for their politics than hard confrontations with reality. They think it political suicide to vote for difficult solutions. In so doing, they sell the public short. Retribution is not visited upon leaders when sacrifice is shared fairly, and when it has a worthy end. In fact, it is the failure to act that is economic suicide and thus certain death for the politicians responsible.

If I could give any gift to leaders of the government in Washington, what I would order for each of them is perseverance and a sense of humor. They will need both if they are to work meaningfully. Overcoming twelve years of presidential advocacy for free lunches is a Herculean task.

15

Making a Difference

I'M WRITING this as I close out more than thirty years in elected office. My father advised me to "leave the party while you're having a good time." I've had a great time.

I even got some favorable reviews. A *New York Times* editorial after I announced that I wouldn't run for reelection as governor said that "Lowell Weicker is blunt, often arrogant. But he is a man of remarkable personal courage. His thirty years of public service have made a real difference."

The *Hartford Courant* also was generous, saying, "He's lifted politics out of the banal. He gets things done, whether straightening out the state's fiscal crisis or battling right-wing ideologues in the US Senate or helping to pass federal legislation to aid the disabled."

That is heady stuff. But truth be told, in the last few years political and media trends have been chipping away at this "excitable kid's" optimism and idealism. Politics is not the joy it used to be, and I don't want that morning ever to come when I rise hating the business I have always loved.

For my colleagues in politics, a word of advice. Live and let live. You're not going to win them all and, indeed, a good legislator must have give as well as take among the tools of his trade. Hate and the annihilation of opposition are no substitutes for everyday, tough, intellectual choices. Stay accountable, not necessarily reelectable.

For my friends in the media: start doing your homework.

News is more and more entertainment, and that is good for a democracy that depends on an informed electorate. But information is no longer the sole province of the erudite and discerning. It belongs to everyone, and accuracy in reporting is essential as never before. Tabloid journalism is a bad common denominator on which to base dissemination of news. For those who practice for profit within the First Amendment, remember, it is not a divine right; it is a shared constitutional responsibility.

What have I learned in a career of government and politics, and does it have application for new generations entering or considering entering upon fields of public service?

Let's start with politics, because that's the fun part and the part most crying out for innovation and breaking the mold.

Aside from convenience and for purposes of identification, why in God's name, in the freest marketplace in the world of things and ideas, do Americans stubbornly insist on preserving and glorifying the intellectual monopoly, or rather, duopoly, called the two-party system? What exempts the two political parties from all the ills, historical and contemporary, that attach to other scenarios of no competition? Whether resultant high prices, bad dictators, or flawed products, monopoly/duopoly has little in terms of achievement to recommend itself.

For American politics, duopoly translates into weak candidates, intellectually neutered officeholders, meaningless party platforms, and ineffectual national policies. It often turns outstanding individuals, dynamic people with altruistic goals, into manipulative agents of collusion. Obedience to a corrupt system is too big a price to pay for the chance to serve.

Does the American public share in the de facto glorification of the two-party system? Certainly not, according to party affiliation statistics. For decades, electoral surveys have shown more citizens describing themselves as independents than as Democrats or Republicans. In other words, a third party with no name, no platform, no patronage, no candidates or officeholders — a third party that is simply none of the above — attracts more people than do the Democrats or the Republicans.

In voting preference, too, the public shows no fondness for the two-party system; the sharp decline in voter turnout since 1960 or so is substantial evidence of that. So is the result of the 1992 presidential election. Ross Perot did not win in 1992 but the election showed that all an independent candidate needs to attract millions of voters is a means of grabbing their attention. Perot did that with money. He got his 19 percent share of the vote with virtually no warmup, no credible ticket, and no mainstream platform. He got in the race late, dropped out, got in again. His explanation for dropping out was regarded as flaky by many.

Perot's vice-presidential running mate, Admiral James B. Stockdale, was admired by those who knew of his courage as a prisoner of war and participant in Vietnam. He is a legitimate hero. But it would be hard to think of any public figure less ready than Stockdale to take the helm of a civilian government.

The 19 percent share came despite Perot's and Stockdale's shortcomings. It also came amid almost universal nattering by alleged political experts, to the benefit of the two main parties, that Perot stood no chance of winning and that, therefore, a vote for him was a wasted vote. Among those carrying the water were some leading newspaper, magazine, and TV reporters and commentators. We can only speculate how many more votes Perot would have garnered had the press treated him as a viable candidate.

Could I have won the governorship in Connecticut in 1990 if every leading news outlet said forget about Weicker, he's not a real candidate? Perhaps not; my margin over the Republican was only three percentage points as it was. But because I was a proved vote-getter, the news media never took the approach that I couldn't win. Perot did not have that advantage.

As far as electability goes, I think it is fair to say that my election as governor was sufficient to prove that a third-party candidate who works at it can defeat the Republicans and Democrats. Period, end of argument — except to comment that what can happen on the state level can also happen with the presidency. A strong, well-known, well-financed independent now more than ever has the potential to win it all.

The two-party system owes its continued existence, not surprisingly, to the self-aggrandizement of Republicans and Democrats and to many in the news media who look upon change as expensive logistically. The public is miles ahead of both the politicians and the press in seeing the irrationality of the present system.

Let me cite two examples — one in Washington, one in Connecticut — of how the two-party system covers its ass. Presidents and Congress have consciously sacrificed the national interest time and again in terms of fiscal responsibility for perceived Election Day gains. Mounting deficits have been real for many years. The executive and congressional solutions, however, have been fantasy. Through aggrandizing and twisted use of tax dollars, leaders in Washington have squandered the nation's hard-earned fortune, making serious debtors of every American today and, in all probability, for generations to come.

Through it all, the public has been left with an assurance of financial stability while the reality was approaching financial disaster. This disaster was so bad that it placed the nation in the worst recession of modern times and in an economic position that imperils national security.

People have little to say about their destiny when seventeen cents of every dollar go toward interest payments and the overall debt still gets larger. That is a terrible bind.

The national interest dictates making sacrifices to bring down the debt. But it is in the political interest of the Republican and Democratic parties, given any difficult and unpredictable issue, to suborn the harshness of reality to the narcotic of a free lunch. The political parties talk a very good game; they've got the rhetoric down pat. But they haven't reduced the debt by a single penny in more than twenty years.

(There are those who criticize President Clinton as having done too little, too late in his attempts to deal with the federal budget deficits. To a degree, I am one of those critics; I think more must be done.* But at least Clinton raised the issue to the level of national and legislative debate, and then did something. That is a far cry from decades of either spend-spend-spend or "Read my lips.")

---

* Despite selective tax increases and spending cuts under Clinton, the budget deficits remain intolerably high. How much is too high? Too high is when, in any given year, there is no money left to help retire the national debt. By that standard we are looking at deficits that will be too high from now to eternity.

In Connecticut, the de facto merger of Republicans and Democrats over tough issues almost resulted in the worst possible collusion during the great income tax brawl of 1991. I have already mentioned the incident, reported in the press, in which as a reward for approving an unbalanced budget, legislators of each party would be uncontested for reelection by the opposing party. This was at a time when the state had a $1-billion real deficit, a $3-billion projected deficit, and only draconian measures of revenue raising and spending cuts could save it from fiscal chaos.

The two-party plot, aimed at defeating the income tax proposal, was not only illegal, it also would have created an even larger deficit. It was a model, however, for avoiding accountability. Political duopoly would replace democracy. Have no doubt, legislative prestidigitation like this is repeated a hundred times over in the nation's capital. Luckily, Connecticut legislators voted down this crooked deal twice, albeit by narrow margins.

How do we deal with such collusion? By competition. In Connecticut a third party was present, around which honest legislators, Democrat and Republican, coalesced. Their decision, finally, to approve the state income tax was based not on the artificiality of party affiliation but rather on fact, vision, and courage. The beneficiaries? The people and the state of Connecticut. And, mirabile dictu, the legislators themselves who ultimately were rewarded by election for their courage in doing the right thing.

The Democratic and Republican establishments would like people to believe that an independent, third-party officeholder cannot get things done. We proved that notion wrong in Connecticut, through the enactment of the income tax alone. As a *New York Times* news story said in April 1994, "Mr. Weicker, most politicians grant, has proved that a governor can govern without a major party behind him. He has accustomed the state to hearing its chief executive say what many people think: partisan politics does not make good government."

Had I belonged to either party, I might not have been able to get the tax through. Members of my party in the legislature would have tried hard to shoot it down. Furthermore, loyalty to the party might have kept me from pushing for an income tax. I got more, not less, support for the income tax because I was an independent.

That is, while it took them time to go along with it, politicians in both parties were able to vote for the income tax and lay the blame on me. I was the lightning rod, a role that is not very pleasant but that is sometimes necessary to achieve meaningful government.

Later, in 1994, I prodded the legislature into enacting the toughest handgun-control statute in the United States. The first step was to have a strong, intelligent bill crafted, and for that I turned to my longtime aide Stan Twardy, who by then was in private practice at a Stamford law firm. Democrats and Republicans in the legislature managed to kick the bill around and let their session come to an end without acting on it, and the chances for handgun control looked moribund. What else is new? But over the summer I called them into special session, and at that point, knowing they would have to do something, the legislature acted quickly and well.

I might also add that at that point not only was I an independent governor fighting the notorious gun lobby, but I also was a lame duck, with only about six more months in office. So don't tell me a third-party leader can't govern; that's only duopoly propaganda.

Some charged that I rammed programs like gun control down the throats of the legislators. What a laugh! I couldn't ram anything through; I had no troops of my own in the General Assembly, not one; my only certain vote was that of Lieutenant Governor Eunice Groark, in the event of a tie. And still we got things done.

By now, American politicians have spent thirty years getting acquainted with a new, changing electorate. Citizen distaste for the two parties is a long-established fact of life. The natural consequence of such distaste, logically thinking, should be the creation of a third major political party, or a third and a fourth. The politicians know this. They just don't broadcast such threatening news.

To be successful on the national level, a third party must be centrist and have a wide appeal, addressing many issues — the broad spectrum — not just one issue. Once established, the third party would produce true competition, resulting in ideas and actions far superior to those in government today.

*   *   *

I have no doubt that a solid third party would rejuvenate the Democrats and Republicans, and make for better government all around. It's the two-party system that has gotten so corrupt, ingrown, self-serving, not the elected officials themselves.

This nation has never had more intelligent elected officials than it does today. That is especially true at the highest levels: in the Senate, the House of Representatives, cabinet officials, governors. It applies also to the feedstocks in politics: the state legislators, mayors, and so on. We have never had more educated individuals, more sophisticated, more informed leaders. What is needed is more courage and less caution. With the exception of a few, integrity is not the problem.

As for the system of representation, it was sheer genius at the time it was created and it is sheer genius today. Where it falls apart is that it rests on the people. If the people are distracted, slumbering, apathetic, or lazy, the system suffers. And probably all those things apply to the voter today.

Many critics say we need this amendment or that to the Constitution to improve the system. They are dead wrong. All their tampering won't improve the system or the Constitution of the United States one bit.

I have been asked, what's so terrible about a balanced-budget amendment or an amendment limiting the terms of members of Congress? The answer, regarding a balanced-budget amendment, is that budgets don't get balanced by amendments, they get balanced by acts of will. Let me point out once more: when I took office in Connecticut, we had a $3-billion shortfall in an $8-billion budget, and that was in a state with a balanced budget provision! Having a balanced-budget amendment, and then violating it, is worse than doing nothing. It is writing a law and disobeying it.

As for other gimmicks, they often add up to one excuse after another to give the appearance of doing something rather than actually doing it. When I was a kid having a medical examination, I knew at one point I was going to get my shots. But I did everything to avoid that moment. "You sure you weighed me? Checked my height? Tested my reflexes?" That is what the nation is doing now. We know exactly what we are coming to eventually, but we are trying to postpone the moment. And the postponing process could be killing us.

When these gimmicks don't work, the system starts to fray and people reach for silly alternatives. The next step is to try more drastic solutions, of which term limits is one. And next would be other measures involving totalitarianism in some degree.

Better by far than gimmicks would be leaders who stand for constitutional principle and governmental reality that unify the nation and lead people to become engaged in public policy and citizenship.

Leaders on the highest levels have enormous personal influence. People look to presidents, governors, other top officials to set the tone. There are so many ways in which high elected officials can help establish a national mood by example. Who else but a governor can say in an address at the opening of the legislature, "We have racial isolation in our school system that must be addressed," and simply by focusing on the problem, help set the agenda for three million people?

Who else but a US senator can take his Down's child at a tender age and, instead of hiding him, show the world a loving relationship that is just as normal as with any other child? (And by so doing, perhaps keep some parents from being ashamed of their Down's child.) I brought Sonny into the Senate cloakroom at the US Capitol when he was an infant; I can't tell you how many people wrote me in appreciation.

Leaders must deal with problems and not always defer hard decisions. Policy soft landings are wrong roads that we have traveled too many times, and they cost us. By 1986, toward the end of my Senate career, for example, there was a widespread demand for tax reform. It was generated by the fact that some corporations and wealthy taxpayers could legally avoid paying their fair share. At the same time, our most pressing problem as a nation was the growing federal budget deficit. That year it reached a staggering $240 billion, sapping our credit markets. (Today a $240-billion deficit gets a ho-hum from leaders in Washington. Clinton's efforts, which I laud, were to bring the deficit down only slightly below that range! But such huge deficits are as dangerous now as ever.)

We had a real chance in 1986 to address both the tax laws and the national debt. The solution was self-evident: make the tax code fairer and at the same time increase revenues to a level approximating our expenditures. One method could have been introduction of a tough minimum tax to take care of the fairness issue and raise a lot of new revenue. Well, a minimum tax was put in effect, but under President Reagan's instructions, the reforms were "revenue neutral," taking in no additional funds.

What we needed was to move toward a balanced budget. Instead we enacted a law that only increased the deficits. I voted against the 1986 tax reform but it was like voting against a tornado.

The biggest taxation–government services problem today is not that the rich aren't paying their fair share, and it isn't that the poor are soaking up all the benefits. The problem is that we have welfare for middle-income America that goes beyond anything that could have been imagined thirty or forty years ago.

This is a difficult message for a politician to make. But the fact is, Middle America has done fantastically well. Let us use Connecticut as an example. Obviously, I am not referring to the thousands who lost work in recent years. They and their families have taken a tough hit. As governor I tried to make these individuals and families whole by bringing new jobs to the state.

At the same time, perhaps 80 or 85 percent of the employed held on to their employment, unscathed, through the worst period. These members of the middle class had it made, getting the lion's share of government benefits that most people are not even aware of. Nursing-home care in the state in 1991, for example, utilized almost totally by the middle-income population — not the rich and not the poor — cost eight hundred million dollars in a budget of eight billion. That is 10 percent by my arithmetic. The higher-education budget and state grants for education in the state's towns take an enormous part of the pie and also go mostly to the middle class. The public parks, highways, environmental programs are among the finest in the land; they are costly and benefit middle-income people mostly because, after all, most of the people are in the middle-income group.

What is true in Connecticut is true in most places. I would

have no objection to this setup if more middle-income citizens understood the situation, and if they had the propensity to take care
of the guy behind them, as did their predecessors in generation
after generation.

The point to be made is that in one form or another we are all
helped by government, federal and state. So stop painting "help" as
a black, Hispanic, or poor problem.

Legislatures and Congress aside, no automatic pilot can
guide the American ship of state as well as the votes of its crew.
And the facts show the crew has been AWOL from the election
front for years. Whether federal, state, or local elections, the statistics of declining participation are appalling. I accept the complaint
of lack of choice as being valid. Indeed, additional competition is
the key to eventual political and governmental reform. Unfortunately, however, millions of Americans, for what they fantasize
to be in their financial interest, have accepted the free-lunch theory of government. That I don't accept.

Nowadays, unless achievement for person or community
comes to pass without cost, it is rejected. Whether local school
budgets or national drug wars, solution does rely as much on dollars as ideas. The past two decades or so show more bellowing and
less accomplishment than any period in our history. In the meantime, investment in humanity's future has become a rhetorical
rather than a fiscal exercise.

Nevertheless, the hope for better times — for less crime,
more and better jobs, et cetera, et cetera — rests with the people.
The people must get into the act. They must become more knowledgeable, more concerned, and then they must reward the courage
of politicians by electing them.

I would admit to being starry-eyed if I were merely calling on
all Americans to pay attention and get involved. That would be
nice, but it is not likely to happen and it isn't necessary, either.
Fortunately for democracy, the cause of better government doesn't
need a new, politically literate majority. But it does need a dedicated, commonsense few. Enough activists to form a wedge. A
small fraction of the 180 million adult Americans to keep things hot
for the 535 people in the House and Senate.

*   *   *

I have said for many years that greater citizen involvement is the key to stronger, more efficient government. Not long ago, cynics used to roll their eyes and make fun of that notion on the grounds that getting people more involved is hopeless. Not even the cynics can say that any longer. The precedent for greater citizen participation in politics was set in 1992, and no amount of cynicism can push it aside. That has been Ross Perot's contribution to American politics, and it is a major one.

My aim in this book has been to describe to some degree how politics works, to appeal to the broad range of people to get off their duffs. In a democracy, the people rule, and too few of the people today are doing their job. There must be a better understanding of and striving for the ideals that have made the United States the hope of the world for so long. Individuals must drop their negativism and make a new assessment of government and their own role as citizens.

We Americans still have abundant reason to count our blessings. We have a constitutional government that has provided the most stable, most open, most free, most generous society ever created. The rest of the world still envies us, looks on us as an incredible phenomenon.

The United States has been lucky. We didn't have to fight a decrepit old social order like the Russians did; we simply started afresh. Our colonial period was short. Our efforts to throw out the British met with little opposition. Our ocean allowed us to avoid the fear of European encirclement. We have achieved what is only a dream in most countries.

The same industrial revolution that freed slaves created a massive working class. This group eventually was elevated and found justice through the labor union movement.

How humane and effective we are in creating human betterment should be the yardstick for public action. The free market is great, assuming everyone can get a foot in the door. This is true whether we are talking about jobs, or education, or health care, or anything else in the United States. Too many Americans, however, are standing outside that door. For some, it is a problem of discrimination based on their age or sex or color of their skin, or their accent, or their need for a wheelchair to get around. For others, it is more a matter of poverty — poor housing, poor nutrition, poor health care, poor day care, poor neighborhoods, poor schools — and the poor self-esteem that too often accompanies poverty.

The burden of poverty in America today is largely being shouldered by the youngest of our citizens who don't get preventive medicine, who populate ramshackle housing or have no homes at all and live in the streets, who drop out of school and into drugs. How can this be when the pride of our country has always been the ability of each generation to pass on to its children a world with more opportunity and less hardship?

Among preschoolers, according to recent statistics, one in seven is at risk of dropping out of high school, one in four is poor, one in five girls is at risk of becoming a teenage parent, one in six is uncovered by health insurance.

Readers may say, those aren't my kids you're talking about, they're somebody else's. But their future is inextricably woven with that of your children, unless the United States takes up the repugnant South African model of reservations for the disadvantaged and guards at the perimeters. Even the South Africans are abolishing that.

Nationwide there are an estimated 20 million to 27 million Americans unable to read or write in any meaningful way. Let's make sure we know the consequences. Joblessness and drug addiction, welfare dependency and crime are illiteracy's companions. It costs $6.6 billion a year just to keep incarcerated the 260,000 people whose crimes have been directly linked to their inability to read and write. Unable to hold a job, these individuals resort to thievery and other forms of lawbreaking to obtain a living. Hundreds of thousands of others have turned to crime or drugs or both because they cannot see their way clear to the something better that literacy and a good education offer.

Every day in America there are signs of a society that may not survive. Crime grows. There are more random killings, more innocent children caught in the crossfire than in any other civilized country, by far. In my lifetime there has been this progression: Careful people used to avoid a few streets in some neighborhoods because they were unsafe. Then they began avoiding a few more streets, then whole neighborhoods, and then — the situation today — large sections of cities.

We are en route to a day when all urban areas will be off limits except to people who live there and don't have the means to get out.

Nowhere is it written that America must survive. To make it happen, all of us had better be about the business of ensuring a good, decent quality of life in this country. Good jobs, good schooling, good health care for everyone. Because if we don't, the poor will continue to pay for it with their lives, and we will all go on paying for it in terms of a society ridden with crime, drugs, homelessness, and disease, including mental illness.

We hear a lot about the politics of compassion, but too often the point is lost that compassion is really an enlightened form of self-interest.

Our problems are serious, and the list is long. But our history is that of a nation able to institute change and thereby to grow and improve. That has been America's singular greatness.

There are those among us, fake rugged individualists that they are, who reached a level of success and are convinced that they did it on their own. To that I say, they hell they did. They had help. They had quality public education, with athletics, libraries, and the arts. They had a GI bill, home ownership with mortgage interest deductibility, nursing-home care for Mom and Dad, Medicare, and so on and so on. The list is endless and all of us have shared in it. So don't expect today's needy to go it alone, they can't.

It has been said of me from time to time that I have been arrogant and tough as a politician. No one likes to think of himself as arrogant. As for tough, I'll accept that as praise. After all, if I was tough, on whose behalf was it? Not for maintaining the status quo. Not, most of the time, for the majority.

I set out in politics to use what power I could for those who had no power of their own. Social improvement is not born easily; it involves much pulling and pushing. That's what I have been tough about, if anything.

Change for the better has been our lot as Americans for more than two hundred years. Most of the time we have handled it well, if haltingly on occasion. A world came to our shores because here lives could change. Country of origin, religion, visage, economics, numbers made no difference. From the Constitution to the Americans with Disabilities Act to a thousand other statutes, we may be proud of the laws of this land and the hospitality, generosity, succor that they signify. They have broadened and strengthened the mainstream.

But laws alone are hollow. Generation by generation, it is changing lifestyles, changing allocation of resources that mark the crossing from concept to reality. Change has been the certainty, the experience, the promise of America. Two hundred years ago, one hundred years ago, the story was the same as it is today. Bringing about visionary, effective change has been America's great achievement and pride. May it continue to be.

Epilogue

January 1995

MIDTERM CONGRESSIONAL ELECTIONS are over. Both houses of Congress are in Republican hands. The presidency has been a focal point of opinion polls, and Bill Clinton is getting knocked around.

Americans are angry as never before, whether they backed the winners or the lowers or whether they just stayed home, which was the case with the large majority.

The Republican gambit of a free lunch, both fiscally and intellectually, scored big. It was a high-risk strategy in that lack of immediate results could turn them out as quickly as they got in.

The idea of cutting taxes while maintaining essential services and entitlements — underline the word *essential* — is not just outrageous, it's dangerous. This nation is already overloaded with debt and deficits. The economic peril from within is far greater than any military threat we have confronted during my lifetime.

Essential services, whatever the definition, must be paid for in cash and not by credit card.

Equally discouraging is the apparent disposition of Republicans to rewrite the Constitution. Such an activity is, admittedly, free and conveys a sense of accomplishment and well-being to the citizenry. Let me respond to any gutting of the Constitution as follows:

If you want to teach *your* child religious values, do it on your time at your home and in your place of worship. That takes effort, but it will be the best expenditure of time you've ever made.

If you want the best in public servants, then *you* hustle down to the voting booth and vote the good ones in and the bad ones out. No term-limit approach can do the job of creating good government better than you.

Lastly, if budgets are to be balanced, it will be done by deed, not slogan. It will be done by elected officials truly cutting services or raising revenues, or both. It won't come simply because some words on paper dictate that it be done.

In any event, I opine that the Republican pitch to the dark side of America will be short-lived, whether by pressures from within the party or by all of us without.

These are not easy days for William Jefferson Clinton. He has made some high-visiblity gaffes and missteps. My own critique, however, is that he has achieved a lot. Even when he has fallen short, as in health-care reform, he has raised important issues to the level of national debate. Sooner or later these matters too will be resolved.

Mr. President, my advice is simple. Don't base your beliefs on the political landscape but rather, as your first instincts told you, on a landscape that is reality in America. Choose two or three beliefs important to you, and for God's sake, stick to them. The perception of leadership is as important as the reality. Right now you look like Diogenes without a lantern.

What to say about Connecticut? A four-way campaign ensued among John Rowland (Republican), Bill Curry (Democrat), Eunice Groark (A Connecticut Party), and Tom Scott (independent). The results were Rowland 36 percent, Curry 33 percent, Groark 19 percent, and Scott 11 percent. (A fifth candidate drew the remaining 1 percent.)

Lack of recognition dogged Eunice at the outset. She climbed steadily but did not have enough time. In integrity and intelligence she was the class act of the field, and I am sure she will be a major winner in the future.

Scott bombed — again! Enough said!

Rowland and Curry both had primaries, which helped them by drawing daily news coverage that put the two traditional major parties back in the forefront of public consciousness.

In the state legislature, Democrats strengthened their majority in the House by picking up four seats, and Republicans took control of the Senate by one seat.

All in all, Connecticut in 1994 was a relatively calm patch in a raging national political sea. That was the case even though an income tax had been instituted, racial isolation addressed, hand guns and assault weapons curtailed — indeed, every hot button of current political controversy pushed!

Why so much less anger in Connecticut than elsewhere? Perhaps because the governing, not the politics, absorbed the feelings of Connecticut's people. Their representatives did business, not hocus-pocus. The battles had been over four years, not four months. Putting aside the defeat of my dear friend Eunice, hooray for the Nutmeg State!

What do the election results portend for 1996? Specifically, has the necessity for third-party competition been obviated by the GOP sweep? The answer lies not in the head-to-head (Republican versus Democrat) stats, but in the turnout.

At 38 percent, the American public has by absence stated its case for alternatives.

It will get its wish in 1996! And unless there is a merger of money and ideas on the independent front, the centrist choices for president of the United States could be as high as four in number. To such a demise of the two-party system, I borrow from my British forebears to say, "Good riddance to bad rubbish!"

For the angry American, this word of advice: Stop whining. If conditions aren't what you want, set about to fix them. As my friend Don Imus is wont to say of injuries intellectual and physical, "Rub some dirt on it and get back in the game."

Nationally, citizens can be proud of how much this country has done for every successful individual in it. Call it entitlement, welfare, grant, opportunity, education, tax deduction — not one of us has made it on our own. We have always helped each other with cash, effort, life and limb. At our best, we have, over many generations, earned hero status by seeing to it that our society is open, by providing opportunity to all.

If the past is prologue, then I'm sure some brave soul will, shortly after the turn of the century, be writing a book not dissimilar to this. My hope for those times is that the author won't have to be a "maverick."

Index